Guiding Young Children in a Diverse Society

Ann Gordon
National Association of Episcopal Schools

Kathryn Williams Browne
Cañada College

Allyn and Bacon

Boston ▪ London ▪ Toronto ▪ Sydney ▪ Tokyo ▪ Singapore

Vice President, Education: Nancy Forsyth
Editorial Assistant: Kate Wagstaffe
Marketing Manager: Kathleen Hunter
Senior Editorial Production Administrator: Susan McIntyre
Editorial Production Service: Ruttle, Shaw & Wetherill Inc.
Composition Buyer: Linda Cox
Manufacturing Buyer: Megan Cochran
Cover Administrator: Suzanne Harbison

Copyright © 1996 by Allyn & Bacon
A Simon & Schuster Company
Needham Heights, MA 02194

Library of Congress Cataloging-in-Publication Data

Gordon, Ann,
    Guiding young children in a diverse society / Ann Gordon, Kathryn
Williams Browne.
        p.   cm.
    Includes bibliographical references and index.
    ISBN 0-205-15798-X
    1. School children—United States.   2. Child development—United
States.   3. Children—United States—Conduct of life.   4. School
children—United States—Discipline.   5. Pluralism (Social
sciences)—United States.   I. Browne, Kathryn Williams.   II. Title.
LB1117.G635   1996
372.18—dc20   95-22395
                                                                                CIP

Photo Credits:
Pages 6, 9, 36, 54, 102, 115, 128, 139, 209, © copyright Robert Harbison; pages 42,
51, 77, 163, 167, 179, 183, 200, © copyright Will Faller; pages 16, 91, 220, 225,
228, Children from San Francisco YMCA's Child Development Center; pages 23,
71, 95, 237, 245, 249, 261, Kate William Browne; page 145, © Jim Pickerell.

Printed in the United States of America

10   9   8   7   6   5   4   3   2   1   00   99   98   97   96   95

Contents

Preface

This is a book that begged to be written. We met as members of the faculty at the Bing Nursery School of Stanford University twenty years ago and began to share stories and strategies of guidance and discipline issues we faced each day. Over the years spent in classrooms with young children, at home with our own, in college classrooms with students, in early childhood settings with new teachers, and in workshops with professional colleagues, we knew that we had developed a point of view that was worth sharing. Each of us recognized in the other a person who was comfortable with children who were challenges and enjoyed communicating our ideas with other parents and teachers.

We hold several beliefs in common, beliefs that influence every page of *Guiding Young Children in a Diverse Society*. They are beliefs that unite us in a common voice on what can be one of the most difficult aspects of teaching: helping children function effectively and behave in positive ways.

- We believe that the best way to prepare children to live successfully and productively is to help them become increasingly responsible for their actions and their behavior.

- We believe that the early years are the most opportune time to help children see others with increasing understanding and to show them how to respect and tolerate ways in which we are all different and unique.

- We believe that each child is a part of a larger community—family, neighborhood, religious, ethnic or cultural group—that influences and shapes the family's values and beliefs.

- We believe in the essential partnership between parents and teachers, that family influences must be considered in sensitive and knowing ways.

- We believe that guiding children's behavior is a far greater challenge to teachers than planning environments or developing curriculum, and that often a teacher's skills are not sufficient to ensure success.

- We believe in the application of child development principles to disciplinary practices, a developmentally appropriate approach, which shapes lifelong practices in guidance and discipline.

- We believe that every student needs to form his or her own point of view about guidance and discipline and this is best achieved when theory is matched with practice.

Our beliefs are translated to these pages in a number of ways. *Guiding Young Children in a Diverse Society* has two sections, with a pivotal middle chapter that flows into and from the three chapters on either side of it. We begin with a general discussion of behavior, its relationship to punishment, and some of the fundamental principles of child guidance. This is followed by a concise yet comprehensive chapter on the major developmental theories on which we base our knowledge of children and their behavior. We feel this is critical information for beginning teachers, and have stressed the relationship of theories to behavior and guidance issues. A wealth of guidance and discipline techniques follow. They are time-tested, developmentally appropriate strategies that work, and give students many tools to use from their guidance tool box. Chapters 5, 6, and 7 are broken into age groups typical of early childhood programs (very young children: infants and toddlers; preschoolers from ages three to five; and school-agers from kindergarten through second grade) to focus on the unique behaviors characteristic of those age groups and to underscore the need for developmentally appropriate guidance.

Each section is influenced by and influences Chapter 4: Issues of Diversity. This chapter is the centerpiece of *Guiding Young Children in a Diverse Society* and expresses our point of view about the need to teach children to interact differently in a world grown small and to prepare them for life in a democratic society. A strong commitment to working with families has been a fundamental practice of early childhood professionals for many years. This chapter stresses that this basic belief must now be seen in the light of multiculturalism in the United States as we approach the new century.

The families in our schools are different from us and different from each other. Teachers of young children have to develop attitudes of inclusiveness as they work with children and their families on the critical issues of guidance and discipline. Cultural sensitivity is called for as parents challenge some of early childhood's most preciously held beliefs. Today's teachers must become aware of their own cultural biases when families object to a school's philosophy as being at odds with their own ways of raising children. We address what guidance and discipline means from a cultural standpoint in this chapter and give students a new understanding of why and how to involve families in the guidance process.

Some of the most uncomfortable guidance situations to handle are those that deal with discrimination. "You're a girl. You can't play here." "We don't like people with glasses." "You're a dummy. You can't read." Legislation continues to safeguard people from discrimination based on ability and gender and our classrooms are becoming more inclusive of children with a wide range of abilities and learning styles. The teacher in the twenty-first century must have a point of view that goes beyond acceptance of differences and that confronts children's prejudices about children with handicaps or ways in which boys and girls play and interact with each other. Chapter 4 does just that.

Another of our beliefs is that teaching college students is an interactive process. We know they do not learn developmental theory or guidance techniques by reading about them, as much as they do by observing and interacting with children and relating theory to their own experience. The first time they say, "You could pick up the blocks or help clean up the art table. Which would you like to do?" and it works, they make that critical connection between theory and practice. Throughout each chapter there are many and varied ways to connect chapter content with experience:

In-chapter exercises offer concrete ways to apply chapter content. Jones (1986), one of the preeminent teachers of adults, states, "People who are going to be teachers of young children should be taught in the same way they will teach." The five educational devices used in each chapter of *Guiding Young Children in a Diverse Society* support our belief in Jones's maxim.

Profiles open each chapter with stories of children and some of the typical behavior and guidance situations teachers face. We all learn from stories, especially those with vivid details, for they help us clarify common issues. These vignettes are referred to throughout the chapter, calling on the student to keep making the connection between the words on the page and a true-to-life experience.

Try It challenges students to take what they are learning directly into the classroom to prove the material to themselves.

Think It Over asks students to reflect about their own childhood and school experiences, providing that link between theory and their own beliefs and values.

Alternative Approaches underscores the notion that there are many ways to handle problem behaviors, many solutions to try, many approaches to take. Just as we want young children to grow up thinking there is more than one right way to solve problems, we want college students to explore options and alternatives.

Observe and Apply ends each chapter with an activity that calls for students to step back and look at a situation, then respond to it, based on their learning from the whole chapter.

Summaries, review questions, and a bibliography further extend the student's knowledge and grasp of the material.

For all these reasons, this was the book we have wanted to write. We hope students take our point of view as a jumping off place from which to develop their own personal theory of discipline based on a thorough exploration of developmental theory and goals.

Acknowledgments

This is the second book we have co-authored and we want to acknowledge the joy of collaboration, of teaching and learning from each other, and of enlarging each other's lives. Writing books together allows us to practice some of the basic principles of good early childhood philosophy. We have differences and we respect those. We like to learn through play, so we have fun with ideas and creatively tackle how to organize, structure, and make sense of a topic such as discipline. In a sense, we are dedicating this effort to the principles of collaboration and cooperation. It has brought about the fulfilling writing partnership we have enjoyed for fifteen years.

A book, especially a textbook, is more than pages bound together. We like to think that the creative process that first expressed itself in questions such as "How will we tackle theory?" and "What do students most need to know about Dreikurs?" gives life and energy that transcends the covers. Along the way, co-authorship gets shared with a number of other creative thinkers whose contributions help to make this material more interesting, pertinent, up-to-date, and accurate.

Our reviewers have been superb. They have come through with clear and precise evaluations of our work-in-progress, offering candid and constructive suggestions. We thank the following reviewers for taking the time and the interest in adding to the life of *Guiding Young Children in a Diverse Society:* Olivia N. Saracho, University of Maryland, Janet Gonzales-Mena, Napa Valley College, Nancy J. Lutz, Clark State Community College, Bob

Schirrmacher, San Jose City College, Billie Thomas, Northern Illinois University.

There is only one Nancy Forsyth, and that's too bad. She has been our editor, guide, and friend for three years. Were she not so brilliant at what she does with authors and books, she would make a wonderful early childhood professional. Nancy knows the field well, is current with developmental theory, promotes alternatives, helps solve problems, and cares about the unique nature of every human being she meets. Our point of view was ours to begin with, but it has been tested and honed, mellowed and redesigned because of Nancy Forsyth's instinct for what the student needs. Thank you from a very grateful Ann and Kate.

Understanding Children and Behavior

Profiles

A mother and her toddler, Sarah, are grocery shopping. Sarah is sitting in the lower area of the grocery cart among the packages. When her mother is distracted, Sarah jumps up and down, holding on to the edge of the cart but coming perilously close to jumping out. "Stop that!" says Sarah's mother, then turns her back to Sarah and walks to the far end of the aisle. Sarah gives one more high jump and, indeed, topples out of the cart, landing on the floor on her well-padded bottom. She cries out, more from surprise and shock than from injury. Her mother rushes toward her, jerks her up to a standing position, squats down while shaking her, saying, "I told you not to stand up! You could have hurt yourself!" She swats her on the backside, gives the child another shake, puts her face up close to her and says, "If you do that again, I won't bring you to the store again." Sarah bursts into tears.

Pete, a three-and-one-half-year old, was found playing quietly in the book corner, writing and drawing on the walls with marking pens. His teacher says, "You bad boy! You can't play in here anymore. And you won't get any treats after nap time." She grabs the pens and slaps Pete's hands.

Theo, a six-year-old, has been in after-school care for six months, ever since his parents divorced and his mother went to work. During the past few weeks, Theo's name-calling has accelerated to the point where the family child caregiver has spent much of the afternoon breaking up fights between Theo and the children he taunts. She mentions this concern to Theo's grandmother, who takes care of him and with whom he and his mother live. Together the two women talk over Theo's behavior while he puts on his coat. He turns to them and screams, "You poopy-heads! You stupid dummies! You don't know anything!"

Think It Over

Do these stories seem familiar? What behavior in the stories bothered you? Why? What changes would you make in the way these situations were handled? Why?

A Guidance Approach to Discipline

Helping Children with Their Behavior

Sarah, Pete, and Theo are behaving in typical ways for children their age. They are experiencing the impact of their emotions on others and having to deal with reactions and responses from others. We meet these children when they are just beginning to learn social skills: how to communicate positively and directly, how to cooperate with others, and how to solve problems. Each of them deserves our respect and understanding as they learn to behave responsibly and respectfully toward themselves and others.

Because children construct their moral and social world from their everyday experiences, we must look carefully at our own approach and response to their behavior. The subject of children's behavior may raise strong feelings. Emotions get high when adults discuss their methods of guidance and discipline. Many adults admit that much of what they do doesn't really work. We may repeat ineffective methods our families and teachers used, because many of our attitudes and discipline practices are derived from our own experiences. How we were raised influences our own discipline style: we may overreact against how our parents treated us or we may respond in the same way, even if we do not agree with their methods. We can repeat what we know or we can change our approach by reflecting on whether or not those methods were appropriate or successful.

Behavior and Misbehavior

All children's behavior has a reason and a purpose; therefore, whatever a child does is simply "behavior." However, certain behaviors are problematic. While we may not always see the same behaviors as difficult, we do agree that all children behave in ways that need to be changed. Behavior that is destructive, inappropriate, and otherwise unacceptable we call "misbehavior."

Behavior—or misbehavior—is to some extent in the eye of the beholder, because how we perceive what children do influences how we respond to them. Some adults may consider a child who persistently asks questions as rude; others may view this behavior as a measure of the child's curiosity and intellectual development.

This notion of the adult's attitude or belief is important, particularly as we work with children from a diversity of families, cultures, and experiences. For it is often when perceptions are mistaken or biased that we respond to children inappropriately and ineffectively. In some cultures, children are taught that looking into an adult's eyes while they are speaking is a sign of disrespect. To others, it is disrespectful *not* to look at adults who speak to you. We must learn the reasons for such behavior and consider its source. There is further discussion of cultural differences as well as behavior issues related to gender differences and disabilities in Chapter 4. Environmental factors and teacher attitudes and techniques that influence guidance and discipline practices are discussed in Chapter 3.

Reasons for Misbehavior

Why do children misbehave? Some of the reasons children act as they do are found in the theories of development in Chapter 2. The work of Driekurs is especially useful when looking at reasons for misbehavior.

Underlying it all, however, is the notion that children have some universal needs. One reason they misbehave is that they are trying to meet these basic needs: (1) for food and shelter; (2) for safety and belonging; (3) to make decisions and be actively involved; and (4) to be heard, understood, and appreciated. When we see children misbehave, it may be helpful to ask ourselves what the child's behavior is telling us about unmet needs and to look at that behavior to gain insight into our own response.

Temperament also plays a role. Some children seem to respond actively and strongly to the world from birth; others tend to withdraw or behave cautiously and fearfully; still others appear to have a more easygoing, flexible reaction to what happens to and around them. Thomas and Chess (1977), in their comprehensive, longitudinal study, identified three types of temperaments:

- The *easy child,* who is generally cheerful and adaptable;
- The *difficult child,* who reacts intensely and negatively and has difficulty adapting to new situations;
- The *slow-to-warm-up child,* who reacts mildly yet negatively and is slow to adapt to new experiences.

At least one-third of the children studied did not fit into any of the distinct categories but blended characteristics from the three styles.

The tendency to have a certain temperament is noticeable at an early age, but, according to Thomas and Chess, temperament is not necessarily permanent. A person's temperament may change over time, especially if childrearing practices are matched to the child's unique style. Thomas and Chess refer to this as the *goodness of fit,* where parents and caregivers accept a child's basic disposition and work with warmth, patience, and consistency to help that child master appropriate behaviors.

It can be useful to take into account a child's first, natural reaction to people and situations. The toddler who is feisty, very sensitive to external stimuli, and irregular in eating and sleeping habits will need a different sort of interaction and guidance than one who is more placid and flexible. The following activity demonstrates how temperament can be influenced by sound childrearing practices.

Try It   Bobby, a highly active kindergartner, refuses to participate in any quiet activities at school, much to his teacher's dismay. He remains constantly in motion, avoiding art, puzzles, and reading activities. At home, his parents are insisting that he spend an hour a day in quiet play, no matter how hard he resists. Applying the *goodness of fit* concept, what could you suggest to help Bobby, his parents, and his teacher? You will want to think about activities that would allow Bobby the opportunity to be active yet relatively quiet at the same time, and what role other children might play in helping Bobby benefit from these new learning experiences. What sort of timetable would you suggest? What would you say to Bobby that acknowledges his individual nature yet supports him in adapting to school?

Family Influences

The family is, of course, the single greatest influence on the young child. It is the context for the child's early life experiences; it is the mediator of a child's culture and ethnicity; it is the interpreter of the child's experiences in the greater world of backyard and neighborhood, supermarkets and malls, center or school.

Families today are defined broadly and include single parents as well as couples raising children; extended families with grandparents, uncles, and aunts; families who have blended following remarriage; families where the mother and father work outside the home, and families where the mother stays at home. What children need from a family remains the same: an adult or adults who care for them and provide for their basic needs. Neglected children may lack the supervision and guidance necessary for the development of self-regulation and prosocial, connected behavior.

The people and the relationships within the family are of paramount importance in developing healthy attitudes toward discipline and guidance.

Family influence has a profound affect on a child's behavior. Teachers of young children do what they can to support the most important relationship in a child's life.

A family's style of dealing with conflict, anger, misbehavior, and authority is communicated to the children and influences their behavior. It is important to help parents see that the whole picture of the child's family life as it is reflected in their discipline strategies is a critical part of their guidance and discipline approach.

It is in the family that the child finds a place of belonging that allows and encourages growth, experimentation, mistakes, and celebrations. The family provides the setting in which children are socialized, where they may try on and refine their social and expressive skills. Here is where the child first tests out, "No, I won't!" to see what happens. Children model their parents' way of working together, solving problems, or disagreeing. They experiment with being dependent and independent, defiant and cooperative, and take the lessons learned out to school and the greater world.

Sources of Conflict

At every age and stage of development there are good reasons why children and adults get into conflict. Erik Erikson was one of the most influential psychoanalysts in this century and his work is discussed at length in Chapter 2. His theory of psychosocial development (1950) proposes a series of stages, or crises, that people face throughout their lifetime. We can see how each of these stages can be a source of tension between children and their families.

Infants must cry to express all their needs—from wanting to be fed to needing to be held or changed. If the adult doesn't respond to the need, the crying persists and the adult and child both end up frustrated, scared, and angry. Erikson teaches that learning to trust begins when an infant is cared for in consistently loving and nurturing ways. This, in turn, teaches them to trust others.

Learning to walk is a landmark occasion in the life of a *toddler*, and that newfound independence is carried into other behaviors. A chorus of "No's" throughout the day identifies toddlers' increasing need to do things by themselves, long after the adult has run out of patience. Erikson suggests that adults should respond to the toddler's cry for freedom in supportive ways: let them choose and decide for themselves when possible and appropriate. When children have some choices and adults do not overly restrict or shame them, conflict is lessened, autonomy is protected, and children can grow in confidence as they gain more control over their own lives.

Preschoolers continue on that path of self-determination as they stretch discipline boundaries, become assertive and persistent, question why, and otherwise test limits. They have a sense of purpose and direction and, according to Erikson, want and need to gain control over their actions. Preschoolers need to learn the limits of their initiative without guilt for their increasing need for independence.

As they move into kindergarten and early elementary years, *primary age* children experience peer pressure and social needs outside the home, which increasingly become areas of tension and conflict as these children find their own strengths and interests. Feelings of incompetency at home or school can cause a sense of inferiority and be at odds with the need to be productive and feel successful.

Throughout their young lives children have an ingrown need to express themselves. Teachers and parents know that a child's drive for self-determination may often come up against our own wishes. If we foster this emerging self, we can give children the skills to express their needs in creative and acceptable ways.

One of the most important lessons young children must learn is to wait—for a treat or a toy or an activity—with a minimum of frustration or anger. We may have experienced the painful scene in stores when parents refuse to buy a screaming child a toy or candy. In the classroom we may have seen children who demand immediate possession of a favorite wagon or tricycle even if it is already in use. Helping children learn to *delay gratification* is an important step in behavior management.

Guidance and Discipline

To Be a Guide

We often speak of guiding a child toward self-control or guiding a child's behavior. The adult's role as *guide* is an important concept. It may help to think about being in a museum or a park or a foreign country where a guide leads the way, explains what direction to follow or what path to take, and tells you what rules apply. When guidance is supportive, clearly articulated, and compassionate, children's sense of self-direction is enhanced. In caring and understanding ways, the effective teacher leads children toward greater self-understanding.

Experience has taught us that we help children the most when we accept their need to assert themselves, are confident in our own guidance approach, and create a climate where self-discipline will flourish. By providing a nurturing environment that fosters healthy attitudes about problem solving and conflict resolution, we help motivate children toward self-reliance. We adults are the guides through the process and throughout this text we explore the kind of guidance that advances children's understanding of their own role as participants.

Discipline Has Many Meanings

The words *discipline* and *disciple* have a great deal in common, primarily the concept of teaching and learning through training and instruction. Too often, the word *discipline* is used in its most negative form: to enforce obedience, to punish or penalize. A guidance approach to discipline is based on the teaching/learning component: to help children *learn* what is desirable and acceptable behavior and to *teach* them empathy and respect for others. Theo's caregiver helps him learn how his behavior affects others ("They don't like to play with you when you call them names.") and what it means to him ("How did you feel when they called you a baby yesterday?" "How do you think they feel when you call them 'dummy'?"). To discipline negatively (punish) excludes the opportunity for teaching and learning to take place. A guidance approach to discipline teaches children how to:

- Channel their impulses into self-controlled and socially acceptable behavior;
- Learn right from wrong;
- View the consequences of their own behavior;
- Become good citizens and members of a group.

Developmentally Appropriate Guidance and Discipline

Children go through stages of growth in certain sequences. The universal ways children are alike at a given age are often labeled "ages and stages"; that is, children tend to behave in ways similar to those in their own age range, and all children go through the same developmental stages. Identifying these periods is helpful in effectively guiding children's behavior, knowing that patterns may emerge related to a specific age or stage, and thus having a context in which to understand the behavior. Toddlers, for instance, touch and explore anything within reach. It is a normal part of their growth and a developmentally appropriate behavior. Knowing this, we keep fragile items out of their reach so that we do not continually admonish the toddler, "Don't touch!"

There are two questions to ask when formulating a *developmentally appropriate* approach (Bredekamp, 1987) to guidance and discipline:

1. Is the guidance technique suitable for a child this age?
2. Is the guidance technique right for this individual child?

Pete requires a different response from the teacher than would Theo, whose caregiver knows children of six are capable of considering others' points of

Effective teachers understand developmental appropriateness. The boys are engaged in a class meeting to solve problems on the playground. These children are old enough to benefit from the discussion. Is this technique useful for toddlers? For three-year-olds?

view. At three-and-a-half, Pete sees only a vague cause-effect relationship and may not yet be able to view how his behavior affects others.

To fully appreciate the developmental point of view, teachers must become familiar with the developmental continuum of the early childhood age range. Children go through stages in a developmental sequence, but they do so in ways that reflect their own rate of growth and background. A child of six may have the language ability of a seven-year-old and the social-emotional skills of a four-year-old. The continuum helps teachers to match abilities with behavior and keep expectations reasonable, key factors in good discipline practices. Table 1.1 on page 11 gives examples of discipline and guidance techniques that are developmentally appropriate.

Developmentally Appropriate Expectations

Adult expectations are another source of conflict when they exceed the child's abilities to perform what is required. It is not realistic, for instance, for a teacher to expect a three-year-old to sit quietly at group time for twenty minutes. Nor should a family child caregiver insist that her own toddler

Alternative Approaches

The adults in the situations on page 11 have other options that are more suitable to the children's ages and levels of development:

1. The teacher can shorten group time or have smaller groups to allow for greater participation. Or, group time could include movement and music, songs and fingerplays, and stories where children will act out the parts. When actively involved and able to physically participate, the needs of three-year-olds are met.

2. The caregiver can provide a special box or private place where her toddler can store special toys and possessions that are brought out only when other children are not present. Together, mother and child could select those toys that are to be shared by everyone.

3. At bedtime, a parent or older sibling can help Wally lay out clothes for the next day, choose a breakfast cereal, and set the table in preparation for a busy morning. Using a kitchen timer to monitor himself, Wally can set a reasonable time to get dressed and to the table. An older sibling, grandparent, or parent can help monitor progress and offer assistance where needed.

| Table 1.1 | | |

Developmentally Appropriate Guidance Practices

There are a number of teaching strategies and good practices that adults use to help children learn how to get along with others, solve conflicts, and act cooperatively. These examples are taken directly from NAEYC's position statement on developmentally appropriate practices (Bredekamp, 1987). Used with permission.

Age Level	Appropriate Practices	Inappropriate Practices
Infants	Adults respond quickly to infants' cries or calls of distress; responses are soothing and tender.	Adults are rough, harsh, or ignore the child's responses. Crying is ignored or responded to irregularly at the convenience of the adult.
Toddlers	Adults say "No" only when the prohibition relates to children's safety. Adults give positively worded directions ("Bang on the floor") not just restrictions ("Don't bang on the table").	Adults are constantly saying "No!" to toddlers or becoming involved in power struggles over issues that do not relate to the child's health or well-being. Adults punish children for asserting themselves or saying "No."
Three-Year-Olds	Adults support 3-year-olds' developing independence, allowing them to do what they are capable of doing and assisting when needed.	Adults expect 3-year-olds to be independent and to entertain themselves for long periods of time; they are impatient, hurry children, and do tasks for children that the children could do themselves.
Four-and Five-Year-Olds	Children are provided many opportunities to develop social skills such as co-operating, helping, negotiating, and talking with the person involved to solve interpersonal problems.	Children work individually at desks or tables most of the time or listen to teacher directions in the total group. Teachers intervene to resolve disputes or enforce classroom rules and schedules.
Five-to-Eight-Year-Olds	When children are exposed to exciting, frightening, or disturbing events, real or imagined, adults help them deal with their emotions and express their feelings. Adults recognize signs of overstimulation and provide an alternative calming activity.	Adults are not sensitive to signs of over-stimulation in children and treat such demonstrations as misbehavior that must be punished, or adults escalate the situation by encouraging children to release pent-up energy in uncontrolled activity.

share all of her special toys with the other children. A family should understand that six-year-old Wally will not get dressed, eat breakfast, and be ready for the school bus without any supervision. When conflicts arise in these situations, it may be that expectations are not *developmentally appropriate*, that children are expected to behave in ways not suited to their age. In this text, we discuss guidance as it relates to specific developmental stages and age-appropriate expectations.

A guidance approach to discipline helps adults focus on behaviors they want to encourage and be aware of long-term effects of their actions. Sometimes adults must change their own attitudes and behaviors to help children grow. Sarah's mother should realize that walking away from the shopping cart left the toddler in danger and that she must bear some of the burden for Sarah's fall. The anger she expressed may also be a form of relief that Sarah was not injured. Sarah's mother should think about ways that Sarah could be occupied while she sits in the cart, especially if leaving her at home is not an option. See Table 1.2 for a summary of what children and adults can learn from a guidance approach to discipline.

Table 1.2

Guidance and Discipline: An Interactive Approach

Guidance is an interactive process in which both children and adults may learn. Everyone benefits from disciplinary practices that foster changes in attitudes and behavior.

We Teach	Adults Learn To	Children Learn To
Values	Express	Internalize
Self-control	Maintain own	Practice
Respect	Give to child	Accord to others
Appropriate behavior	Model	Observe and imitate
Limits	Be clear and consistent	Accept consequences
Feelings	Accept own and child's	Identify and label
Problem solving	Offer meaningful choices	Make decisions
Self-esteem	Protect and enhance	Respect and appreciate self
Rule setting	Share power	Participate in creating behavior controls
Taking another's viewpoint	Be sympathetic and understanding	To be empathetic
Collaboration	Involve child in solutions	Problem-solve cooperatively

Think It Over

Do you use the same guidance and discipline techniques that your parents did in raising you? Have you changed any of these methods? Why? Do you remember a time when you were expected to behave in a way that seemed more appropriate to an older child? What did you do?

Discipline and Guidance Concepts

The Importance of Behavior Models

Discipline, from the word *disciple,* suggests that a pupil or learner is to follow an example (Gordon & Browne, 1993). A guidance approach to discipline provides adults who teach by example and who are *role models* for behavior. Children care deeply for their parents, teachers, caregivers, grandparents, and other significant adults, and they come to internalize the values these adults exemplify. *Modeling* is an excellent teaching tool. It works because children want to be like the adults they love and will follow their example. What children see others do tends to become part of their own behavior. The power of being a behavior model for young children cannot be underestimated.

One of the most important aspects of being a behavior model is that adults can model the acceptance of feelings as well as modeling actions. Parents and teachers can show children that strong feelings can be expressed in constructive ways through a variety of outlets. To be a model for children, we first have to learn these skills ourselves, recognize and label our feelings, and demonstrate acceptable means to alleviate our frustrations. Verbalizations help. "Sometimes I get so angry I want to hit something! When that happens, I go into the bedroom and hit my pillow as hard as I can!" Sharing ways of coping with feelings lets children know we too have had to learn self-control.

Recognizing and accepting feelings is good for children, and it is beneficial to adults. Many adults were raised to suppress or deny their feelings and were told that being angry was "bad" or "not nice." Yet we know our anger exists and that living and working with children causes us to be angry at times. As we recognize ourselves as models of behavior, it is important that we learn socially and developmentally appropriate ways to express our feelings as adults.

If we fail to come to a self-understanding about the way we deal with anger and frustration, we are more likely to teach children inappropriate and dehumanizing methods of behavior. Hitting a child is the most obvious example. At the start of this chapter, Sarah's mother resorted to hitting and threatening her child, in part because she had not yet learned to channel her own anger. Had she learned that when she feels angry at Sarah she could count to ten, take three deep breaths, and walk away for a few minutes, her immediate response might not have been to hit Sarah. Had she taken the opportunity to examine what caused her anger (possibly her own neglect for leaving the cart unattended) she might discover that her anger is really at herself as much as toward her child. That could influence the way she disciplines Sarah.

Through adults who care for them, children can learn to respect their own feelings and be exposed to ways to cope with them. They can also learn from us to deal with feelings in violent and shameful ways. As adults who serve as models for children we have to learn to deal with our own feelings in order to be the most exemplary models of behavior for children.

Guidance Is Related to Self-Esteem

Self-esteem is an individual's sense of personal worth and is developed as a reflection of the way other people respond to you. Early in life, self-esteem is primarily influenced by family, friends, and other important people, such as teachers. Children express the way they feel about themselves through their behavior, and the type of discipline they experience can either enhance or damage their self-esteem.

In any guidance situation it is important to take into account how the situation will affect the child's self-esteem. Theo, in the third example, undoubtedly feels his young world has collapsed, and his self-esteem has been badly threatened as he confronts the many changes in his life over the past six months. Theo's grandmother might have picked him up, given him a quick hug, and then told him, "I really do like coming to pick you up but I want you to use my name, Grammy, the name you always call me. No one likes to be called names that hurt. If you want to make up silly names, we'll get your stuffed animals out when you get home and you can call them silly names." Theo now has a limit set (no name calling), alternatives (use his stuffed animals to call names), reassurance that he is still loved (hugs), and reasons why his behavior was stopped (names hurt).

Self-esteem and self-control are related. Children will not try to control and direct their own behavior if they see themselves as worthless and unimportant. When they see themselves as capable and have a sense of self-worth, children are more likely to take responsibility for their actions and respect the rights of others. Children are robbed of their self-esteem when they are treated harshly and made to feel that they have no ability to control themselves, as Pete experienced when his teacher called him "bad." Shame, disgrace, and embarrassment have no part in good discipline procedures.

Coopersmith's seminal work in the area of teacher behavior and self-esteem (1975) shows that confident and motivated children who function independently were the by-products of teachers with high self-esteem who gave positive feedback and based classroom management on joint cooperation and respect. Teachers lacking in self-confidence, on the other hand, tend to be critical of children, who in turn become passive, dependent, and defensive. Grouping children according to their abilities, such as having the most accomplished readers be the Red group (Bukatko and Daehler, 1992) lowers self-esteem. Respecting children, believing that what they say makes a difference, and allowing them to express their feelings creates a climate for strong self-esteem to emerge.

The Ultimate Goal: Self-Discipline

The goal of discipline is for children to achieve self-control. This happens over a period of years as the child moves from the early protective controls set up by parents and caregivers to an internalization of the family's standards and values. This transference of control from adult to child is achieved through techniques that gradually decrease the child's reliance on external controls.

For the first few years, children need outside controls, primarily to keep them safe as they become mobile and interact with their environment. Gates are put across stairways, the yard is fenced, and cabinets are outfitted with latches that children cannot open.

During the preschool and primary years we see the development of a conscience, when children begin to internalize right and wrong. By being freed from some of the outer controls, children can come to accept responsibility for their own actions and find the limits of their own behavior. The first grader can do her homework alone; the preschooler doesn't hit his little brother even when his parents are out of the room. When we gradually hand over to children the opportunity to govern their own actions, we communicate trust. For young children, with their urge to prove themselves and their drive for independence, this is an important step to take.

To foster responsibility and self-discipline, we set up the environment as an educational experience that teaches self-direction, decision-making, and independence. Table 3.1 on page 70 shows examples of ways to achieve this.

At each age level, children need to learn strategies that help them gain control over their behavior. How do we help this girl protect her place on the tire swing? What do we say to the boy who hasn't hit out at her, but may want to?

Freedom and Discipline

There is a reciprocal relationship between responsibility and freedom. The more people assume responsibility for their own behavior, the more freed they are from external controls. Freedom is not something we award children; it is the natural consequence of their becoming self-directed and self-controlled. Responsibility for one's own actions is learned through experience and by being held accountable. Children do not learn the extent of their capabilities until they are given the freedom to test their own resources. We must provide situations and use guidance practices that allow children freedom to test their safe boundaries, assert themselves, and make their own decisions. If children always operate with external controls provided by adults, they will never know how much freedom they can handle.

Acting with Authority

"I just can't control Carla. No one can." "Derrin has a real authority problem." When we hear adults make comments such as these we are hearing from people who have exhausted their usual methods of discipline and are unclear about their responsibility to be in charge. It may also mean that the adult is about to lose control and may be on the verge of using power assertive techniques and other damaging methods of punishment.

The control issue is not really one of learning how to "control" children; rather, adults must learn to direct their energies toward a problem-solving, limit-setting, modeling approach to discipline. Adults are bigger and stronger and can gain control of children in any number of ways. Wise adults learn the proper use of authority by understanding their own feelings and developing an awareness of their own response to authority. Calm and confident adults who face their own feelings about dealing with unacceptable behavior help create a climate in which children are better able to master their impulses. That is the constructive use of authority.

Authority can be one of the most intimidating concepts for beginning teachers to grasp, yet authority and appropriate management are legitimate concerns, essential to the teaching role. Teachers, after all, have the responsibility for the safety and well-being of the children in their care. It is the adult's job to ensure that children will not hurt themselves or others and that they learn how to be responsible members of a group. Inexperienced teachers often tend toward extremes: ignoring the authority that comes with the teaching role or using authority as superiority and power. Both of these extremes miss the point and create environments for children that may be harmful.

The key to proper use of authority is having the self-confidence to truly be in charge without overpowering others. Teachers must put the interests of the children first by assuming their rightful role as protectors, and they must be in charge of their emotional responses. Teachers who understand the appropriate use of power and authority base their interactions with children on mutual respect, care, and confidence.

Think It Over

Can you think of a time when you were aware that a child was observing how you reacted to a problem? How did it make you feel? How do you think you handled being a behavior model? Do you remember the first time you were allowed to make a very important decision on your own? How has that affected your ability to allow young children to make some of their own decisions?

Negative Discipline: Punishment

Discipline and Punishment: A Distinction

Discipline, as discussed in this text, means guiding and directing children toward acceptable behavior. It is an interaction that involves the child as much as the adult, emphasizing the positive ways a child can grow and change ("You can learn to ask Jeremy for a turn. I'll teach you some ways to say it."). Punishment, as it is often used, generally refers to on-the-spot adult reactions to misbehavior, often focusing on what the child is not supposed to do. (*To Sarah:* "I told you not to stand up in that cart!" *To Pete:* "You can't play in here anymore. You won't get any treats.") It is often a one-time response stemming from the adult's anger and frustration and varies in degree according to the depth of that anger.

All children must learn to realize the consequences of their behavior, so some form of guidance and discipline is usually in order. Consequences can range from mild ("You can't play at your friend's house because you didn't do your chores") to violent (being slapped or beaten). Most punishment falls in the middle range. Table 1.3 distinguishes between guidance and punishment.

Table 1.3

Guidance and Punishment: A Distinction

Discipline and punishment are two distinct concepts and can have opposite effects on children. A thoughtful and considered guidance approach to discipline can create a more positive atmosphere, which fosters responsibility and self-control. Punishment, taken to extreme, may have a serious impact on children's development. (Adapted from Gordon & Browne, 1993).

Guidance	*Punishment*
Emphasizes what to do and sets an example to follow	Often emphasizes what *not* to do by adults who frequently insist on blind obedience
Is an ongoing process of interaction between adults and children	May be a spontaneous on-the- spot reaction of adults who decide and act
Is seen as a positive response, which helps children develop responsibility and self-control	Is often negative and punitive in ways that may undermine trust, autonomy, and initiative
Fosters a child's ability to think, which bolsters self-esteem	Has the potential to diminish self-esteem when adults depend on external controls
Is based on a caring, nurturing approach, which protects children's feelings	Frequently spontaneous and impulsive, often causing feelings of shame and humiliation
Viewed as a collaboration	Often results in power assertion by adult

Types of Punishment

Punishment may be broken down into several categories:

1. That which is *physically or emotionally hurtful:* hitting, pinching, spanking, kicking, threatening, shouting, cursing, name-calling, ridiculing, humiliating. Sarah's mother and Pete's teacher used several of these methods.

2. That which *denies freedoms or withholds/deprives:* denial of privileges or activities, or limiting activities ("I won't bring you to the grocery store again"); being grounded ("Because you couldn't stop running into the street, you can't play outside after school for a week"); withholding affection ("Daddy doesn't like little boys who won't clean their plates").

3. That which *isolates:* sent out of sight, sent to room, time out ("Stay in your room until you quit crying").

4. That which takes some form of *restitution:* assigning added chores ("You'll have to take the garbage out for an extra day because you forgot to do it today") or being given responsibilities in excess of behavior ("Because you didn't put your bike away, you won't be able to go to the movies with us on Saturday"); repay monetary losses ("That was Grandma's dollar. You will have to repay her out of your allowance"); replace or repair damage ("Mr. Harmon loves his flowers. You'll have to buy him some new ones to replace the ones you picked").

When a consequence becomes punishment seems to be a matter of degree. A consequence moves into the realm of punishment when it is not logically connected to the offense and a punitive aspect is added. Which of the examples just cited are reasonable results of the misbehavior? Which are not?

Any consequences for inappropriate behavior should be brief, swift, and limited to the mildest form. To avoid becoming punitive, there should be no carryover, no continuing reminders of the child's misbehavior, and no delaying of consequences. Children should see the direct and immediate connection between their behavior and the punishment. Sarah's mother responded right away, but she did so in ways that did not help Sarah change her behavior. She offered no alternative behaviors that would have been acceptable, such as walking alongside or sitting in the seat provided at the front of the cart and helping her count out four oranges or find their favorite cereal.

Pete, on the other hand, can't understand why he is in trouble, does not know how to handle his urge to draw with the new pens, and feels rejected by the teacher. The teacher is exerting external control over the situation rather than attempting to teach Pete some self-control. Another teacher might have responded, "Oh, no, Pete. You drew on the walls. That's not good for the walls. Those pens are for paper only. Let's go get the sponges and cleanser so you can clean the pen marks off the wall." While scrubbing together, the teacher adds, "Next time, use the paper on the easels or take some off this shelf. You've done a good job of scrubbing. The marks are almost off now." Giving Pete a form of restitution is appropriate for a preschooler.

In this scenario, Pete comes out of the situation with greater understanding of how his behavior affected others and of his own ability to correct that behavior. He is empowered by the information the teacher gave him to act differently the next time. His self-esteem is intact, and he has been supported in his efforts to help restore the situation. This is a marked contrast to the first teacher's reaction and to that of Sarah's mother.

Chapter 3 further discusses natural and logical consequences and techniques for handling behavior without resorting to punitive measures.

Research Support

Research supports the method of the second teacher in the example of Pete. Patterson (1975) suggested three components to be most effective in disciplining children: (1) intervention must happen early in the act of misbehavior; (2) intervention must occur at the lowest possible emotional level; and (3) intervention must involve the mildest form of punishment. Minimum response coupled with minimum punishment is further supported by Roedell et al. (1977) as a way to help children regain their composure and be able to learn from the experience. Other studies (Patterson & Reid, 1984; Youngblade & Belsky, 1990) of aggressive children found that when their aggression was not stopped as soon as possible, parents became ineffective in their demands for good behavior.

Try It   Go back and read the Profiles at the beginning of the chapter. Write down the ways Sarah's mother, Pete's teacher, and Theo's caregiver would have responded if they had followed Patterson's three components for effective discipline.

Power Assertive Discipline

The more harsh and punitive methods are referred to as *power assertive techniques*, relying on physical punishment and use of force. They rely on a child's fear of being punished rather than the use of reason, understanding, and appropriate limitations, which is called *inductive guidance.* (See Chapter 3 for more discussion on inductive guidance.) There is some research to support the view that aggressive punishment on the part of the adult begets more aggression in the child. Sears, Maccoby, and Levin's (1975) early study of childrearing practices found that punishing five-year-olds for aggressive acts had the opposite effect: children in fact became more aggressive. Coming at it from a different direction, Denham, Renwick, and Holt (1991) show how children's behavior is influenced by positive social interactions with their mothers. Mothers who support a child's autonomy and mastery of skills by modeling, reinforcement, and verbalization have children who show prosocial and nonaggressive behavior.

Spanking

Spanking and other corporal punishments are the most controversial forms of power assertive methods. Using corporal punishment is an abuse of power. Most significantly, when an adult spanks or hits a child, the opportunity for teaching and learning new ways of discipline is lost. Corporal punishment interferes with the guiding and teaching components of good discipline practices.

For years research studies have pointed out the ineffectiveness of corporal punishment and its relationship to a cycle of family violence (Patterson, DeBaryshe, & Ramsey, 1989). Bandura's research (1977) demonstrates that children whose parents use a high rate of physical punishment are frequently aggressive themselves. Emery (1989) supports the premise that adult models of aggression foster aggressive behavior in children.

The arguments against spanking are persuasive. Spanking and hitting do not alter behavior over the long term, damage the child's self-image, model inappropriate behavior, expose the adult as out of control, may provoke even more aggression in the child, and undermine self-control. Table 1.4 distinguishes between good and harmful guidance practices.

Think It Over

How did your parents punish you? Would you do the same with (1) your own children or (2) the children you teach? Why? Were you ever punished unfairly? How did it make you feel? Do you think you have ever punished a child unfairly? What would you do differently? Are there times when spanking is called for? If so, under what circumstances would you spank a child? What alternatives can you think of?

Table 1.4	

Guidance Practices

Some discipline methods are harmful to children and defeat the goals of good guidance practices. Other methods promote good discipline practices and should be a part of every adult's repertoire.

Always Try To:

Have a plan based on child's needs	Include the child in finding solutions
Think before you react	Be consistent and respectful
Take a deep breath, calm yourself first	Acknowledge your own feelings
Ask for help when needed	Be prepared to be flexible
Remember what you want to teach	Adapt to the needs of the child
Have faith in the child	Provide direction and guidance
Protect the child	

Think Carefully About:

Removal from the group	Overreacting
Isolation	Moralizing

Never:

Criticize	Humiliate
Blame	Use cruel humor
Discourage	Withhold affection
Shame	Scream or yell
Use sarcasm	Use physical punishment: slap, hit,
Ridicule	choke, punch, shake
Belittle	Threaten with another person

Fundamental Principles of Child Guidance

A guidance approach to discipline fosters the growth and development of the individual child in the socialization process. Adults and children interact with one another and the environment as part of an interdependent system. Six essential principles form the basis for developmentally appropriate guidance attitudes and techniques.

Effective Guidance and Discipline Practices Are Based on Knowing Child Development Theory

These insights help us realize the individual nature of each child in relation to the total development. A basic understanding of how children grow and the predictable patterns and stages through which they develop is necessary if teachers are to guide effectively. Matched with a teacher's own observations and experience, knowledge of normal stages of development provides an understanding of what to expect, the variations in behavior and capacities of young children, and the confidence to support their growth.

Emphasis Is on Guiding and Teaching

This emphasis requires an interactive approach with a strong problem-solving component. Control of a child by an adult is not the ultimate goal; self-discipline is. Everything adults do and say—directly or indirectly—affects what children do. We want to be able to trust children to solve their own problems and sense their own competence by learning to monitor themselves. We want to help children learn to cope with problems by allowing them to work out solutions without undue interference. We want them to make judgments based on the inner controls they learn as they interact with others. We want to teach them through our own example and behavior. We use the environment as a guidance tool and adhere to a well thought out philosophy of discipline.

Guidance Is a Process

The results of this process will be achieved over a period of time. It is not a single act but a process developed slowly in the life of a child, step by step,

Children learn to be resourceful and responsible when guidance has a strong problem-solving component. What do you say to help this child come out of the tree with her dignity intact?

from the infant over whom the adult has complete responsibility to the adolescent's emergence into a self-reliant adult. Guidance is the constant and ongoing procedure of helping children learn to regulate their basic impulses, express their feelings, channel their frustrations, and solve their problems. A teaching and learning process, guidance is the creation of a system of strategies that fit the child, the home, and the school. It is integrated into a way of living and behaving with children. There are no quick fixes, nor is there a single strategy that applies to all circumstances: Children and situations are as different as the teachers, parents, and caregivers who deal with them. We first define discipline for ourselves, according to sound developmental theories, then set appropriate goals for the individual children we teach. We also weave in the cultural values of children's backgrounds. The process becomes defined by what we believe children should learn and by being intentional about each discipline and guidance moment. Figure 1.1 on page 25 outlines the relationship of these variables.

Guidance and Discipline Have Long- and Short-Range Goals

Guidance and discipline help children become self-disciplined and independent problem solvers over a lifetime. Short-term goals deal with the current crisis or newly exhibited behaviors and require immediate action. Meeting long-range goals begins with the small steps taken by short-term resolutions to conflicts. Teaching children to pick up blocks and return them to the shelves is a short-term skill that has implications for the long-range goals of group responsibility, cooperation, and self-help skills. When long-range goals are clear, adults can respond to short-term problems in ways that are growth enhancing.

Guidance May Require Changes in Behavior of Both the Adult and the Child

Guidance is a working partnership between teacher and child or parent and child, where both may learn, is noted in Table 1.2. Many people think discipline is something done just for and to children, that it is only the child's behavior that needs to be changed. In fact, when adults use good guidance practices they are often encouraged to change their own behavior as well. Part of the teacher–learner relationship is to give children legitimate opportunities to participate in choosing their course of action, and with each choice, the adult also has to choose a response. This tenet is really about the *relationship*—the give and take between adult and child that is respectful of both of their viewpoints and their ability to change.

Figure 1.1

The Guidance Triangle

In establishing effective guidance practices, adults take into consideration three important elements: the child, the adult, and the situation. For instance, a two-year-old needing assistance is more likely to respond to the intervention of a familiar teacher than one who is substituting for the day.

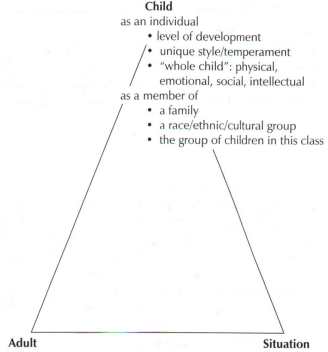

Child
as an individual
- level of development
- unique style/temperament
- "whole child": physical, emotional, social, intellectual

as a member of
- a family
- a race/ethnic/cultural group
- the group of children in this class

Adult
- the role (teacher, parent, coach, advocate, friend)
- relationship to the child
- values, biases
- skills and guidance techniques

Situation
- the physical environment
- time of day
- who, what is involved
- what else is happening
- what is unique about it

Guidance Is Influenced by Many Factors

Guidance is influenced by many factors such as individual style and temperament, culture, race, nationality, family background, and personal experiences. They affect how we deal with children and the discipline philosophy we adopt. Most of us have developed a teaching and/or parenting style based on these influences. Figure 1.1 elaborates the relationship among some of these factors. The expertise and education of a teacher or parent, the cultural and religious values of the child's family, and society's values all affect our approach to child guidance. We all have varying expectations, motivations, and attitudes toward childrearing, as the examples of Sarah's mother, Pete's teacher, and Theo's caregiver demonstrate. As adults, we must be aware of how a child's life is shaped by these often diverse forces.

These six basic tenets take into consideration the needs of children, parents, and teachers, respecting the interactive nature of the discipline process. They suggest that the child's self-worth is intertwined with appropriate guidance practices and that parents and teachers must have a partnership with the child and with each other to succeed. Most important, these guidelines imply that good discipline practices teach life skills: the development of attitudes and behaviors that teach children how to live in harmony with other people.

A Point of View

The six fundamental principles of child guidance, in effect, create a road map for this text. They are the foundations on which the content of this book was created, and they suggest the form and structure for each chapter. The first principle, knowing child development theory, is basic; our understanding of why children think, learn, and behave as they do influences our interactions and relationships with them. Theories challenge us to think about how children learn and grow, to wrestle with our own beliefs and values, and to emerge with a personal point of view. By placing a chapter on developmental theory next, we underscore our commitment to the application of child development theory to disciplinary practices.

The next four principles outline the philosophical approach to the rest of the text. The guidance process is defined as interactive and integrated. It is interactive in the sense that we teach children about behavior through our own example and behavior, and we engage them in the process as active participants in solving problems. This guidance approach is integrated because we know that how we guide children will be affected by their age, stage of development, individual temperament, family profile, and cultural and ethnic background. Process implies a period of time. The guidance techniques we suggest in Chapter 3 are a series of actions and changes that bring about results over time. Our point of view is that there are no quick fixes to guidance and discipline; instead, it is an ongoing, lifelong process.

The final fundamental principle dictates the pivotal chapter in the text, which focuses on issues of diversity. Guidance is influenced by many factors, and one of the most powerful is family. The statistics in Chapter 4 leave no question about the need to understand family childrearing patterns or cultural values as we teach a culturally diverse generation. Classrooms that are inclusive of gender, ability, and culture need teachers who are sensitive to how these factors play themselves out in the lives of children. This chapter includes strategies to assess the effect of our own biases on our teaching interactions and helps to develop a point of view from another's perspective.

Theories, techniques, and a broader sense of the child's world create a background for the final three chapters, which are devoted to specific age groups. Theories come alive, techniques seem more plausible, and the child's history is seen in real-world situations. Focusing on a small age range provides an opportunity to explore developmentally appropriate guidance practices so that our point of view matches their level of growth and development.

To help you develop your own point of view, concepts and theories are translated by examples and suggestions for practical application throughout the text. Learning devices such as "Try It," "Think It Over," and "Alternative Approaches" help you to think through the material and use the information in ways that relate to your own teaching. Use the practical features in these chapters to analyze problems and develop solutions that reflect a grounding in the fundamentals of guidance and discipline.

Think It Over

Do you agree with the six principles of guidance? Which is most important to you? Least important? Why? Which one seems to be the most difficult to do? Why? Write a seventh principle with some of your classmates.

Summary

Young children are just beginning to discover ways in which people interact with one another. Their behaviors and attitudes are influenced by their individual nature, adult expectations, and their family culture and structure. Everyday experiences form the basis from which they learn the necessary skills to think, problem solve, communicate, negotiate, and cooperate. Their behavior and innate temperament may be seen as the raw material from which they build self-confidence, self-respect, and self-discipline.

A guidance approach to discipline is effective because children learn to take responsibility for their own actions and come to understand how their behavior affects other people. A guidance approach takes into consideration the age and development level of the child. An important part of the process is that adults learn to focus on the long-range implications of their own response and the importance of their role as behavior models.

Punishment differs from guidance and discipline because it is often carried out in negative and punitive ways. It may not be connected to the behavior, and therefore loses its intended impact on the child. Children should emerge with greater understanding of how their behavior affects others and a growing ability to exert self-control. Power assertive techniques, which rely on force, physical punishment, or threats, are ineffective in helping children learn self-discipline. Spanking and other forms of corporal punishment damage a child's self-esteem and often reinforce aggressive behavior in children.

There are fundamental principles on which an effective child guidance approach is based, beginning with an understanding of child development theory and an emphasis on guiding and teaching appropriate behaviors and attitudes. Guidance is a process with long- and short-range goals, which may require changes in both the adult and the child and is influenced by many factors. These principles help us create developmentally appropriate guidance practices and techniques. They foster healthy attitudes toward responsibility and respect to self and others as children learn to become contributing members of society.

Observe and Apply

Observe a teacher who acts as a guide in helping children learn appropriate behavior. What are some of the ways she sets out rules and expectations that enhance her role as a guide? How are children supported in their need to assert themselves? To make some of their own decisions? To respect others? How does the teacher help children become aware of how their behavior affects others? In finding alternative solutions? Contrast her role as guide with another observation of a teacher who takes a different approach to guidance and discipline.

Review Questions

1. What are some of the reasons children misbehave?

2. What is meant by "developmentally appropriate" guidance and discipline? Use examples from classroom or home observations to demonstrate what you mean.

3. Why are behavior models important?

4. Describe how guidance and self-esteem are related. Use specific examples from your observations.

5. What are four types of punishment? Which are most appropriate for toddlers? for preschoolers? for children from six to eight? Justify your response with child development theory.

6. What does research say about punishment? Do you agree with the findings? Disagree? Why?

7. List and define the six fundamental principles of child guidance. Use examples.

Bibliography

Bandura, A. *Social Learning Theory.* Englewood Cliffs, NJ: Prentice Hall, 1977.

Bredekamp, Sue, (Ed.). *Developmentally Appropriate Practice in Early Childhood Programs Serving Children from Birth Through Age 8,* expanded edition. Washington, DC: National Association for the Education of Young Children, 1987.

Bukatko, D., & Daehler, M. W. *Child Development: A Topical Approach.* Boston: Houghton, Mifflin Company, 1992.

Coopersmith, Stanley. *Developing Motivation in Young Children.* San Francisco: Albion, 1975.

Denham, S., Renwick, S., & Holt, R. "Working and Playing Together: Predictions of Preschool Social-Emotional Competence from Mother-Child Interactions." *Child Development,* 62, no. 2 (1991): 242–249.

Emery, R. E. "Family violence." *American Psychologist,* 44 (1989): 321–328.

Erikson, E. *Childhood and Society.* New York: Norton, 1950.

Gordon, Ann Miles, and Browne, Kathryn Williams. *Beginnings and Beyond: Foundation in Early Childhood Education.* Albany, NY: Delmar, 1996 (4th ed).

Patterson, G. R. *Families: Applications of Social Learning to Family Life.* Champaign, IL: Research Press, 1975.

Patterson, G. R., Debaryshe, B. D., & Ramsey, E. "A Developmental Perspective on Antisocial Behavior." *American Psychologist,* 44 (1989): 329–335.

Patterson, G. R., & Reid, J. B. "Social Interaction Processes within the Family: The Study of Moment-by-Moment Family Transactions in Which Human Social Development is Embedded." *Journal of Applied Developmental Psychology,* 5 (1984): 237–262.

Roedell, W. C., Slaby, R. C., & Robinson, H. B. *Social Development in Young Children.* Belmont, CA: Wadsworth, 1977.

Sears, R. R., Maccoby, E. E., & Levin, H. *Patterns of Child Rearing.* New York: Harper & Row, 1975.

Thomas, A., & Chess, S. *Temperament and Development.* New York: Brunner/Mazel, 1977.

Youngblade, L., & Belsky, J. Social and emotional consequences of child maltreatment. In R. Hammerman & M. Hersen, (Eds.), *Children at Risk: An Evaluation of Factors Contributing to Child Abuse and Neglect.* New York: Plenum Press, 1990.

2

Theories of Guidance and Discipline

Profiles

Beth and Janine are preschoolers in a parent cooperative. Beth brings a special necklace to school one day, and Janine is very interested. First, she watches Beth as she parades around the classroom, showing everyone her "pretty-pretty." She thinks about grabbing it, because she really, really wants it so much she should have it. But if she grabs it, Beth will scream, and then everyone will yell at Janine and she'll have to give it back. "I know what I can do!" Janine says aloud to herself. Going to her cubby, she takes a chocolate cookie from her lunch and offers it to Beth for the necklace. When Beth refuses, Janine gets angry and they begin calling each other names. Finally, Janine cannot stop herself: she grabs the necklace and runs outside.

Suneela and her classmates arrive at the after-school care room after a full kindergarten day of high structure and academic lessons. Their uniforms flying in the wind they create from running down the hallway, the children are noisy and reckless; often there are collisions and fights as they enter the room. The parents have asked that the after-school time include time to do homework, as the children are often picked up as late as six P.M. and school obligations are difficult to fulfill with so little "at-home time" before bed.

Zachary and Amal are young children in a local children's center. Although they are the same age and have similar family structures, they behave very differently. A demonstrative, energetic child, Zachary is easy to redirect and to understand. Amal is more withdrawn and distrustful; as a toddler she had a particularly difficult time separating from her mother with the caregiver, a babysitter, even her grandmother. Now she is not particularly verbal, and often stays away from children or overpowers them.

Why, in a discipline book, learn about theory? Teachers are too busy "doing discipline" to spend much time with theory. We need to deal with the children immediately, and have precious little time for reflection. After all, isn't discipline really about how we respond to the children's behavior, and not about how we think of it?

Although the previous statements may be true, there are three good reasons to have your personal philosophy of discipline solidly grounded in theory. First, *the major thinkers of development, learning, and guidance have something valuable to contribute to our knowledge of children.* The five theories selected here add greatly to what we know about how children learn, think, and behave. By having a better understanding of children in general, teachers are better prepared to deal with children's behavior.

Second, *learning about theories can help teachers develop better programs and techniques.* Teachers who are more experienced with children can plan appropriate programs that avoid problems, and can respond more accurately to those that commonly arise. In doing so, good teachers (1) build a framework for dealing with children that takes into consideration development and theory; and (2) keep an open mind, staying flexible and prepared for the unique, idiosyncratic, unexpected behavior of individual children. To do both well, teachers need to understand and be able to use the major theories.

Finally, *teachers develop their own personal theory of discipline through a "sifting" process.* That is, they need to learn enough about major developmental and learning theories to see that there are different perspectives. In presenting different—and sometimes conflicting—theories, teachers must decide what makes sense to them. It is often uncomfortable, because working through different viewpoints and techniques can reveal our own biased thinking. When we are in this uneasy state of mind, however, we can see how our own values and beliefs act as filters and cloud our vision of a child, a family, or a situation. This critical thinking is valuable, because it asks teachers to tolerate a diversity of thought while developing their own theory of discipline.

As you read these theories, pay attention to your own responses and experiences. Once you understand a theory, take from it what you think useful. Although we cannot cover every detail of every theory, a review of them strengthens teachers' theoretical base for guidance. Compare what these theories say about children and guidance with what you may already know and with what you do every day with young children. In other words, "sift" through them, and separate the wheat from the chaff. Often, you may conclude that an eclectic approach, based on the situation, the child, and the adult, is best. And no matter which one you find most useful, you have a more solid foundation for your own personal theory of discipline.

Think It Over

What developmental theory would inform the teacher about what is happening with Beth and Janine and what to do? What learning theory would prescribe the optimal learning environment and positive experiences in Suneela's after-school program? Which theory of guidance might help a teacher with the difficulties with Zachary and Amal?

Psychodynamic Theory

Overview of the Theory

Psychodynamic theory was first developed by Sigmund Freud, and was elaborated on by Carl Jung, Alfred Adler, Erik Erikson, Anna Freud, and others. In general, the theory posits that development proceeds through a sequence of stages that produce qualitative changes in an individual. Psychodynamic theory considers both inborn instincts and the appropriate environmental and interpersonal supports. Furthermore, its proponents view the child's own perceptions of an experience to be as important as the experience or environment itself in shaping the child's behavior.

The stages or developmental periods are determined partly by maturation and biology and partly by the experiences (environment, family, school, society, and the like) in which a child grows. Because the stages are determined by the age of the individual, any unresolved issues from one stage are carried forward and affect the person's ability to deal with subsequent stages. According to this theory, such "excess baggage" can lead to deviant or abnormal personality patterns.

Key Player: Erik Erikson

Erik Erikson, who followed Freud in the psychodynamic viewpoint, focused on how society affects the person. In particular, Erikson's theory proposes that human development progresses through a series of stages in the form of psychological dilemmas or crises. The major crisis at each developmental stage originates in the demands of society on the individual. These demands differ from one society or culture to another. Furthermore, in the early years, such demands or expectations are rooted in family and school. Finally, demands change as the person gets older and changes. Thus, each stage is characterized by a crisis. At the time of crisis, the child is particularly vulnerable to the challenge but also has the potential for increased personal strength, or psychological growth, in that area. Erikson's stages of development, as shown in Table 2.1 on page 35, can thus be seen as a series of turning points, as the person over the life span engages in a prolonged search for a sense of identity. The child's success in meeting the challenges of each stage depends on the interactions between the child and important adults.

Applying the Theory to Discipline

Erikson's theory has certain important implications for teachers of young children. First, *adults serve a critical role as an emotional base and social*

Table 2.1

Erikson's Stages of Psychosocial Development

Erik Erikson's theory of psychosocial development describes the basic crises of life, from birth through old age. In the early childhood years, children face challenges at each stage of development, and need adults who can respond effectively to those issues.

Age	Crisis	Guidance Needs from Adult
Infancy	Trust vs. Mistrust	Responsiveness, warmth Positive and affectionate adults Predictable environment Consistent caregiving
Toddler	Autonomy vs. Shame and Doubt	Give child the strength of will Encourage play and exploration Toileting encouraged with care Clear limits with flexibility
Preschool (three to six)	Initiative vs. Guilt	Allow "all by myself" Establish small set of logical limits Plenty of social experiences Encourage "good ideas"
Elementary (six to twelve)	Industry vs. Inferiority	Emphasize skill building, working on gaining and improving, not perfection Refrain from competition Include group experiences

mediator. They must understand the particular vulnerabilities and challenges of the children they care for and educate, and must translate their understandings into successful ways of working with children and their parents. For example, consider the activity of building and destroying a tower. Many teachers and parents think that the child is being "destructive" or even has a "mean streak," because after building a tower, the child does not save it or even stand back to admire it, but gets almost manic pleasure from kicking it over and watching it collapse. The teacher with an Eriksonian viewpoint sees this as the continuing push and pull of active mastery and power. It makes the child feel stronger to know there is someone or something weaker. And the tower cannot cry and call for Mommy as a little brother can. So, a teacher with this theoretical bent most likely is rather tolerant of such "build and destroy" activities. In the block corner, in dramatic play, in the sand area, the teacher puts a limit on the destruction of others' creations, but not of one's own.

Adults serve as an emotional base for children, understanding the unique challenges of each child in their care.

Second, *the psychosocial needs of children at different developmental stages tell teachers what role they need to play in guidance.* For instance, infants are classified in Erikson's first stage: *trust and mistrust.* Research on attachment (Ainsworth, 1982; Bowlby, 1969) indicates that infants are genetically wired to form attachments to the people who care for them. As discussed earlier (see Chapter 1, "Understanding Children and Behavior"), they signal adults very early on and continue to build relationships with those who respond most sensitively. Whether a child develops a secure or insecure attachment depends on the adult giving responsive feedback. Infants need adults to pay attention to their signals, interpret them accurately, and respond with appropriate feedback. As babies grow, this attachment is expressed as fear of strangers and preference for those primary adults, as the ideas and research of Bowlby and Ainsworth have amply proven and Chapter 5 discusses further.

A good example of how to apply Eriksonian theory to children's real behavior comes in the case of Beth and Janine. When Janine sees the necklace, she first thinks like a toddler ("I want it; I'll take it"). She then realizes that if she acted on that idea, she would get into trouble, and stops herself. Her new ideas—bribery, then name-calling, and finally grabbing—are all part of the seesaw of initiative versus guilt. A teacher can intervene effectively by stopping the chase, holding the beads, and getting the two children to tell what they want and how they feel. If Janine feels understood by her teacher ("You really like that necklace . . . You were trying to think of some ways to get a turn") she is then more able to hear and think up some other ideas ("Can I wear it for five minutes, *please*? You can have a turn with my magnet toy.").

Third, *an Eriksonian teacher plans programs that include children's ideas.* In terms of discipline methods, they employ a problem-solving method of resolving interpersonal differences in which the children brainstorm their own good ideas for how to deal with the conflict. An example of including children's thoughts illustrates the school-aged challenge of *industry and inferiority.* Kindergarten and primary-grade children encounter new expectations, as well as novel opportunities. They find that they are going to and from school with less adult supervision, are expected to listen, to sit at a desk or table, to bring their own lunchbox, to read, to print, to add and subtract, to be out on the playground, to try a sport or club. There are so many things to try and feel useful about! Still, this profusion of new opportunities and expectations brings with it chances for feelings of inferiority and failure. "Can I do it?" and "I'm not sure" are heard along with "I can join in" and "I can make that." Because five to eight is also a time of increased peer involvement and a sense of privacy and self-containment, caring adults may need to work at keeping a child in close communication, so that feelings are shared and worries dealt with. Busy lives, high-paced programs, overcrowded classes, and/or impoverished conditions often discourage such times. A teacher with an Eriksonian framework is likely to involve the children in making the rules and deciding the consequences for misbehavior. *Reasonable* expectations are in order. Guidelines that are too slack or inconsistent do not allow children to feel useful or in control. At the same time, expectations that are too high create anxiety and anxious behavior. Eriksonian teachers keep track of the demands placed upon the children; allowing children to see the results of their actions is different from feeling overwhelmed or shamed into a sense of inferiority.

In conclusion, Erikson's psychosocial theory gives teachers a strong theoretical basis in paying close attention to the parent-child relationship and the child's culture as determinants of what is expected of the child. Eriksonian teachers plan discipline methods with the teacher-child relationship in mind, and are sensitive to the child's growing sense of self in terms of social interactions. In addition, Erikson's theory supports teachers in developing programs with elements of choice and free play. Finally, this theory states strongly that the teacher must be involved in a child's affective world, being an emotional base and a spokesperson for what is expected of the child at any particular age.

> **Think It Over**
>
> Do you remember what fun it was to knock down a tower or break apart a sandcastle? What was it like to look longingly at another child's toy, balloon, or lollipop? Did you ever just grab for it? Did any grownup in your life understand the thrill of such power, or were you admonished to "play nicely"? In Eriksonian theory, the balance of "taking initiative and doing what you want" and "going too far and feeling bad about it" is a natural part of a preschooler's psychosocial development. Adults may need to set the appropriate limit so the child learns the social rules, but they also need to be an understanding ally for the child.

Social Discipline Theory

Overview of the Theory

The social discipline model, which has been of particular interest in its application to guidance, stems from the social discipline or individual theory of Alfred Adler. Books written by Dreikurs (1990, 1991), Dinkmeyer (1989), and Nielsen (1987) all flow from Adler's work. This social theory holds that all behavior is purposeful and directed toward a goal of belonging, or social recognition. A child's outward behavior always emanates from this inner goal, and children's misbehavior and even neurotic behavior comes from this same wish to belong or to compensate for feeling inferior (a sense of not belonging). The social discipline model for dealing with children's behavior has the rationale of teaching children some form of social acceptance; teachers observe what children do, analyze what goals they are trying to reach, and show children how to belong.

Key Player: Alfred Adler

Alfred Adler was a disciple of Freud. Like Erikson, Adler gave psychodynamic theory his own interpretation. And like Erikson, Adler felt that it was the social rather than sexual aspects of experience that were of primary importance. His theory, that of individual psychology, concentrates on the individual as embedded in the social world, and as a positive agent for change. He believed that the central motivation of the human being is to belong and be accepted. Adler felt that every human being has the potential for being different, for changing behavior, for learning how to fit in. As Dreikurs and Cassell (1991) put it, Adlerian psychology has five basic premises:

1. *Humans are social beings and their main desire is to belong.* This is true for adults and children.
2. *All behavior is purposive.* To understand the behavior of another, one must know to which goal it is directed. If children misbehave, it indicates that they have wrong ideas about how to be significant.
3. *Humans are decision-making organisms.* They decide what they really want to do, often without being aware of it. They are not victims of forces such as heredity, the environment, or other outside influences.
4. *A human is a whole being who cannot be understood by some partial characteristics.* The whole is greater than the sum of its parts.
5. *We do not see reality as it is, but only as we perceive it, and our perception may be mistaken or biased.*

Children learn early a style of life that helps them feel like they belong or have some place in society. Adler believed that children are striving to reach their highest potential, and their notions about how to succeed determine whether their behavior becomes useful and socially acceptable or useless and destructive.

Key Player: Rudolf Dreikurs

Rudolf Dreikurs is probably the most well-known and prolific writer on the social discipline model. He has expanded and applied Adlerian psychology to the daily living struggles of children in their two most important social settings: the home and the school. Like Adler, Dreikurs contends that all behavior is for the purpose of belonging, and, optimistically, all children are capable of rational thought and of changing their own behavior and attitudes. Also like Adler, he believes that the educational setting must include a strong social aspect of learning; adults and peers need to interact with children and direct their ways of living, or redirect their mistaken goals.

Dreikurs gives specific instructions for how adults can learn about a child's goals and mistaken beliefs, and offers strategies for redirecting mistaken goals and using the group (class, gang, family) to get the child to learn. Teachers and parents play an active role in helping children learn their place in life. Table 2.2 on page 40 charts young children's typical misbehaviors, teachers' reactions, the questions to diagnose the problem, and corrective procedures in Dreikurs' social discipline model.

Table 2.2

The What and Why of Children's Misbehavior . . . and What to Do

Dreikurs' social discipline model gives guidelines for how to correct children's misbehavior. By observing a child and paying attention to one's own reaction, a teacher can ask important questions and diagnose the child's problem behavior. This process guides the teacher's response and gives important clues about how to help the child.

Child's Behavior	Teacher's Reaction	Questions to Ask	How to Proceed
Nuisance	*Annoyed*	*Goal: Attention*	*Never give attention when child demands it*
Show-off	Does for child	"Could it be that you want special attention?"	Ignore the misbehavior
Clown	Reminds, nags		Do not show annoyance
			Be firm
		"Do you want me to do something special for you?"	Give lots of attention at any other time
Stubborn	*Defeated*	*Goal: Power*	*Don't fight, don't give in*
Argues	He can't do this to me.	"Could it be that you want your own way?"	Recognize/admit the child has power
Wants to be Boss			Avoid power struggle
Temper tantrums	I won't let her get away with this.	"Do you want to be the boss?"	Give power where child can be productive
Tells lies			Respect child, ask for her help
Does opposite to instructions			Take your sails out of his wind
Vicious	*Deeply hurt*	*Goal: Revenge*	*Never say/act hurt*
Sullen	Outraged	"Could it be that you want to hurt me?"	Apply natural consequences
Defiant	Dislikes child		Do the unexpected
		"Could it be that you want to hurt others/get even?"	Persuade child that she is liked
	How can I get back at her?		Use group encouragement/get a buddy
Hopeless	*Helpless*	*Goal: Inadequacy*	*Encourage when he makes mistakes*
Gives up	Throws up hands	"Could it be that you want to be left alone?"	Praise her efforts
Rarely participates	Don't know what to do with her		Make him feel worthwhile
Inferiority complex		"Could it be that you feel stupid and don't want people to know?"	Say, "I do not give up with you."
			Get class helpers.

(Reprinted with permission from Dreikurs and Cassell, 1991)

If our main goal in life is to belong, then striving for social acceptance plays a major part in our early interactions. Let's look at Zachary and Amal from our chapter opening. As preschool children, they have very different experiences. Zachary is outgoing and flexible, so his actions are quickly accepted by the other children and teachers. Amal is less trusting, and is irritable with the tension that comes with uncertainty. She tries grabbing what she wants, or taking over the play when she wants to join. Children protest, the teacher frowns, and Amal feels unsuccessful in obtaining acceptance. These experiences start a pattern of misbehavior. She then tries to fulfill the need to belong and feel important by being annoying, destructive, hostile, even helpless, in the mistaken belief that this can gain her acceptance. This misbehaving child, claims Dreikurs, is only a discouraged child trying to find her place. The subconscious goals that motivate misbehavior are attention, power, revenge, and inadequacy (or helplessness).

To recognize which goal the child is using, teachers have to understand the meaning of the behavior. Teachers use a four-step process to determine which of the four mistaken goals is motivating the child:

1. Observing
2. Being psychologically sensitive to your own reactions to the behavior
3. Asking the child questions
4. Making some directive statements to the child (confronting the child with the four goals), and watching for the child's reaction

The teacher watches Amal carefully (Step 1). She sees that whenever she tries to help Amal get involved, so to show her another way to play, Amal gives up and withdraws. The teacher's first reaction is helplessness, that if Amal won't try there's nothing the teacher can do (Step 2). This makes the teacher wonder if Amal's mistaken goal is one of inadequacy, so she asks, "Could it be that you feel bad and don't think you can play with them?" (Step 3). Amal nods silently. Now the teacher keeps going, "It can be hard to know how to get started. Children often worry that the others will say 'You can't play.' You are someone with lots of good ideas, and you can have fun. I don't give up on you; I think together we can figure out how to get you playing with them. Let's ask Zachary to show you how to use the gear toy" (Step 4). Having observed the child and her own reactions, the teacher finds out Amal's mistaken belief, and applies the corrective techniques that correspond to the child's mistaken belief that is motivating the misbehavior.

Applying the Theory to Discipline

Both Adler and Dreikurs believed that the teacher and parent play a crucial role in helping children learn both how to behave and how to feel accepted in society. Dinkmeyer and McKay (1989) have applied this model to the development of children's self-esteem, both at home and in classrooms, noting that these are the "techniques of encouragement." Nelsen (1987) advocates this approach as one of "positive discipline." Wolfgang and Glickman (1995) describe the theory as using several important tools to change and improve children's behavior.

For those working in early childhood education, the theory applies to guidance and discipline in several ways. First, all children are guided by the teacher, who observes the behavior closely. This is a fundamental principle of good early childhood teaching practices and is the basis for developing programs that meet children's individual needs. Second, everyone's capacity to learn and change is based on the optimistic premise that young children are *trying*—to learn, to do it right, to go forward. Children's misbehavior is taken as a clue to their thoughts, ideas, and attitudes, not a sign that they are bad or vicious people. The teacher's job is to understand the child, and use discipline techniques that avoid criticism or demeaning actions. Rather, they involve the child and actively and directly work with the child in a friendly relationship. Third, the techniques for diagnosing children's behavior include the child, the teacher, and the setting. Taking all these into consideration is a holistic, integrated approach, which acknowledges the ways children perceive and learn.

Children's behavior is taken as a clue to their thoughts and attitudes, not a sign that they are bad.

Teachers adapt these social discipline techniques depending on the age of the children. The very young child who has little or no language comprehension is still given positive guidance through the behavioral theory techniques of observation, modeling, and reinforcement. Physical intervention and isolation are used rarely and only as a logical consequence (such as removing a child in times of danger to self or others), not as a form of punishment that would drive a child away from social involvement. Chapter 3 elaborates on all techniques.

The preschool child is guided with the teacher's involvement through questions and closeness, thus pairing a cognitive approach (see the section on Cognitive-Developmental Theory) with a psychosocial one. Asking a question, "Could it be that you want to be the boss? To hurt them?" helps focus the children's attention first on themselves, an approach that validates the essential egocentric nature of this age. Reinforcement through natural and logical consequences lets children learn first-hand what happens as a result of their behavior, avoiding the autocratic punishments that alienate children and often end in hostility and defiance.

Children in kindergarten and the early elementary years look to teachers for encouragement, as they begin to focus on the end-product of their efforts. Encouragement emphasizes improvement rather than perfection, and stresses the child's developing an internal sense of how to behave. Two cognitive theories—Bandura's modeling and Vygotsky's zone of proximal development—are at work in this psychodynamic-like model. Rather than praise, too much of which can make a child dependent on the teacher, primary children learn behavior that achieves the social recognition of cooperating with and considering others. Classrooms and programs for this age can be arranged to include experiences in democratic and participatory living. Each of the discipline techniques noted here—physical intervention, questions and closeness, natural and logical consequences, reinforcement, and encouragement—are all described at length in Chapter 3.

Cognitive-Developmental Theory

Overview of the Theory

A third major tradition in the study of human psychology is the *cognitive-developmental approach* of Jean Piaget and his followers. Although most explanations of development, particularly in guidance, emphasize relationships with people rather than interactions with objects, cognitive-developmental theorists emphasize the development of how children think. This line of thought includes children's interactions (with people and with objects). Two forces are at work, these theorists claim. Of primary importance is the active nature of the child. Children experience the world and do something with it; that is, they *construct* a reality based on what happens to them, and they continually make adaptations to this knowledge as they experience more. The second force is equally strong: the development of cognitive structures, which is determined by maturation. Basic processes and internal structures affect the child's construction of a world view, and these change with time because the body and brain mature.

Key Player: Jean Piaget

Few individuals have influenced the area of child development as has Jean Piaget, the central figure in cognitive-developmental theory. Struck by the great regularities in the development of children's thinking and their mistakes, Piaget's detailed observations and consequent theories have transformed our knowledge of children's thinking and behaving.

At its core, Piaget's theory sets forth that the child is an adaptive organism, changing with the environmental conditions and the child's own experiences. Children are active, not passive, learners, constantly attempting to figure out their world to understand and live in it. Therefore, children explore, manipulate, and reach out to objects and people.

Additionally, Piaget proposes that children think sequentially, their knowledge growing in stages. Using several thinking processes, children work on a series of understandings or "theories" of how the world operates. Piaget believed that humans are born with certain built-in strategies for thinking, which change as they grow. These built-in strategies affect their encounters with common environmental conditions. What we expect children to do changes over time. All children seem to discover the same kinds of elements about their world, make the same sorts of mistakes, and arrive at the same solutions. For example, preschoolers tell you that if you pour water from a short, fat glass into a tall, thin one, there is now more water. They see the water level is higher in the thin glass than it was in the fat glass. By seven years of age, children now know there is still the same amount of water in either glass. A two-year-old cannot find her teddy bear, because her method of looking is haphazard and erratic. Her nine-year-old sister, however, is much more systematic, retracing her steps or looking in one room after another. Table 2.3 explains Piaget's stages of thinking in the early years.

Table 2.3

Piaget's Stages of Thinking in the Early Years

Piaget's theory of cognitive development shows a sequence of development in children's thinking. These stages will determine children's capacity to think about the world, other people, and how to behave.

Age	*Stage*	*Characteristics and Guidance Implications*
Birth to two	Sensorimotor	"Touch, taste": infant and toddler use all senses to explore and learn about the world
		"Out of sight, out of mind": infant, until nine to twelve months, has no object permanence
		"See it, grab it": infant and toddler work to coordinate the perceptual and motor functions

Guidance Implications: Allow child to explore with all senses; be responsive to infant both verbally and in your actions; use redirection.

Two to six	Preoperational	Acquisition of language
		Symbolic behavior: pretend play with objects and people; lines and dots stand for words
		"Me do it, I want it": child has an *egocentric* viewpoint, sees self as center of things, difficult to understand others' opinions.
		Judgments made on appearance: if it *looks* like more, then it *is* more.
		Difficulty in thinking about two concepts simultaneously: "If I share, then it won't still be mine." "You can't be my friend and his friend at the same time."
		Moral absolutists: rules are fixed, unchangeable
		"Imminent justice": punishment inevitably follows from breaking a rule; good/bad judged by consequences more than intent

Guidance Implications: Give child just a few rules (to keep self safe, to care for others' bodies and feelings, to keep from destructiveness); establish interactive relationship to become a trusted ally and guide; encourage children's use of language to communicate feelings and wants.

Six to twelve	Concrete Operational	Can "conserve": understands that quantity, size, etc., will remain the same no matter how they may be arranged.
		Can handle several ideas at the same time: you can still be my friend even though you are playing with someone else.
		Less egocentric: can apply some logical thinking to a situation.

(continued)

Table 2.3   (Continued)

Age	Stage	Characteristics and Guidance Implications
Six to twelve	Concrete Operational	More sociocentric: peers become important, consideration of fairness, group rules.
		Autonomous morality: social rules are acceptable but are seen as more arbitrary, subject to change, broken rules not always punished.
		Morality of reciprocity: rules made by agreement or trade; intention or motive makes a difference in judging morality of an action.
		Guidance Implications: Begin with children's articulation of their feelings and viewpoint, then lead to understand others'; establish group "rules" that include consequences; work on children's negotiation skills.

Key Player: Lev Vygotsky

Cognitive theory has undergone some changes and reinterpretations in recent years. Bandura's social cognitive theory adds behavioral and modeling aspects to the theory. Vygotsky, a Russian psychologist from the first half of the century, has been rediscovered for his beliefs in how language and culture affect cognitive development.

To Vygotsky, language is crucial for the development of thinking. In the form of private speech, it guides children as they learn to think through what they do. We hear these mutterings often in the younger ages, particularly in two- to four-year olds. Vygotsky claimed that inner speech simply becomes inaudible with age, and is a positive factor with difficult tasks and in social interaction with others.

According to Vygotsky, children of any age are faced with problems they may be on the verge of solving, but are just beyond their grasp. With some structure from another, particularly an adult, a child can pick up clues to figuring it out, and can be led to keep on trying. The area where children cannot solve something on their own but can be successful with some guidance is called the *zone of proximal development*. With a teacher, older friend, or parent, a child is tutored toward success.

Social interaction offers just the sorts of problems that put the child in a zone of proximal development. The younger sister with the lost teddy bear might be helped to find it if the older sister walked her through the house, or if her dad asked her questions about where she had it. Preschoolers trying to decide who gets to play with a favored toy could use a teacher's guidance in brainstorming ways to share or take turns. Many elementary schools now offer a kind of "buddy" program, where older children have a special kindergartner or first grader with whom they read, play, or engage in other activities. The role of private speech fits into the notion of the zone of proximal development, as the older person uses verbal prompts to guide the child. By reducing these prompts as the child takes over, the guide thus helps the child's reach go beyond the normal grasp, and develop new solutions and thinking skills.

> **_Try It_** If you teach in a program with "family age grouping" or for multiple ages, try using a "buddy plan" or "each one, teach one" for a project. For instance, pair readers with nonreaders and have the two choose a picture book. After reading the story, the reader then turns the pages while the nonreader re-tells it. Then the two of them together can "Read-Tell" the story to the whole group. Try your plan with an interpersonal problem. Tell the whole group, "Here's a problem some children had. They got a new piece of equipment in the playyard, and all of the children want to be on it at once. There have been several fights, hurt feelings, and even some injuries." Now, divide the children into pairs, with class leaders or master players partnered with nonplayers or socially inept children. Ask them to think of what the children could do, and then have the partners tell their ideas for you to list with the kids together.

Key Player: Lawrence Kohlberg

Another interpretation of children's stages of thinking comes in developing ideas of right and wrong. In fact, Piaget himself described stages in children's moral reasoning, with the very young child considered premoral, those from three to six being "moral realists" in a world of absolute and fixed rules, and the school-aged child moving into autonomous reality, in which children accept social rules but see them as more arbitrary and changeable.

Lawrence Kohlberg's work expanded and overlapped that of Piaget, and extends into adolescence and adulthood as well, although in this book we will look only at the first stages as they relate to young children. Kohlberg began by developing a series of dilemmas, stories with someone in difficult circumstances, and asked children to state what the person should do and why.

Kohlberg's levels of moral development have undergone considerable scrutiny. Over a thousand studies have been conducted to test the validity of the theory, and strong criticism abounds. Several other models have been posed in recent years. Nancy Eisenberg (1986) proposes a model of Prosocial Reasoning, insisting that most of Kohlberg's dilemmas were about wrongdoing rather than on children's reasoning around doing good. William Damon (1980) describes two components of moral reasoning, justice and authority, as being the key elements in how children develop levels of judgment about what is fair and why a person should obey. Carol Gilligan (1982) points out the value judgments made in Kohlberg's stages, contending that the two sexes are socialized differently and thus develop slightly different moralities.

Nonetheless, it can still be said with some certainty that there seems to be a sequence to the development of moral reasoning. The early stages seem dominant in the early childhood years. Young children defer to the superior power of adults or older children, doing right so that they won't get into trouble, or because bigger and stronger people can tell them what to do. As children mature in elementary school, they may move to a notion of doing something to satisfy your own needs; doing good because you want to, and it can get you something you want. Children seem to move from a self-centered orientation to a more "other-centered" or at least "others-considered" viewpoint with age and experience. Cross-cultural research indicates this same pattern of development, although the rate and "endpoint" of moral reasoning varies. There does seem to be a clear set of stages in the development of moral reasoning, and this appears universal.

Applying the Theory to Discipline

The theories of Piaget, Vygotsky, and Kohlberg offer important implications for teachers of young children. Let us consider the general points of these three together and how they affect educational practice.

- *The theory helps teachers realize that changes in a person's behavior are closely attached to a person's knowledge.* A child is in the process of learning and acquiring knowledge gradually and constantly. Children are actively involved in their own development. Knowledge is acquired as a result of the interaction between the child and the environment. Children learn, think, and behave as a result of certain inborn, cognitive structures that are determined by heredity and maturation. In guidance terms, we need to know the child's developmental level to match our techniques with their understanding. Furthermore, children need both experience and knowledge (information, reasoning, and the like) to become more self-disciplined.

- *Teachers of young children need to plan programs that give children much "food for thought."* A rich physical environment should also be supported by an engaging "Thinking-Doing-Talking-Interacting" environment. Children need plenty of time to explore their own reality, especially through play, both spontaneous and planned. Most important, teachers with a developmental viewpoint are ready to deal with the particular kinds of behaviors that correspond to various stages of development. In guidance terms, teachers need to give children reasons for why they are expected to behave, to ask children's opinions and ideas for how to solve discipline problems, and to allow children to have a say in what happens to them both when they behave well and misbehave.

- *Very young children (under three) are likely to concentrate their energies on developing the senses and motor skills.* Grabbing, hair-pulling, and biting are as common as putting everything into the mouth or pulling and pushing themselves and objects around the room and yard. Children begin to judge and change their actions based on what adults do about it. In guidance terms, a child relies on adults' responses to learn about right and wrong. For example, a child needs to notice, "When I grab his hair, a grown-up takes my hand away, and shows me 'Gentle touching.' Again and again, they smile when I do the gentle part."

- *The preschool child is gradually acquiring language, and "egocentric thinking" is the hallmark of this age.* These children see the world from their own viewpoint, and are best guided if teachers can help the child articulate this viewpoint before being asked to listen to another's. The child who sees the teacher as someone who listens and understands how it is for him, rather than being told what to do or lectured, will then be able to generate other ways to get what he wants, or help someone feel better, or even comply with adult demands. In guidance terms, preschool children need clear limits and guidelines, as with the very young child, and also need to be encouraged to see what might be fair, helpful, a "good deal."

- *In the primary years, children become more able to handle several ideas at once.* They begin to understand other points of view, moving out of total egocentric thought toward a more sociocentric outlook. The family, classroom, and small group become important. Children will start to do something to live up to others' expectations. Friendships matter, and how one looks in the eyes of one's classmates becomes important. Teachers who develop positive relationships with children can see them trying to do what the teacher thinks is right. At the same time, the "class clown" or "outcast" develops, and it is the adults' challenge to help each child develop a sense of interpersonal connection. In guidance terms, teachers elicit children's opinions and ideas about social and discipline problems that encourage the development of moral reasoning beyond simply one's own needs. Classroom problems become vehicles for seeing more than one person's viewpoint.

- *Children learn a tremendous amount from others.* Children learn from direct interaction with other children, as well as from older children as guides. They can learn to stretch mentally if given encouragement and some strategies from teachers and parents. In guidance terms, we plan our discipline methods that involve the child or group of children rather than implementing a "top-down" or "because I say so" set of rules.

Try It   To find out what your children think about what is right and wrong, try some scenarios with them. Best used at a small or large group time, write up these situations on cards that can be drawn out of a hat, or with sketches that can be "read" without words. Finding some that really happen in your program (names changed to protect the innocent, and guilty!) is particularly relevant, but make up some of your own. *For instance:* Megan finds some money on the bus. She is saving for a special toy and this money will give her enough to buy it. What should she do? *Another idea might be:* Tyrone and James come to school through the back gate. Some days big kids tease them. It's scary, and the worst thing is the big kids grab their lunches and take whatever they want. James and Tyrone don't like it, but the kids say if they tell, they'll really get it. What should they do? Ask the kids to tell you how they feel, what they think the kids should do, and what might happen by following that advice. See what level of moral development the children seem to have, and listen for how they make their decisions. Be ready to show them the plausible results of their ideas and to share with them the reasoning behind some of your own.

In conclusion, Cognitive-Developmental theory gives teachers a strong theoretical basis in paying close attention to the child's emerging thinking and learning. In addition, this theory supports teachers in developing programs with elements of choice and free play, with a rich environment for active manipulation and a set of interpersonal experiences that help children learn about right and wrong.

Finally, teachers and parents can be most helpful if they are aware that all children have a capacity for reason within their particular stage of development.

Children learn a tremendous amount from others, and will acquire the behaviors based on what they see and what is valued by the culture in which they live.

Behaviorist Theory

Overview of Theory

Behaviorist theory is a *learning* theory, as opposed to a developmental theory such as Erikson's or Piaget's. Developed during the 1920s, behaviorism is considered more pragmatic and objective than psychodynamic theory. What is known today as "behaviorism" begins with the seventeenth century philosopher John Locke's notion that a child is born with a "clean slate," a *tabula rasa* on which events and experiences are written throughout life.

Behaviorist theory holds that the conditions of those events determine all important human behavior; that learning is the main determinant of behavior.

In contrast to psychodynamic theory, most behaviorists insist that only behavior can be treated, not feelings or internal states. They posit that learning takes place when a person interacts with the environment, and through experience, behavior is modified or changed. The learning comes from outside the learner: the environment shapes the person by controlling or modifying the experiences through the rewarding and reinforcing of explicit behaviors.

Behaviorist theory tells teachers to pay close attention to the environment. The environment includes the physical setup (such as the arrangement of furniture and materials or the positioning of playground equipment) and careful planning of the daily schedule. Small, intimate spaces beckon children in for quieter play; a certain number of chairs at the table indicates how many people can fit there; a long hallway or open area invites running. By taking these ideas into account, teachers acknowledge that the external environment will affect children's behavior. Chapter 3 details the relationship between the physical and temporal environment and children's behavior.

In behaviorist theory, three types of learning occur: classical conditioning, operant conditioning, and observational learning or modeling. The first two are based on the idea that learning is mostly the development of habit and that people learn through a series of associations, forming a connection between a stimulus and response that did not exist before. The third is based on a social approach of learning through observation and imitation.

Key Player: B. F. Skinner

Early behavioral theorists, Pavlov and Watson, experimented with *classical conditioning,* using stimulus and response associations, most notably chronicled in the example of the dog who is taught to salivate at the sound of a bell. The organism (dog) is a passive participant whose behavior is changed by an external stimulus. Watson highlighted the effect of purpose, intent, and control of the environment as the criteria for changing behavior. Teachers, he would have said, control the environment so as to control children's behavior. Behaviorists then noted that behavior which leads to satisfying results tends to be repeated. This reinforcement theory uses rewards and punishments to support or eliminate a specific action. If teachers want children to "do good," they need to reward those good behaviors so that the children will do them more. Any behavior a teacher doesn't like can be extinguished by ignoring or with punishment.

B. F. Skinner was the foremost speaker for behaviorism and differed from his colleagues in his belief that human emotion and motivation are very much related to human behavior. He advocated positive reinforcement as far more humane and effective than punishment. His principles of *operant conditioning* focus on the response rather than on the stimulus. The process that makes it more likely that a behavior will reoccur is called *reinforcement,* and the stimulus that increases the likelihood of repeated behavior is called a *reinforcer.* Most people are likely to increase what gives them pleasure (food, attention) and decrease what gives them displeasure (punishment, pain, withdrawal of food or attention). The behaviorist can influence the person's behavior by controlling the reinforcement.

Reinforcers can be positive, negative, or nonreinforcing. A *negative reinforcer* is removal of an unpleasant stimulus as a result of some particular behavior. Madeleine consistently interrupts circle time, even though it is one of her favorite activities. Before conditioning, she is told that if she talks to her neighbors and shouts answers at the teacher, she will be asked to leave the circle. When she begins to shout, she is told to leave, and to return when she can sing without interrupting (negative reinforcement). She can end the negative reinforcement—her isolation from the group—by controlling her own behavior. A *positive reinforcer* is something that increases the likelihood of the desired response (praise, attention). During the conditioning period, Madeleine is praised whenever she pays attention, sings along with the group, and keeps her hands off those around her. A third way to respond to Madeleine is with *nonreinforcement.* This is the deliberate withholding of a reinforcer, a planned refusal to pay attention to a child during an episode of undesirable behavior. Ignoring Madeleine's outbursts would be an example of nonreinforcement, and should tend to diminish the behavior.

There is a distinct difference between a negative reinforcer and punishment. *Punishment* is an unpleasant action designed to make the behavior *less* likely to occur. If Madeleine were spanked when she shouted, the shouting would be the punished behavior and she probably would shout less. However, if leaving the group is the result of the shouting, she tries to stop shouting to increase the likelihood of staying at circle time. Negative reinforcers thus *increase* the chance of the desired behavior being repeated (not shouting) and removes attention from the less desirable behavior (shouting).

It is important to note here that not all reinforcements are external. Some actions are intrinsically rewarding to a child. Intrinsic reinforcements of satisfaction (in completing an assignment), pride (in one's creation), pleasure (in working cooperatively with a friend or group), and discovery (in creating a new color by mixing other colors together) are powerful reinforcements, and have implications for teachers and classroom use. One behaviorist who considered the internal world of the child or learner was Albert Bandura.

Key Player: Albert Bandura

Bandura takes the behaviorist approach along another track, called *social learning theory.* In a departure from traditional behaviorists, Bandura believes that reinforcement is not always a necessary component for learning. Children learn many things for which they are not reinforced and, in fact, learn many behaviors by watching and observing others and then imitating those behaviors. The major contribution of this theory is the concept of *modeling,* or observational learning (see Chapter 1). *Learning and teaching by example* are powerful tools for the teacher, and have serious implications for parents as well. Children are more likely to imitate a model whom they perceive as being similar to themselves, having status, and being nurturant, helpful, and affectionate (Bandura, 1973; Harris & Liebert, 1992). This includes television and cartoon characters as well as the real-life models of parents, caregivers, teachers, and peers. Bandura's early work on the effects of modeling on aggression in the preschooler is discussed in Chapter 6.

If children learn behaviors from observing others, what do you think children will learn from watching this event?

More recently, Bandura (1986) has emphasized Piagetian or cognitive aspects of the child's thinking and reasoning capacities. He now labels this the *social-cognitive theory,* combining the reinforcement aspects of the environment on behavior and the notion that behavior comes from the child's early social and cognitive experiences. This newer approach acknowledges children as active participants whose "social experience shape their expectations—their 'inner working model' of themselves—which, in turn, shape how they process subsequent social experiences" (Youngblade & Belsky, 1990). The early childhood experiences create the image children have of themselves, which is further reinforced by positive or negative interactions with parents, teachers, and peers. In other words, the social skills children learn during the preschool years have been shaped by interactions with people and the environment. These determine how children experience the world in later life, how they choose friends, share materials and ideas, and get along with others. Early behaviors tend to maintain themselves (Schickedanz et al., 1993).

Applying the Theory to Discipline

The implications of behaviorist theory for teachers are far-reaching. Behaviorist theories make a strong case for the ways the environment influences our behavior. A teacher can use this knowledge to arrange all aspects of the environment in such a way that positive learning is enhanced, or can ignore the physical surroundings or daily schedule and see the results. Close attention to the arrangement of furniture, materials, and daily schedule pays off (See Chapter 3).

Using behavioral techniques, adults can influence changes in children's behavior. That is very good news for teachers and parents! Adults can set up a structure that helps children learn new behaviors and ways to respond to the environment. Together, teacher and child actively participate in helping children succeed. For instance, the teachers in Suneela's after-school program at first simply told Suneela and her classmates to "slow down" and "calm yourselves" and "take it easy." They then realized that they were inadvertently reinforcing the unruly behaviors they were trying to curb. They then rearranged the environment.

Instead of . . .	They did this . . .
Funneling all the children into a tight space . . .	Opened both doors to the room as entrances.
Standing them in line to sign in . . .	Offered the sign-in sheet at the snack table later.

Starting with a grouptime to tell about the day . . .	Made a "Choice Chart" posted at the kids' cubbies.
Telling them what not to do . . .	Gave "good goin' " slips to all who were focused and constructive, to be turned in at the day's end in exchange for turns at the "grab-a-toy" basket.
Having a homework time first thing . . .	Made "Homework Haven" the activity right after snack, later in the afternoon.

Table 2.4 gives examples of how using behaviorist techniques increases desirable behavior and decreases what is undesirable.

Still, there are problems with applying behaviorist theory. Application of behaviorist theory requires precision in defining the exact nature of the behavior desired and keeping a factual account of the child's progress. This is hard to do, but it is essential to be effective. Otherwise, it is easy to have an emotional response that interferes with your ability to proceed without bias about the amount of improvement the child has made or needs to make.

Another problem with behaviorist guidance techniques is that adults sometimes use reinforcements that are meaningless to children. For instance, suppose you want to get kids to stop tearing around the classroom, and you decide to try some reinforcement. You decide to frown at the children when they run and praise the children when they walk. After a week, your facial muscles are tired, but the behavior hasn't changed. It turns out that these particular three-year-olds are so busy running that they are (1) somewhat unaware of your smiling and frowning in the first place, and (2) not particularly interested in your emotional reactions in general. Smiling is a social reinforcement and requires that the child want or like the smile and approval; a frown is a social negative reinforcer and a child would have to feel badly about seeing it, and thus want to avoid getting frowned at. If these young children are not especially attached or attentive to you, your approval (or disapproval) won't be a reinforcer. You need to think more about these particular children: what "turns them on"? What would they want to avoid? In this case, getting them to stop and retrace their steps with "walking feet," rearranging the environment to eliminate a runway, or a redirection back outdoors where you want running to occur might be more effective at changing their behavior.

Moreover, good observational skills are necessary for all early childhood teachers, and are used in a behavior modification approach. All teach-

Table 2.4

Behaviorist Techniques for Guidance

Behaviorist theory offers several helpful discipline techniques to increase desirable behaviors and decrease undesirable ones.

Technique	Definition	Example
Cueing	A reminder to the child before the behavior occurs.	"Madeleine, on that last song you almost yelled. Remember how you want to use your voice when you sing."
Ignoring	Nonreinforcement to remove the trivial, small annoyances from daily interactions.	Juan, a chronic whiner, is ignored when he whines; when he doesn't, you give full and positive attention, saying, "Juan it's so easy for me to listen to your great, full voice."
Targeting one behavior	A focus on only one bothersome behavior prevents a teacher from constantly admonishing a child and perceiving that child as more difficult than is the case.	A teacher decides to focus on Lew's hitting other children as the primary behavior to address, and ignore his dawdling at snack time or hoarding all the Legos™ for the time being.
Shaping	The reinforcement of small steps toward a desired behavior.	If the goal is to help Gina participate in a group game, the teacher begins by reinforcing watching others play, then for walking near the children playing, then encouraging her to do it with a friend (or the teacher), then choosing to do it herself.
Modeling	The application of a model as example to be observed and imitated.	Adults and other children serve this function. A teacher helps Eben learn table manners by using them herself, and drawing his attention to other children when they use a napkin, pass the snack plate, chew with their mouths closed.

ers do not necessarily have these skills, and considerable effort may be needed to train oneself to be an accurate and objective observer. With poor observation comes either an overreaction or an ineffective technique that results in teacher frustration, such as the three-year-old runners. Table 2.4 describes some of the observation techniques teachers need to use behaviorist theory well.

Finally, overreliance on behaviorist techniques may backfire. If children are doing things that are intrinsically interesting to them and are given external reinforcers (such as rewards), they may end up only doing those things for the reward, and not for the internal pleasure or satisfaction of

Alternative Approaches

Daniel is having trouble following the rules about not hurting others, and generally in developing self-control. As an older preschooler, he is still prone to violent outbursts, usually against other classmates who either won't do what he wants or give him what he demands. Daniel is a challenge for teachers, who find themselves frustrated and exhausted by his behavior. What theoretical model best advises teachers what to do?

Point:

The *cognitive-developmental view,* which has dominated much of the thinking about early childhood, gives one idea about how to understand children's antisocial behavior. Piaget and Kohlberg both concluded in the 1960s and 1970s that children's moral behavior paralleled the development of logical reasoning and their ability to engage in social perspective-taking. Because young children are still relatively incompetent at following adult logical explanations and are still quite egocentric, it naturally follows that they will have a poor grasp of social rules. Reason, claim those of the cognitive-developmental tradition, is the key point of moral development and is learned later in childhood. This view tells teachers that children cannot be expected to understand rules very well, and won't be able to see how grabbing or hitting hurts someone else.

Furthermore, the Piagetian model of learning champions hands-on, concrete experiences. In the social realm, teachers are advised to give children plenty of time for peer interaction and, contrary to Eriksonian or humanist opinion, to stay relatively uninvolved. Finally, in direct opposition to behaviorism, this approach advocates that teachers avoid praise (as well as punishment) and allow children to construct their own path of moral development.

From this viewpoint, Daniel cannot be "taught" morality about the right/wrong of hitting others. Teachers should redirect him to other activi-

having done something (Deci & Ryan, 1985). Children who are used to getting a reward for certain behaviors may become dependent upon such rewards, becoming other-directed and not self-reliant.

Still, the interactive nature of social cognitive theory has implications for guidance. We can ask children to become responsible for their own ac-

ties, and encourage his peers to respond to him directly when he bothers them. Daniel will learn over time to incorporate their reactions into his developing sense of morality.

Counterpoint:

A *psychodynamic-humanistic view* offers another way to look at both Daniel's behavior and teachers' responses. Children develop an awareness of others' feelings and thoughts early in life. Witness very young children's attempts to comfort someone in distress, offering a blanket or patting them. Preschoolers often point out others' transgressions, evidence of some social awareness of right and wrong. School-age children and some preschoolers can demonstrate their social competence by generating ideas to resolve interpersonal conflicts.

This viewpoint claims that emotion and conscience, rather than logical reasoning, cause a child to stop their own antisocial impulses. The child internalizes societal standards by being connected in meaningful ways with caring, consistent adults who teach empathy and social skills and point out wrongdoing and prohibitions.

From this viewpoint, Daniel can and should be taught how to behave and to control his behavior. In fact, adults play a central role in teaching him. Research in attachment and parenting styles confirms adult influence on children's social and moral behavior. When he hits, the teachers must emphasize the effect on others, without holding a grudge or being punitive. They teach him prosocial behaviors in many ways—by telling him, doing it themselves, and pointing out when others do so—and demonstrate to him how good it feels to engage in appropriate behavior. Daniel learns what to do and what not to do, and how each of those feels to himself and others as he develops a sense of morality and self-control.

tions as we see them observe, think, and reflect on the actions of others. We can guide them in ways so that they can bring their own resources and capabilities into play. Teacher responses to children's behavior can influence their images of themselves as being good or bad. A self-fulfilling prophecy can confirm the inner working model a child has for good or ill.

Specifically, teachers of young children who use a social cognitive behaviorist theory in their classrooms are sensitive to the public nature of discipline. When a child misbehaves, everyone is watching. For the child in question, the teacher's words and actions can either reinforce the notion that "I'm a good boy, but I did a bad thing" or the belief that "I'm a bad girl and don't do anything right." Moreover, every other child in the classroom wonders what will happen to them. The observing child learns by the example of the child who is being disciplined.

Many teachers use some of the behavioral theory techniques without acknowledging their origin. Such techniques are useful tools in classroom management. They influence children to modify their behavior because they place responsibility where it belongs: with the child. The adult who uses behaviorist techniques well carefully informs children of the results of their actions and trusts their willingness and ability to cooperate in a solution. The child's self-respect is left intact because no punishment or blame is used. By integrating these methods into a disciplinary approach, teachers can enlarge the child's capacity to become increasingly self-directed, rather than fearful of excessive punishment or overdependent on praise.

The convergence of behavioral and cognitive theories bodes well for educators. As Bee (1992) states, ". . . the cognitive elements in Bandura's theory seems to me to offer the possibility of creating . . . a genuinely *developmental* social learning theory." The closer relationship between development and behavior theories can give us a more accurate picture about how children grow and learn, as shown in the next theory about how children think.

Think It Over

Were you punished as a child? How did this occur? Did you stop doing those things to avoid future punishment? Or, were you ever ignored when you did something rude or interrupting? If so, your parents or teachers were using behaviorist discipline techniques, even if they didn't know it!

Ecological Theory

Overview of the Theory

One of the most significant changes in recent years has been the evolution of an ecological perspective regarding children's development. The trend is to view the child in the context of a broader family system rather than as a single entity, taking into account many of the forces that affect and influence the child's life. This approach emphasizes the interrelationship between children and their environments. Children are viewed not just as a part of a family system, but that family system is seen within the context of the neighborhood and community, and cultural and other institutional systems.

Learning and development take place through the complex interactions of these systems, each of which has an impact on the child. A more comprehensive and integrated picture of the child emerges, which includes the family's values, resources, structures, and needs (Bailey & Wolery, 1992).

Key Player: Uri Bronfenbrenner

A systematic approach that views individuals, families, and organizations as components of an organized network, which is interrelated and interdependent, is generally credited to the work of von Bertalanffy (Bailey & Wolery, 1992). It was Uri Bronfenbrenner's application of general systems theory to human development, however, that made this information accessible to educators. Just as we are developing a greater consciousness about the effects of our presence on the environment, we need to raise our awareness of the various influences that affect children's behavior. The thought here is that the child is influenced, directly and indirectly, by many factors. Bronfenbrenner (1979) describes four levels of the environment, nested within each other like a circle of rings. With the child at the center, these four are *the settings* in which the child spends a significant amount of time, such as home and school/child care; *the relationships* of those settings, such as parents and caregivers/teachers; *the societal structures*, such as church, neighborhood, and the media; and *the larger contexts* in which the other systems operate, such as federal laws that affect children, and societal attitudes, values, and ethics.

Applying the Theory to Discipline

The point made by the creation of these four levels of the environment is that systems operate at many levels and in a hierarchy, and the profound effect they have, directly or indirectly, on children's lives must be taken into account as we look at how children grow and develop. Those who work with young children must be aware of the ecological framework in which the child lives: the family unit, its emotional tone, the way in which control is exercised, and the quality and quantity of communication and cognitive stimulation (Bee, 1992).

The family is the main source of values for the child, and discipline practices outside that context (for instance, teachers) will be effective only to the extent that they fit in with the values, expectations, and attitudes established in the home. Thomas and Chess (1977) referred to this as the "goodness of fit," the respect for and understanding of the unique system composed of the child, the family, and the total ecology in which they live (Bailey & Wolery, 1992). This certainly underscores the need to have a working partnership with parents, and especially those families whose cultural and ethnic backgrounds differ from ours. Many issues that might fall into the category of discipline have different interpretations, depending on one's cultural background. In some instances hitting and slapping are considered acceptable; in others, they are taboo. In one case, a child looking adults in the eye is considered disrespectful; in another, it is considered polite to look at adults when they speak to you. To be truly effective teachers, we must be aware of some of these variations and how they might affect the life of the children in our classrooms. Chapter 4 explores some of these issues.

The ecological theory is a transactional model; that is, there is a reciprocal relationship within the various interactions and between people. The individual and the environment are interdependent; each affects the types of experiences and how they are perceived. Children are continually interacting with the environment, and their behavior is a result of not just the transactions, but how they perceive and understand these experiences. A child's behavior affects the adult and is, in turn, affected by the adult over a period of time. For instance, imagine that Zachary consistently disrupts the class. After awhile, you as his teacher may begin to feel inadequate or incompetent in classroom management skills, if you are unable to deal with him effectively. Your feelings may affect other areas of your interactions with him, and you may even mistakenly conclude that he has other social problems because he is so difficult with you. His successes in learning may be overlooked or not recognized because of his social behavior problems with the teacher.

Guidance and discipline that takes into account the behavior of only one of its participants will be less effective than exploring the several systems involved in the interaction between teacher and child. Trying to help Zachary's interrupting may fail if we do not consider "the bigger picture," such as the teacher's attitude toward the child, the child-teacher relationship, the child's own family setting, or the culture in which these two are operating (the school setting). Altering symptomatic behavior (class disruption) may fail if the child's ecological context is ignored.

Think It Over

Did you watch much television as a child? What were your favorite shows? Did you or your friends ever "mimic" them? Consider the "lessons" learned while watching, both what the show intended to do (keep your attention, even "sell" you a product) and what else you saw and tried as real behavior. How important were these images of the larger culture to you? In an ecological view, where did TV fall in influencing your behavior? What do you think of the role of television in children's lives and learning today?

Summary

Theories about learning, guidance, and interaction inform teachers about how to develop effective programs for and techniques with children. Major contributions are made from a diversity of theoretical disciplines:

Theory	*Key Player(s)*
Psychodynamic	Erikson
Social Discipline	Adler, Dreikurs, Nelsen
Cognitive-Developmental	Piaget, Vygotsky, & Kohlberg
Behaviorist	Skinner, Bandura
Ecological	Bronfenbrenner

Learning about developmental, learning, and guidance theories helps teachers apply valuable knowledge to their work with children. Five major theories inform educational thought about constructive guidance. The *psychodynamic theory* of Erik Erikson is a stage theory of psychosocial crises that children face as they mature. These stages affect the role a teacher plays in guiding children and spotlight the strong influence of the parent-child relationship and culture on children. *Social discipline theories* of Adler, Dreikurs, and Nielsen are grounded in the belief that children are trying to belong, and make decisions about what they do based on their own perceptions about reality. In striving for social acceptance, children misbehave in understandable ways; teachers are most effective if they match their discipline strategies with children's internal beliefs. The *cognitive-developmental theories* of Piaget, Vygotsky, and Kohlberg emphasize children's thinking structures, underscoring the active nature of the child in constructing a personal reality and rules. *Behaviorist theory* focuses on the conditions and environment. Skinner's emphasis on operant conditioning defines the role of reinforcement in changing children's behavior, whereas Bandura stresses learning by example, or modeling. Finally, the *ecological theory* of Bronfenbrenner emphasizes the interrelationships of a child's social systems: family, school, and community all play a part in how a child behaves.

Although there are important differences among the theories, all imply that teachers must take into consideration how children think and their efforts towards positive discipline.

Teachers who are well grounded in theory are better able to develop a repertoire of guidance techniques for the children in their care.

Observe and Apply

Do the psychosocial crises of Erikson's theory or the need to belong and be understood of Social Discipline theory make sense in real children? Observe a group of children for instances of high emotion—excitement, anger, sadness, surprise, fear, joy. Instead of immediately intervening to stop or correct a child's outburst, try saying, "It looks like you're feeling _____ (sad, glad, bad, mad)." Watch the child's reactions. What happens to the child? The tension of the moment? The outcome of the situation? Does your connecting with the child's feelings help the child or the situation? Acknowledging a child's feelings is part of Erikson's claim that the adult is an emotional base, and Social Discipline's theory that humans have a strong desire to belong and their place be understood. Of course, if a child is doing something harmful, be sure to stop the violence or destruction before talking about feelings.

Review Questions

1. Give three reasons why a teacher's personal philosophy of discipline should be based on theories of child development, learning, or guidance.

2. Name five theories that are major influences in the development of effective discipline strategies.

3. Match the theory/theorist with its guidance implication.

Erikson — The family is the main source of values and discipline practices for the child, and so must be taken into account by teachers.

Erikson — Teachers need to develop techniques of encouragement to guide children well.

Social Discipline — The psychosocial needs of children at different stages inform teacher guidance.

Social Discipline — If teachers believe a child is trying, they can see misbehavior as clues to a child's attitude.

Cognitive-Developmental — Children can change their behavior based on what they know.

Cognitive-Developmental — Adults serve as an emotional base and social mediators.

Behaviorist — Children are a clean slate upon which events are written.

Behaviorist — The environment influences behavior.

Ecological — The hallmark of preschool is "egocentric" thinking.

Bibliography

Adler, Alfred. *Understanding Human Nature.* New York: Premier Books, 1957.

Adler, Alfred. *The Education of Children.* Chicago: Henry Regnery, 1970.

Ainsworth, Mary. Attachment: retrospect and prospect. In C. M. Parkes & J. Stevenson-Hinde (Eds.), *The Place of Attachment in Human Behavior.* New York: Basic Books, 1982.

Bailey, Donald B., & Wolery, Mark. *Teaching Infants and Preschoolers with Disabilities.* New York: Charles Merrill, 1992.

Bandura, Albert. *Aggression: A Social Learning Analysis.* Englewood Cliffs, NJ: Prentice Hall, 1973.

Bandura, Albert. *Social Foundations of Thought and Action: A Social Cognitive Theory.* Englewood Cliffs, NJ: Prentice Hall, 1986.

Bee, Helen L. *The Developing Child.* New York: Harper Collins, 1992 (6th ed.).

Bowlby, John. *Attachment and Loss: Vol. 1. Attachment.* New York: Basic Books, 1969.

Bronfenbrenner, U. *The Ecology of Human Development.* Cambridge, MA: Harvard University Press, 1979.

Damon, William. "Patterns of Change in Children's Social Reasoning: A Two-Year Longitudinal Study." *Child Development,* 51 (1980): 1010–17.

Deci, E. L., & Ryan, R. M. *Intrinsic Motivation and Self-Determination in Human Behavior.* New York: Plenum Press, 1985.

Derman-Sparks, Louise. *Anti-Bias Curriculum: Tools for Empowering Children.* Washington, DC: National Association for the Education of Young Children, 1989.

Dinkmeyer, Don, & McKay, Gary D. *The Parent's Handbook: Systematic Training for Effective Parenting.* Circle Pines, MN: American Guidance Service, 1989.

Dreikurs, Rudolf, & Soltz, Vicki. *Children: The Challenge.* New York: Plume Books, 1990.

Dreikurs, Rudolf, & Cassel, Pearl. *Discipline Without Tears.* New York: Plume Books, 1991.

Eisenberg, Nancy. *Altruistic Emotion, Cognition, and Behavior.* Hillsdale, NJ: Erlmbaum, 1986.

Erikson, Erik. *Childhood and Society.* New York: WW Norton, 1963 (2nd ed.).

Gilligan, Carol. *In a Different Voice: Psychological Theory and Women's Development.* Cambridge, MA: Harvard University Press, 1982.

Gordon, Ann Miles, & Browne, Kathryn W., *Beginnings and Beyond: Foundations in Early Childhood Education.* Albany, NY: Delmar, 1996 (4th ed.).

Harris, Judith R., & Liebert, R. M. *Infant and Child: Development from Birth to Middle Childhood.* Englewood Cliffs, NJ: Prentice Hall, 1992.

Kohlberg, Lawrence. Stage and sequence: the cognitive-developmental approach to socialization. In D. A. Goslin (Ed.), *Handbook of Socialization Theory and Research.* Chicago, IL: 1969.

Nelsen, Jane. *Positive Discipline.* New York: Ballantine Books, 1987 (2nd ed.).

Schickedanz, Judith A., Hansen, Karen, & Forsyth, Peggy D. *Understanding Children.* Mountain View, CA: Mayfield Publishing, 1993 (2nd ed.).

Schickedanz, Judith, A. "Helping Children Develop Self-Control." *Childhood Education,* Wheaton, MD: Association for Childhood Education International, 1994.

Thomas, Alex, & Chess, Stella. *Temperament and Development.* New York: Bruner/Mazel, 1977.

Wolfgang, Charles H., & Glickman, Carl D. *Solving Discipline Problems: Strategies for Classroom Teachers.* Boston, MA: Allyn & Bacon, 1995 (3rd ed.).

Woolfolk, Anita E. *Educational Psychology.* Boston, MA: Allyn & Bacon, 1993 (5th ed.).

Youngblade, L., & Belsky, J. Social and emotional consequences of child maltreatment. In R. Hammerman & M. Hersen (Eds.), *Children at Risk: An Evaluation of Factors Contributing to Child Abuse and Neglect.* New York: Plenum Press, 1990.

3

Guidance Techniques

Profiles

At the art table, Yuriko and Cammy, both three, are seated across from each other, drawing pictures. Cammy looks around for a yellow marker and finding none, reaches over and grabs one out of Yuriko's hand. Yuriko looks startled but grabs it back from Cammy and begins coloring. Angered, Cammy picks up a black marker, reaches across the table, and scribbles on Yuriko's papers. Cries and howls of protest bring the teacher to the scene.

Roxeanne and Julian, both four-year-olds, are working steadily at a table with baskets of buttons, shells, and rocks. They have been sorting and counting for over twenty minutes. Reggie approaches the table, sits down, and reaches for one of the baskets. "We don't want you here," states Roxeanne. "Yeah, we don't want dummies here. Just buddies. Only real buddies can play here." Reggie pulls out a chair and starts to sit down. Roxeanne leans toward him, shouts "No!" and returns to the activity. Reggie, on the verge of tears, continues to sit. A nearby teacher notices and walks over to the table.

"He was in my way!" cries Eddie. "Well, he pushed me first!" responds Marco, as the teacher separates the two fighting six-year-olds. "It wasn't my fault. I didn't do anything," continues Eddie as he lunges at Marco again. "My Dad said to hit back if somebody hurt me," explains Marco. The teacher takes a deep breath and sits down with the boys.

Think It Over

What have these children done that might be called "misbehavior"? What age-related circumstances or family or cultural influences might have affected any of these situations? Is there a single approach to use in solving all three episodes?

Indirect Ways to Influence Behavior

Subtle factors, such as room arrangements, daily schedules, and quantity and types of materials, affect children's conduct. The wise teacher learns to use them to advantage and avoid unnecessary problems. The size of the group and the number of teachers also affect behavior in a classroom. Less obvious influence are exerted through the environment, the curriculum, and the techniques teachers employ that support children's growth and development of social skills.

Messages from the Environment

Indoors and outdoors, environments for children should give clear messages about what is to take place there. An area should invite a child to "run and make noise here" or to "sit, listen, and read." Children can be free to explore and master the space and materials if they have choices, opportunities to be self-directed, and clear guidelines for behavior. When children are busy and in control of what they are doing, the likelihood for misbehavior diminishes. Environmental cues serve as tangible reminders of behavioral boundaries, freeing teachers and children to respond to the program and to one another in meaningful, positive ways. Table 3.1 on page 70 has many examples of how the environment can be arranged to let children know what behavior is expected when they play or work there.

Modify, Enrich, and Enlarge

Throughout the day, teachers who are sensitive to the impact of the environment on behavior modify the classroom, enriching and enlarging the children's experiences. Props may be added to the block area to encourage greater social interaction, or to give a new dimension to the play already in progress. When children seem overstimulated by too many choices, the teacher may remove some of the materials, limiting their choices to a more acceptable level. If a group of children are too noisy or if a child needs a place to concentrate, teachers can create and rearrange space to accommodate their needs. Modifying the environment simplifies the situation so that it is easier for children to behave appropriately.

The Temporal Environment

The temporal, or time-related, environment can add stress or reduce friction, depending upon the amount of time allotted for important daily functions. Being hurried through play, routines, or transition times may cause tension within the classroom. No one likes to feel hurried. We allow time in the schedule for children to play and work at their own pace; to discover, inquire, plan, create, evaluate, change direction, solve problems, and complete a project takes more than twenty minutes. Active learning, which reinforces a child's right to relevant and meaningful curriculum, requires

Table 3.1

Messages from the Environment: Creating a Setting Where Expectations Are Clear

The Classroom	Fosters Behavior That
Is set up with a variety of learning and activity centers	Promotes choice, self-direction, and provides opportunity to move about
Has low, accessible open shelves with age-appropriate equipment and materials	Invites children to care for equipment and materials, to put away when finished
Is equipped with a sufficient amount of materials and equipment for the size of the group	Provides choices for children to practice decision-making; can play with materials until they are finished, lessening the potential for fighting over equipment and waiting
Centers are set up for several children to participate in an activity, and tables and chairs are arranged so children can see one another	Encourages social interactions, cooperation, sharing, problem-solving and self-direction
Provides space large enough for classroom gatherings in an uncongested area	Builds community among the group; fosters discussion and group problem solving
Has quiet, small, private areas	Allows children to retreat and reflect, be alone, or interact with just one other person
Is uncrowded; has space to work and play at the tables, on the floors	Encourages movement and exploration; avoids conflict over lack of space
Has well-defined spaces that clearly indicate what activity takes place there	Lets children know what is expected of them; messy, noisy, or quiet play
Uses low dividers to separate areas	Teachers can observe and supervise with ease
Provides individual cubbies or lockers, open and within easy reach	Suggests that children are responsible for their private possessions; respect for others' privacy

Outside	Fosters Behavior That
Is safe and secure; climbers, slides, swings are appropriate size, height, and complexity	Provides choices; few limits so children are free to explore, take risks, make noise
Has variety of large motor equipment that can be used in many ways	Calls on children to use muscles, act cooperatively with others, problem solve
Has covered area for rainy day play	Allows children opportunity to make noise, use excess energy, have active play on daily basis
Has large, open spaces	Uses full body motion, freedom to run, expend high energy levels
The schedule provides large blocks of time for uninterrupted play	Encourages children to become involved in their play; promotes self-direction; respect for child's need to play and work at own pace
Includes a wide selection of activities	Leads to competence and independence; enhances decision-making skills
There are enough adults to supervise	Responds to trust and support
Provides children with equipment that is movable and flexible so children can create new play spaces	Supports growth and mastery of self-control

uninterrupted time. Clean-up, bathrooming, and transitions to new activities should be given the extra five or ten minutes in the schedule to reduce the potential for resistance, anxiety, and a general loss of control.

Teacher/Child Ratio

Good discipline begins with the teacher, but one of the most significant aspects of a quality program for young children is *how many* teachers and *how many* children are in the class. Guidelines of teacher/child ratios common in the field of early childhood education are based on the age of the children in the program (Bredekamp, 1987):

- For infants: One teacher for every three children
- For toddlers: One teacher for every five children
- For preschoolers: One teacher for every eight to ten children
- For school-agers: One teacher for every twelve to fifteen children

These standards provide enough adults per child per class so that children may experience individual attention during the course of their school day. A good teacher/child ratio helps to ensure that an adult is available not only to teach in appropriate ways, but to help solve problems and work through solutions. Guidance moments are not scheduled; they occur throughout the school day, the result of constant interaction among children with their peers and with adults. To meet program and guidance goals, there must be a sufficient number of adults to care for children's needs, to staff the activities, and to be available throughout the setting.

The teacher-child ratio has an influence on indirect guidance. In order to give attention to individual children, whether they are hurt, angry, tired, or frustrated, there must be a sufficient number of adults to meet their needs.

The size of the group as well influences children's behavior. If the group is too small, children may be limited in their choice of friends. The exception seems to be in family day care, where the benefits of a mixed age group negate this issue. Too large a group can cause overstimulation and fatigue (Hildebrand, 1980) and prevent teachers from making those all-important connections with parents. Research suggests that smaller groups and age-appropriate teacher/child ratios affect behavior positively, increasing teacher/child interactions, cooperation among children, and involvement in activities, and decreasing the amount of aggression. Guidelines developed by the National Association for the Education of Young Children (NAEYC) recommend the following group sizes:

Ages of Children	Group Size
Infants	Allow for one-to-one interactions and child relating to no more than two adults per day. (Hildebrand [1980] suggests no more than six.)
Toddlers	No larger than twelve, with two adults
Three to five-year-olds	No more than twenty children with two adults
Five to eight-year-olds	No larger than twenty-five children with two adults; fifteen to eighteen children with one teacher

Appropriate Curriculum

The kindergartners are in their reading groups. Julio and Enrique are punching at each other under the table; in exaggerated bounces their legs move the table with each hit. Sung Mi snaps the crayons in half, lining them up in two rows in front of her. As he finishes in the bathroom, Kyle picks up a sponge and begins to squeeze water down the wall next to the sink. Elise and David are taking blocks off the nearby shelf and stacking them between their chairs. They giggle as the tower nears table height; the teacher admonishes them to get back to their basal readers.

What's happening here? A glimpse around this kindergarten classroom provides some answers. Only two learning centers are available and they are closed during "reading time." Materials children need are stored on high shelves; tables clutter the room. The blocks are in short supply and have no accessories. Books and puzzles are limited to the ten-minute "free choice" periods at the beginning and end of the day. The class has just finished their reading worksheets and is waiting for the teacher to show them how to write the letter "S." Recess will not begin for another fifteen minutes. These children are bored, restless, overcontrolled, and underchallenged by the curriculum.

When the curriculum is appropriate and invites children into meaningful interactions, behavior problems diminish. When children are engaged in activities that hold their interest and stimulate their learning, they are less inclined to react as the children in this example. Appropriate curriculum, designed for the developmental needs of the children in the class, is not only the backbone of any quality early childhood program, it is one of the best discipline and guidance measures as well.

The NAEYC and the National Association of Early Childhood Specialists in State Departments of Education (NAECS/SDE) have established guidelines for appropriate curriculum for children from ages three to eight (Bredekamp & Rosegrant, 1992). These standards reflect practices that enhance positive behavior by fostering developmentally appropriate learning and teaching strategies for each age level. Children are challenged, their needs and interests are met, and potential discipline problems are avoided.

Play as Curriculum

Julio, Enrique, Sung Mi, Kyle, Elise, and David have, through spontaneous play, created their own curriculum. When the challenges of the program were not obvious, they did what children do naturally to learn: they began to play. Using the materials at hand in new ways, the children found meaning and interest by manipulating and experimenting, finding ways to meet their own needs. Some might consider these children behavior problems; others would see the creativity and desire for learning as a suitable response to the inappropriate curriculum.

Developmentally appropriate curriculum is planned to meet the cognitive, emotional, social, and physical needs of children in equal measures. If each area of growth is considered as we plan our programs, children are assured of challenges in all developmental areas. Appropriate curriculum allows for individualization and differences in learning styles, abilities, and interests; the materials and curriculum we develop reflect our acceptance of that principle. When children's programs offer materials and activities suitable for a wide range of abilities, every child in the class can be productive, not disruptive. Even if all the children in the class are the same age, they do not have the same physical or cognitive skills. Therefore, a variety of materials allows children to select activities that challenge their unique and varied skills.

A fundamental strategy in curriculum planning, which eliminates many negative behaviors, is the use of play and playful activities to support learning. Children learn through active involvement with materials and with one another. As they play together in small groups they learn to cooperate, to help others, and to ask for help themselves. Active play supports problem-solving skills as children learn to lead or follow, to take turns, to verbalize their needs to one another, and to respect each other's rights. Aside from the much-needed opportunity for children to express their strong physical drives, play teaches children group responsibility and rules of society. During these play periods, teachers have the greatest potential for guiding and directing children's behavior in positive and supportive ways. An underchallenged child is often one who misbehaves simply because the curriculum is neither interesting nor constructive. The overchallenged child also responds by misbehaving when materials are too difficult or too advanced. Thus, the kindergartners created their own curriculum.

Try It   Make a note of where and when behavior problems consistently occur in your classroom. How would you alter the arrangement of equipment, the materials, or the schedule to better support appropriate behavior and effective guidance strategies?

Teaching Techniques

Teachers can influence children's behavior without direct intervention, encouraging positive or negative behavior through more nondirective, subtle techniques. These strategies can prevent a situation from becoming critical, and help maintain a supportive and positive atmosphere in the classroom.

Modeling, one of the most important indirect strategies, may be reviewed by looking at Chapters 1 and 2. Children learn by observing, and are more likely to follow the example of people they love and admire. Modeling is one of the primary tools for parent or teacher to instill appropriate behavior.

Nonverbal Guidance

Mere *physical presence*, without words, can deter misbehavior. Moving close to a situation that seems potentially volatile can remind children to examine their actions. Some children are reassured by a teacher's proximity and feel more secure in handling the problem. By moving closer, a teacher becomes more alert to the children's behavior and gains a better understanding of what is happening. In turn, the children can be positively reinforced by the attention, and their play and work may become more positive. Your physical presence signals to a child, "I see you. I see what is happening." By simply being there, you indicate your awareness and availability, and you remind children, without words, of appropriate behavior and limits.

Glances and *direct looks* often defuse problem situations in ways that words cannot. A raised eyebrow may ask, "What seems to be going on here?" and indicates to children your awareness. A knowing look can communicate that you know what is going on, yet trust the child to work it out before a crisis occurs. Reassurance, approval, concern, sadness, and disapproval are some of the feelings that teachers can communicate in a look without taking direct action.

To be truly effective, a teacher's *body language* must convey support and caring. Get close to the child's level—and the action—by kneeling, sitting, or squatting. Eye contact is critical as you help children learn to develop social skills. Facial expressions of interest and concern let a child know you understand and want to help.

A *touch* can convey support, awareness, caution, or praise, depending on how it is used. A firm grip on a child's hand when it is poised to hit someone else needs no words. A gentle touch on the shoulder or arm can remind Charlie that he needs to exert some self-control before he goes out-of-bounds.

Learning to listen—really listen—to children is a useful skill for teachers. Nods of the head and questioning looks convey your serious concern, and let children know that their problems are important and real, and that you are available to help them learn ways to solve them. Faber and Mazlish (1980) suggest four steps to take for really listening to children: (1) listen with full attention—at eye level, nodding as they speak; (2) acknowledge their feelings with a word—"I can see you are upset"; (3) give their feelings a name—"You sound so sad"; and (4) give them their wishes in fantasy: "I know you would like to spend every day at school outside—and never come in!" This puts the adult in the child's frame of mind before requiring a child to hear the adult's position.

Obviously, one of the most powerful tools at a teacher's command is to *pay attention* to a child. Behaviorist theory reminds us that positive reinforcement, attending to behavior that you want to see repeated, is a useful guidance technique; reinforcement does not always have to be verbal. *Ignoring* behavior, when possible, can also be effective. Positive reinforcement and ignoring are discussed in the section on Behavior Modification.

Teachers' *attitudes* reveal much about their discipline approach and are embedded in the nonverbal aspects of their behavior. This is particularly true for young children, whose command of or attention to language may not be as strong as their skills of noticing people's faces, body, language, and voice. When we have confidence in children's growing abilities to develop social and problem-solving skills, this is conveyed nonverbally as surely as if we spoke the words. There are cultural differences in the way teachers use nonverbal guidance with children. See Chapter 4, "Issues of Diversity: Family, Culture, Gender, and Ability."

Guiding Indirectly with Words

Social learning theory tells us that children learn behavior through verbal instructions, thinking and deducting, and reflecting on their thoughts, feelings, and actions. The words we choose, then, should encourage children in these traits. Use a normal voice level that conveys genuine and sincere interest, and avoid letting emotional reactions influence your tone.

These strategies promote active problem solving by engaging children in exploring their differences and working toward satisfactory solutions. The teacher must strike a balance by guiding children toward solutions without solving the problem for them. A key ingredient is to involve children in monitoring their own behavior.

State the obvious: "Looks like there are two people who both want to be first." When you recognize and label the problem with nondirective statements, it states the situation openly and allows for children's continued involvement and problem solving. The observation and statement, "You are both really mad" opens up the possibility for dialogue between Cammy and Yuriko and also lets them know the effect of their behavior on others.

Ask open-ended questions to help children think about what they are doing and to express their thoughts and feelings. "What would happen if you hit her?" "How many other ways can you find to carry those clothes?" "What can we do when it gets too noisy inside?" "How else could you play that game?" "How do you think he might feel?" These often suggest alternatives for children to consider, or provide them the clues to a variety of ways to solve their problems. We accept their suggestions, help them look at the consequences, and provide a meaningful experience in how behavior influences and affects others. The teacher might have asked Julio and Enrique, "How else can you tell each other what you want without using your hands?"

Whenever possible, *provide a choice*. This allows a child to feel in control and gives an opportunity to practice self-direction and self-discipline. To be truly effective, the choices must be valid and you must be prepared to accept the child's stated preference. "Do you want to go home now?" is not a choice at the end of the school day. "Do you want to carry your jacket to the car or put it on before you leave the class?" is a reasonable choice for a child to make, weather permitting. Providing choices works well in cases where resistance is likely, and leaves children with the implicit understanding that you expect them to comply with one option or the other. Kyle's teacher, when she found him sponging water on the bathroom wall, could have asked him, "Do you want to mop up the water on the floor first or dry off the wall with a towel?"

When we *make positive statements,* children know exactly what is expected of them, and the emphasis is on guidance rather than negative prohibitions. "Hector, if you come over here I will be able to hear you better," tells Hector of the teacher's interest in what he is saying and avoids a negative response such as, "Don't yell, Hector." To encourage children to finish a task we can *use indirect suggestions* or reminders, for instance, "I see you have nearly finished your lunch. We'll be ready to go as soon as you put your dishes away." It is often a good idea to *give reasons* for what we ask children to do; they are more likely to cooperate when they understand our goals. "If you put those papers over here, you will have more room on the

Since toddlers are avid explorers redirection may be a useful strategy to use when trying to intercept and direct a child toward a more acceptable activity. "John, there's another blue car over here waiting for you."

table for your work," communicates a positive approach that is missed if we just ask a child to "Move those papers."

The words we use must *be brief, direct, and clear.* Short, matter-of-fact verbalizations keep children's attention. "Come closer. I really want to hear what you have to say" is a good response to a child who is calling from across the room, rather than a string of sentences indicating that you cannot hear. Excessive explanations, lectures, and moralizing cause children to lose sight of the issues. A good teacher never uses methods that are demeaning to children's self-esteem and confidence, such as threats, sarcasm or name-calling.

> **Think It Over**
>
> What nondirect measures do you think would work with Eddie and Marco? Are there indirect suggestions that would help Roxeanne and Julian include others in their play? Which of the indirect influences on behavior are you most comfortable using? Least comfortable? Why?

Direct Ways to Influence Behavior

Behavior problems vary in degrees and not all situations are of equal importance. Often the indirect approach is enough to modify the children's behavior. The least intrusive method may prove to be successful, and should be tried first. At times, more direct measures are called for, especially if the behavior could harm a child or seriously disrupt the classroom.

There are a number of direct techniques that work well. Each must be examined in the context of overall goals and discipline philosophy of the school. Familiarity with several workable methods helps teachers become confident in using effective discipline techniques. A developmental approach to guidance implies that expectations, consequences, and, therefore, choices of techniques change as children grow and learn.

Inductive Guidance

The most effective methods rely on *inductive guidance* (Hoffman, 1988), which communicates the expectation that children cooperate once they understand the impact of their behavior on others. By asking children to look at how their behavior affects other people, we are helping them move from an egocentric to a sociocentric phase of development.

Inductive guidance is effective because children are actively involved in the process of figuring out what went wrong. Through asking leading questions, adults help children examine their behavior in light of its effect on others (taking responsibility for own actions); in terms of how it makes others feel (arousing empathy toward others); and in the context of what behavior is appropriate (learning to internalize reasons, rules). The Profiles at the opening of this chapter provide opportunities to practice inductive guidance:

"Cammy, when you take someone else's marker, it can make them mad." "How do you think Yuriko felt when you grabbed it out of her hand?" "Where do you think you could find another yellow marker to use?"

"Roxeanne and Julian, how do you think Reggie feels when you call him names? When you tell him he can't play?" "How could you make your game one that three could play?" "Reggie, why do you think they told you not to play here?"

"Eddie, how do you think Marco felt when you pushed in front of him?" "What else could you have done without pushing or hitting?" "Marco, what happens when you hit other children back if they hurt you?" "Why do you think Eddie pushed in front of you, Marco?"

Without threat or fear of punishment, children are challenged to think about how their behavior is causing problems and how they might resolve the situation. In treating children as capable, reasoning beings, the adult communicates a sense of trust and confidence in children's ability to control their own behavior. Children are supported in learning thinking and reasoning skills as they pursue appropriate alternative actions. "That's right, Reggie. You could just sit here and play without talking to Roxeanne and Julian. What else might you do if you wanted a friend to play, too?"

When children are given reasons why their behavior is inappropriate and examples of what their behavior should be, it is easier to internalize the rules. This leads to the formation of a conscience and the ability to use this information in the future. Inductive guidance is also discussed in Chapter 6.

The following methods have many of the components of inductive guidance, calling for children to be held increasingly responsible for their actions. They promote problem solving in varying degrees and foster consequences that are predictable, immediate, and related to the problem behavior. These techniques work well because they help the adult move into a nonjudgmental framework from which solutions can emerge. First and foremost is the setting of appropriate limits.

Setting Limits

Limits are a necessary part of group living; they help define the boundaries of behavior and set up a framework in which everyone knows the rules. According to Gordon and Browne (1993), there are generally two reasons for setting limits: to prevent children from injuring themselves or others, and to prevent the destruction of property, materials, or equipment. They go on to say, ". . . limits are like fences; they are protective structures that help children feel secure," defining the boundaries of behavior just as fences define property boundaries. As children grow and learn to handle more freedom and responsibility, the boundaries also change.

Limits need to be firm yet flexible, and because there are only a few, relatively nonrestrictive. Teachers plan curriculum, design room arrangements, and follow positive guidance practices so that a lot of limits are not necessary (Gordon & Browne, 1993). When children are secure within limits, they can move about freely, make choices about activities and playmates, and play and work as they like. When they encounter a boundary, they learn how people want them to behave and how to get along with others.

To use limits effectively, teachers must learn to set and maintain them with confidence and consistency. Table 3.2 details some guidelines, examples, and reasons for setting limits. Children feel safer when the same limits always apply and when the adult acts in charge.

Distraction

A useful technique with toddlers is to divert the child's attention from the problem that is causing the difficulty. When eighteen-month-old Ruby grabs Larry's toy, distract her with an alternative: a nearby rattle, a book, or perhaps the involvement of another adult. The younger the children, the more likely they are to have their attention moved to something new and equally as interesting. Because children in this age group have short attention spans and their interests shift quickly, they can be easily engaged in a new and not necessarily related activity.

Redirection

Earlier in the chapter we met Sung Mi, who was breaking crayons in half and lining them up on the table. When a child is engaged in an activity you want stopped, it is often helpful to examine whether the behavior is merely annoying, potentially harmful, or the result of boredom or curiosity. Talking to Sung Mi reveals that she wanted to create a rainbow and used the materi-

Table 3.2

Setting Limits

Reasonable limits help children feel safe and learn self-control.

When Setting Limits	*For Example*	*Reasons for Limits*
1. Make sure the limit is appropriate to the situation	"Andy, I want you to get down from the table. You may finish your snack by sitting in your chair or standing next to me. You may not stand on the table."	Child's safety; respect for property
2. Fit the limits to the individual child's age, history, and emotional framework	"Sheila, you've interrupted the story too many times today. Find a place at the puzzle table until we are finished. Remember, I told you earlier that you wouldn't be able to hear the end of the story if you yelled again." "Jamal, I know it's your first day back since your broke your arm, but it is time to listen to the story now. You and Sascha can talk together in a few minutes."	Disturbing other children
3. See that the limits are consistently applied by all adults	"I know you wanted to go outside now but both teachers have already told you that you will have to wait until one of them is able to go out with you."	Child's safety
4. Reinforce the same rules consistently	"Judy, remember everyone walks inside. You can run outside."	Child's safety
5. Follow through; support your words with actions	"I can't let you tear the books. Since this is the second page this morning, you'll need to make another choice instead of the book corner." If child does not leave, begin to pick up books. Lead child to another activity, if necessary.	Respect for property
6. Use simple statements; be clear and state limits positively	"Roger, use a gentle voice indoors. When your voice is too loud, people can't hear one another. You may use your biggest, loudest voice outside."	Disturbing other children
7. Respect the child's feelings and acknowledge them when you can	"I know you want your mom to stay. She has to go to her job right now. I'll stay with you while you feel sad and I'll take care of you until she comes back."	Child's safety and security
8. Act with authority; be sure of your purpose and be confident	"I can't let you hurt other people. Put the block down."	Child's safety

(continued)

Table 3.2   (Continued)

When Setting Limits	For Example	Reasons for Limits
9. Maintain the limit but be ready to accept the consequences; have a plan for the next step, if needed. Don't avoid the situation or give in if the child threatens to fall apart or create a scene	"I'm sorry, Shanna, but you can't take Lenny's notebook. You may ask him if you can look at it for a while but you cannot put it in your cubby. Crying and hitting Lenny won't get you the notebook. Come over here and sit down and let's think about how you can handle this."	Respect for others' property
10. Have children help in defining limits	"We'll be taking taking the bus to the museum next week. What are some of the rules we should follow so that we can enjoy our trip? Wally, do you have an idea?"	Children's safety; foster self-discipline

Adapted from *Beginnings and Beyond: Foundations In Early Childhood Education* by Gordon & Browne. (Delmar, 1996). Used by permission.

als closest to her. Exploring alternatives with her that allow the goal of the activity to be met, but with more acceptable materials, leads to redirection of the activity. "I think we have a box of broken crayons we were saving for another project. Let's go find them, Sung Mi, and you can use them for your rainbow." Redirection, therefore, honors the child's intent but changes the expression or form of activity. "Climbing on the cupboards is unsafe, Tia, but you could climb on the jungle gym when we go outside." "Throwing blocks is dangerous. If you feel like throwing something, let's find a ball." The substitute activity must be valid and acceptable to the child. This method is useful with a broad age range and helps children begin to problem solve.

> **Try It**   In either a home or school setting, use both *distraction* and *redirection* with a child. Were they equally as effective? Why? How would you adjust your strategy the next time?

Natural and Logical Consequences

Based on Dreikurs' work (see Chapter 2), this method involves the child in anticipating the results of certain behaviors, then reflecting on the experience. A *natural consequence* is a direct result of the child's own action and a natural outcome of the behavior. "Lamont, if you take your special toy out of your cubby, it may get lost." At the end of the day when Lamont realizes his toy is gone, he is faced with the consequences of his own behavior and can begin to take some responsibility for his actions.

Logical consequences are similar, but need adult intervention to ensure success. A logical consequence of frequently disrupting a story could be removal from the group. "If you interrupt again, you will have to find another place to play." The consequences are not meant to be punitive; they are the logical outcome to certain behaviors; therefore, they are related to the event and not communicated in anger. The connection to the consequences must be immediate and clear, and must occur each time the unacceptable behavior occurs. We are attempting to give children an opportunity to choose a course of action with the understanding of what will happen if they persist.

This method is especially useful for children who are old enough to see the cause/effect relationship between their behavior and its consequences, but it is an important concept for all children. Experiencing the consequences is the way they learn to see cause and effect. As children gain the ability to discern right and wrong, and can begin to think about their experiences, they are prime for this technique. Natural and logical consequences foster self-discipline, develop cooperation, and help children take responsibility for their own behavior.

Active Listening

Listening carefully to what children say helps them to clarify the problem and begin to seek their own solutions. The adult's role is to show concern, but not to solve the problem for the child. To do this, teachers reflect the child's feelings as well as the words, asking no questions and offering no solutions: "You didn't want your mommy to leave" (to a child in distress over separation). "You feel like you'll never learn to read" (to a child who says, "I'm a dummy.") "You feel sad that your favorite toy is lost, Lamont." When Lamont responds with a plea that you help him find it, continue to clarify his feelings: "You wish I would drop what I am doing and help you right now, but I can't." Lamont then suggests that perhaps Sadie will help him look for his lost toy, and begins the process of seeking solutions.

Young children are able to solve more of their own problems than most parents or teachers are willing to recognize. Often, a teacher moves in on the children before giving them an opportunity to sort through their differences without an adult. We might stand back and allow children who are squabbling a few minutes to see if they begin to negotiate their conflict. Active listening can be used with very young children in simple problem-solving situations, as well as with older, more verbal youngsters, enhancing independence and critical thinking.

Active Problem Solving

Related to active listening, this process engages children in confronting their differences and working together to solve their problems. Again, the adult models concern and interest, and encourages children to come up with alternative solutions. When the teacher sees that Reggie is crying after being rejected by Roxeanne and Julian, she might ask the three children to help solve the situation. Asking Reggie open-ended questions, such as, "What could you do when Roxeanne says things that hurt?" "What might happen if you just sat here anyway?" "How can you let Roxeanne and Julian know how you feel?" To Roxeanne and Julian, similar questions are asked: "What would happen if you had someone else playing here?" "What could you do to help Reggie feel better?"

With active problem solving, blame is avoided and alternatives are created. Teachers help children think through the consequences of the various options they propose, and help them see how their behavior affects and influences others. When a solution is agreed on, it carries the commit-

Alternative Approach

Because excluding other children from play is a fairly common concern, an optional solution for dealing with Roxeanne and Julian is to involve the entire class in working out solutions. At group time, the teacher poses the problem: "I've noticed a lot of people are having feelings hurt because sometimes they aren't being allowed to play where they would like to play. Does anyone know what that feels like? What do you think we can do about it?" A general discussion follows where the children suggest alternatives ("We could sign-up for people we want to play with"). All reasonable suggestions are discussed and weighed as the teacher guides the children toward an equitable resolution that gives children experience in problem solving.

ment of the children involved to make it work. Children emerge with a sense of control and independence, and a feeling of self-worth.

"I" Messages

Parent Effectiveness Training, a child guidance technique popularized over twenty-five years ago (Gordon, 1970), introduced two useful ideas. The first is discussed in the section, Active Listening. The second is the use of "I" messages.

Just as active listening is intended to reflect back to children what they are feeling, "I" messages reflect back how a child's behavior has affected others. They are honest, nonjudgmental statements based on observation and consequences of the behavior. They can be useful in helping adults articulate their own anger and frustration in nonthreatening ways. "When I'm not being listened to, I feel frustrated because I will have to repeat these instructions again." "When I see someone being hit, I get angry because I don't want children to be hurt." "I feel sad when I'm told I'm not liked." Many times children are simply unaware of why something bothers us.

"I" messages are particularly useful for adults to define problematic behaviors and to state them clearly and calmly. This opens up the opportunity for discussion, modeling constructive ways of interacting with each other.

Behavior Modification

Derived from the work of Skinner and Bandura, behavior modification is based on the premise that children learn through repeated reinforcing interactions with the environment. We identify and use positive and negative reinforcement or rewards, knowing that children tend to repeat behavior for which they are positively reinforced, and are likely to avoid behaviors that result in negative reinforcement. The key is to find the appropriate reinforcement for each child and apply it consistently until the behavior has changed.

Reinforcers

Reinforcers must be individualized to meet the needs of the child and the situation. Social reinforcers, such as smiling, hugging, and giving time and attention, are effective as positive reinforcers with young children. Food, tokens, toys, or money are used in some home and school settings as positive reinforcement for older children. Negative reinforcers are unpleasant responses and may include withdrawing the child from play, scolding, and other more severe reactions. Most strategies focus on the use of positive reinforcers to change children's behavior.

Reinforcers may be set up according to a schedule of regular or intermittent use. Initially, a child may be reinforced every time the desired behavior is exhibited. The reinforcement is contingent upon the behavior and is given frequently to increase the behavior's occurrence. Once the behavior is happening often enough, reinforcing may be scheduled at greater, and somewhat more random intervals. In other words, once you have increased a desired behavior and established it as a habit, you needn't reinforce it every time. It tends to continue on its own.

Nonreinforcement, or ignoring the behavior, is useful for less serious problems that may be annoying but are not particularly harmful. A whining child, one who cries easily, or one who teases or swears, is a good candidate for this method. The teacher does not respond in any way to the child when the behavior is evident and may even become occupied elsewhere if the behavior persists. When the child sees that there is nothing to gain—no reaction from the adult—the behavior is likely to cease.

Intrinsic reinforcement refers to the inner satisfaction that in and of itself serves as the reward. We want children to discover the inner strength that can help them in similar situations. Although positive reinforcement may be used to help Ava learn to ride her two-wheel bike, the achievement and success she has as she practices becomes self-reinforcing.

Allen (1992) refers to a *positive reinforcer* as a pleasant consequence that leads to an increase in the behavior it reinforced. Adult social reinforcement is one of the most powerful and important reinforcers available, and it seems to increase those behaviors that it immediately and consistently follows (Allen, 1992). Helpful, cooperative behaviors are likely to follow when a teacher comments, "I saw several children helping Betty move her wheelchair through the doorway today. That is being a good friend!"

The following incident is a good example of the caution needed when using behaviorist techniques. You are tired of being interrupted at story time by a couple of unruly kindergartners. You decide to intervene with a time-out when they talk during the story, and you tell the children in advance what to expect if they interrupt you again. You discover, after a few days, that they are no longer interrupting at story time, but neither are they participating in class activities. Your vague definition of "interrupting" also included comments about the story. Your time-outs have diminished their positive contributions as well as the negative ones, and the children are now discouraged and somewhat hostile. Furthermore, they say that you are unfair and you don't give anyone else time-out. Your emotional reaction to these two children affected your definition of the behaviors and elicited an overgeneral response. Once definitions are clear about what behaviors will be targeted for improvement, all can proceed with the same understandings.

For Classroom Use

Behavior modification can be effective in altering behavior that is disruptive in the classroom. This year's group of kindergartners were lax about cleaning up the room. At a group meeting, the teacher expressed her concern and invited the children to work with her getting more cooperation during clean-up time. Together, they defined what "clean-up" meant: how much to put away and how much to leave on shelves and tables. They chose a portion of the room in which to begin and agreed that when the materials were off the floor and placed in the appropriate shelves, the rubbish thrown away, and the chairs placed against the table, the area would be considered "clean." Before this discussion the teacher had recorded the number of children who participated in clean-up the previous week. This number served as a baseline so that the children could measure progress in the amount of people participating in clean-up. During the next week, the teacher complimented all of the children who spontaneously began to clean up the area and did not mention the portion of the classroom that was not being cleaned. Each day the number of "cleaner-uppers" was printed on the board. Soon the clean up activity became a source of pride and accomplishment to the class, and they began to clean the rest of the room. The goal became its own reward.

Encouraging Positive Behavior

Encouraging positive behavior is one concept of behavior modification technique that can be applied universally. As busy teachers, managing groups of children, we often forget to acknowledge the positive, desirable behaviors in children. Too often, our attention is drawn to negative behaviors. Behavior modification encourages us to find opportunities to let children know when and how they are meeting our expectations and behaving in ways that please us. "Hurray for you, Jordy. You pulled that sneaker on by yourself!" "LaTarsha really helped Mimi write her story today. That was great teamwork, girls!" We reinforce what children do right, what we like, and what we want to see repeated.

Praise

Reinforcing positive behavior and praising children in the hopes of motivating them is linked to behavioral theory. There is a difference, however, between encouraging and praising children's behavior. When we encourage children, we help them focus on what they are trying to achieve. "You are really being careful where you place those blocks, Danielle. Your tower is getting very tall! I can see that you are thinking carefully about where you put each piece." This very specific comment communicates a supportive attitude and lets Danielle know that the effort and thought she is putting into the project is helping her to succeed. No judgment is placed on her work. The danger with praise is that too often teachers tend to use pat phrases ("I like the way Tonya is listening." or "Good job!") that seem to lack sincerity and real interest, and can set up a competitive dynamic with other children in the classroom.

Teachers praise children to (1) foster self-esteem; (2) reinforce learning; and (3) promote appropriate behavior (Hitz & Driscoll, 1988). Praise, as it is used in many early childhood settings, tends to be very global: "You have a beautiful building, Danielle." This comment does not give Danielle the information she needs, omits the learning that she can gain from the experience, and does not reinforce any specific behavior.

Ineffective praise, according to recent research (Hitz & Driscoll, 1988), may have a negative effect on self-esteem, discourage children's efforts, and lead to overdependence on adults. A good example of this is Piero, described later in this chapter, who relies heavily on a teacher's praise for his sense of accomplishment. In fact, Piero has become quite successful in pulling praise from teachers by smiling and beaming at them as he proudly shows off his cleaning efforts. Piero's sense of self-worth is not being enhanced by these interactions, and his autonomy is undermined by his dependence on the teacher's approval.

Managing Transitions

Transitions are periods between activities, or at the beginning and ending of the day, when children move from one place or activity to another. Each day has several transitions, often accompanied by a rise in boisterous activity and inappropriate behavior. Voices rise, children become aggressive, uneasy, anxious. Teachers dread these times because they seem to set children off. Transitions can be managed, however, to encourage positive behavior. Table 3.3 outlines a positive approach to transitions in the daily schedule.

Table 3.3

Ten Tips on Transitions

Planning for smooth, unhurried transitions will benefit everyone: children stay focused, teachers remain calm, and the time between activities is used to good advantage.

Tip #1   *Plan carefully* for each daily transition. Allow plenty of time in the schedule for the flow of action to begin and conclude.

Tip #2   *Control yourself first* and children will stay in control. Keep a calm voice and manner. Speak softly and move in an unhurried way to communicate that this is an orderly process.

Tip #3   *Prepare the children and the environment.* Make sure that the material and equipment you need for the next activity are available and ready for use. Walk quietly through the room to warn children that the change in activity is coming. Speak softly. "It's almost snack time." "You have five more minutes before clean-up time." "Pretty soon we'll be going inside."

Tip #4   *Remind and inform.* Let children know what is happening now and what will happen next. "We're going to clean up so we can all go in and hear the firefighter who has come to visit." "Remember, go to the bathroom and wash your hands before snacks." "While you are waiting for story time to begin, you can join Andrea on the rug and sing some favorite songs."

Tip #5   *Eliminate waiting.* Begin with a small group of three or four children and send them to the bathroom while others are still playing. Other children can then follow as the first group returns to the room and begins to help clean up. Rotate children through situations that require waiting (toileting, washing hands) in easy-to-manage numbers.

Tip #6   *Explain changes.* When the routine will differ, prepare the children ahead of time, if possible. If not, let them know at the beginning of the transition what will be different. "Today, we are doing something different. When you finish in the bathroom, come back out on the patio for a special music activity."

Tip #7   *Involve children easily and early.* At morning group time, ask for volunteers to help with specific jobs. Use a job chart that children can manage by themselves and place their name under the task they want to perform. "Jason, you signed up for table moving today. I'll be ready for you to help with that in just a few minutes. Anyone else ready to help Jason?"

Tip #8   *Target children who need it.* Watch for the children who have difficulty when routines are broken and who seem uneasy or anxious with a great deal of activity going on at once. Involve them early in a task; ask them to be your assistant, giving concrete directions. "Noah, it's nearly time to go outside. I need help in setting up snacks. Can you carry this over to the table for me?"

(continued)

Table 3.3   (Continued)

Tip #9   *Dismiss in small groups.* When a large group is breaking up to move onto other activities, send them off a few at a time. "Everyone who has on a green shirt can get a coat and go outside." "Mrs. Jenson wants all the children whose name begins with 'M' to follow her."

Tip #10   *Promote self-direction and self-control.* Create a climate where mutual acceptance and responsibility for group living is clearly a value. Allow children to choose their method of participation in transitions and eliminate those parts of the process that require them to sit, stand, or wait for the next activity.

Time-Out

Almost every sports event has a period of time when the players, in need of respite from the intensity of play, call for a "time-out." All activity stops for a cooling-off period while the team rethinks its playing strategy. The idea has merit when applied to early childhood classrooms, but too often "time-out" is used as a punitive measure, humiliating the child and escalating the tension.

Time-out is a controversial method. Removing a child from what is reinforcing unacceptable behavior, Allen (1992) believes, is a measure of last resort and should be reserved for the most serious behavior problems. This technique is to be used carefully, if at all (Gordon & Browne, 1993; Mitchell & David, 1992). It can easily leave a child with a sense of rejection when employed by a teacher who is too frustrated and angry to choose more effective and helpful strategies. Nelsen and Glenn (1992), on the other hand, find that when time-out is used in supportive ways, children can feel empowered and confident in their ability to control their own behavior. Using it before a child goes out of control is a key concept in their approach.

There *are* times when children need a quiet place to go, away from the overwhelming emotion of peers and play. At such times, modified version of the classic "time-out" could be useful. A "talk it over" chair or bench could give the child an opportunity to gain self-control before rejoining the group. Supportive, firm, and confident teachers view a child's removal from the group as a positive approach to discipline rather than as a punishment, and treat the child accordingly. "Genna, can you tell me what is upsetting you?" Depending on the age of the child, teacher and child may use this time to discuss ways to avoid extreme behaviors and strategies for keeping emotions under control in more appropriate ways. "What can you say to Brad when he makes you angry?" "How can you tell him without using your fists?" Children should never be humiliated, or isolated in small

areas that could frighten them. As Nelsen and Glenn make clear, time-out may be useful when the adult has distinguished between the desire to control a child (using inappropriate time-out measures) and encouraging a child's ability to gain control by cooling off nearby.

Behavioral and social learning theory helps us communicate to children what behavior is desirable and what learning needs to take place. Time-out does not teach a child new behavior; no real learning takes place if a child is isolated from everyone. Children must be involved with each other, with teachers, with materials and equipment to learn how to work and play harmoniously. What do you think?

Aggressive and Disruptive Behavior

Every teacher has experienced the child who disrupts story time, who knocks over block structures, who provides wear and tear on equipment, materials, and the adult's patience. Children with a high degree of energy, short attention spans, and who are easily distracted, challenge our skills in guiding behavior. These children need extra support as they learn to live in a group and become responsible for their behavior. Table 3.4 on page 92 highlights some areas on which to focus as you work with the more demanding and aggressive child.

Helping Children Resolve Conflicts

Today's child is raised with images of violence and war. Cartoons created for their enjoyment spawn entire industries of products ranging from cereal to sleepware, keeping the message of violence in their consciousness. This

When children disagree, feelings run high and fighting often occurs. Learning social skills means identifying and accepting feelings and finding acceptable outlets for emotions. A teacher who guides young children toward cooperative play relies on patience and opportunities to learn new ways to behave.

Table 3.4

Managing Aggressive, Disruptive, High-Energy Behavior

Four main areas of focus when guiding children who need extra support in managing their behavior.

Area of Focus	*What You Can Do*
Observations	*Collect information* about the behavior: Identify the components that cause children to lose control. When does Nan throw a temper tantrum? Only before snack time? Just after her mother leaves? What prompts Rudy's resistance? What precedes it? How long does it last? How much attention does Arturo get when he interrupts story time? How many teachers intervene? For how long? How has his attention been sought prior to his disruption? Observe and learn also when these children are behaving appropriately and record what and how much attention they receive from teachers at that time.
Modify the classroom	*Evaluate the classroom,* based on the observations you made. Is it orderly and free of clutter? Are there legitimate opportunities to move about and use large muscles? Can children self-select their own activities and make choices about where they will work and play? Is the curriculum challenging and appropriate to the age level? Is there advanced warning when activities will change? Is there an established routine that children can count on? Is there a clean up time where the children help restore the play areas?

> *Examples:* Materials should be stored in low, open, easy to reach shelves that are labeled (scissors, crayons), and placed in containers that children can handle.
>
> Remove puzzles if they are crowded on a shelf, leaving only a few. Rotate them frequently.
>
> Display blocks and block accessories (trucks, people, etc.) clearly. Block sizes and shapes on the shelves give children the necessary cues to assist them with clean-up. Provide protected area for block building, away from quieter activities.
>
> Check to see if the dividers between the activity centers are low enough for ease Fof supervision.

Teacher attention and language	*Give minimum attention* to child during aggressive episode, taking care of any injured party first. Use short, direct sentences, without judgment and without lecturing. *Look at and speak to child at eye level.* Do not shame, ridicule or use physical punishment.

> *Good Example:* "No. I can't let you hurt children."
>
> *Poor Example:* "It's not nice to hit other children. They don't like you when you are mean. Why can't you play nice like they do? I'm gonna have to tell your momma you were bad when she comes. Can you promise me you won't hit anybody else today? Now tell Tomi you are sorry."

Table 3.4 (Continued)

Area of Focus	*What You Can Do*

Pay attention to disruptive, nonattentive, aggressive children *when they are behaving appropriately.* Talk over with them alternatives to their nonappropriate behavior.

> *Examples:* "Next time, tell someone you are angry instead of hitting." "When you are finished playing with the blocks, call me and I will help you find another place to play." "What else could you do if you don't want to hear the story that wouldn't bother other people who want to listen?"

Follow through. Help child return to play, giving choices when possible, with activities that require energy (clay, woodworking, climbing) or those that are more calming (water play, painting), depending on what the child seems to need at the time. Support the child's involvement with relevant comments, interest, and suitable challenges.

> *Examples:* "Let's decide where you want to play now, Faisal. There's room for you at the water table or pounding the clay. I'll help you get started." (Later) "You look like you are having a good time with that clay, Faisal. I bet you can squeeze it so hard it oozes out your fingers! I'll watch while you try."

Interacting with children

Start with a child's known interests. Through observations, determine which activities consistently hold the child's attention so that you can reinforce positive behavior while the child is engaged. This technique also helps to increase attention span.

> *Example:* "You sure have been having fun at the water table, Jessica. Here are some funnels and tubes. What could you do with them?"

Help child plan where to go next and assist in getting started, if necessary. This is effective if the child's activity is changed before he loses interest or before he loses control.

> *Example:* "Jay, it is nearly clean up time and I know that sometimes it is a hard time for you when we stop playing. How about you helping me organize the children who want to move the tables. Could you be my assistant today and show everyone where to put the tables?"

Give time for response; take time to teach. Children need adequate time to respond to requests without being nagged and may need assistance in learning a skill or getting started with what was requested. Make the task manageable. If, after a reasonable time has passed and Shaquille still hasn't put his jacket on, the teacher restates the request and offers assistance.

> *Example:* "You may go outside as soon as your jacket is on, Shaquille. If you put the jacket down on the floor like this, and slip your arms in here, you can pull it over your head."

Help children focus their attention. Get down to their eye level, call them by name, look at them, and speak directly to them. Give advance warning, clear, simple directions, and choices when possible. Do not overwhelm with rules and instructions.

> *Example:* "Coretta, it will soon be time to go home. When you finish writing your story, you may choose to come over to the rug to sing songs or you may find a favorite book and look at it in the book corner."

(continued)

Table 3.4   (Continued)

Area of Focus	*What You Can Do*
	Point out the consequences of their actions to help them understand others' feelings and become responsible for what they do.
	Examples: "Linda is sad because you won't let her play with you."
	"Other children won't be able to use the paint when you mix the colors in the paint jar."
	Remind children of the rules and expectations. Rehearse them in remembering appropriate behavior. Use positive phrases.
	Example: "Before you go to the block area, remember how much space you need for the roads you like to build. Look around and see who else is playing and find a safe place for your road."

Adapted from *The Exceptional Child: Mainstreaming In Early Childhood Education* by K. Eileen Allen. (Delmar, 1992). Used with permission.

influence is felt in the classroom when children model behavior that teaches physical aggression as a way of resolving differences. Conflict resolution strategies can help children learn joint problem solving, ways to disagree, how to negotiate, and how to resolve issues.

Adults who plan to work with children in resolving conflicts must first reach their own level of comfort with conflict and disagreements. Reflect for a moment on your own behavior when you have a difference of opinion with someone, negotiate for a salary increase, or see someone take a parking place from you. Admitting we are wrong, changing our opinions, and viewing our situation from another's point of view are skills we must all learn. We must be aware of our own history of dealing with controversy and examine how we interact with adults and children when dissension arises before we attempt to teach these skills to children.

Conflict is a part of daily life, and children should come to see conflict and disagreement as a matter of course, a natural part of interpersonal relationships. They need to experience conflicts to find out how people solve their differences in nonviolent ways, and to learn alternatives that will work for them.

Teaching conflict resolution skills enhances a child's ability to appreciate and respect others' opinions, to express and value one's own feelings and those of others, and fosters a tolerance for differences in respect to culture and traditions. Conflict, with its multiple solutions, can lead to growth and learning and teach us new things about ourselves and others. Children can learn specific skills, matched to their level of development, that teach a

1. Rip up
2. Keep on dresser and not tear up or throw away
3. Let mom have it
4. throw away
5. Leave alone
6. Let dad have it

Children are often capable of solving their own problems. This group has been exploring the ownership of a group painting. Each suggestion is taken seriously, written down, and a final decision is made by the group. Do you agree with their choice?

wide range of possible ways to resolve conflicts. Gender differences in conflict resolution reveal that girls tend to negotiate and compromise, but boys will settle a disagreement with a fist fight or not give in (Maccoby, 1990; Miller, et al., 1986).

The most effective guidance measures, noted throughout this text, involve children actively in the solutions to problems. They are crucial to the process of conflict resolution: cooling off, talking and listening, and brainstorming solutions, plans, and strategies. This involvement gives children the power and responsibility to act in their own behalf, reinforcing their self-confidence and ability to learn new social skills.

Conflict Resolution: A Problem-Solving Process

Most successful approaches to teaching children conflict resolution skills include a process of identifying the problem or issue, generating a number of potential solutions, then testing them out. This process works with pre-schoolers and is especially appropriate for school-age children. Following are some of the customary steps through the conflict resolution process.

1. *Stop the aggressive behavior.* Separate children who are in conflict and give them an opportunity to cool off.

2. *Gather data and define the problem.* Find out what happened by asking what occurred, who was involved, and how each child is feeling. Ask open-ended questions ("What happened?" "Why did you . . . ?" "How do you feel about . . . ?" "What happened next?") that encourage children to talk about the situation so that the problem can be clearly identified.

3. *Brainstorm solutions.* Encourage children to think of many options by asking, "What other way could you do that?" "How do you think we could do that without . . . (hitting)?" "How do you think you could solve this prob-lem?" Accept all responses without judgment; this is a time to think of cre-ative solutions, so all ideas are valued. Often, children will suggest silly or seemingly unreasonable alternatives, and these should be included.

4. *Experiment with solutions.* Evaluate the ideas generated by the brainstorming session. "Which ideas might work best?" Help them look at the implications of their solutions, decide the workability of the option, and choose the ideas they want to test out. Remember that children's solutions are not necessarily our solutions, but may work just as well.

5. *Help children carry out their plan.* More than likely the agreed-on solution will be modified as children work through what they want to do. Walk through some of the initial steps with them by asking questions such as "Who goes first?" "What happens next?" "Who will be in charge of that?"

6. *Evaluate the results.* Observe children as they put their plan into effect. Encourage them to revise their plan if it doesn't work or to find an-other solution. Reinforce their ability as problem solvers.

Table 3.5 demonstrates an approach similar to these six points in help-ing children learn problem-solving skills. In either approach, the adult neu-tralizes the situation by intervening, showing support for working through the problem, and making statements or asking questions that prompt the children to think about what is happening. No blame is assessed, and chil-dren are encouraged to come up with solutions. The adult then monitors the success of the agreement and assists the children in finding alternative so-lutions, if necessary.

Table 3.5

The Six-Step Approach to Problem Solving

Using these guidelines to help children solve problems, teachers listen more than talk, allow children the time to make mistakes and figure out solutions, and point out that a diversity of viewpoints is natural, normal, and workable.

Scenario: Two children run outdoors to get the available wagon. They reach it simultaneously and start pulling on the handle, yelling "Mine!" One child starts shoving the other child out of the way.

Step 1: Approach (Initiate Mediation):

—Approach the conflict, signaling your awareness and availability.
—Get close enough to intervene if necessary; stop aggressive behavior or neutralize the object of conflict by holding it yourself.

Step 2: Make a Statement:

—Describe the scene.
—Reflect what the children have said.
—Offer no judgments, values, solutions
    "It looks like you both want the wagon."
    "I see you are yelling at each other."

Step 3: Ask Questions (Gather Data, Define the Problem):

—Don't direct questions toward pinpointing blame.
—Draw out details; define problems
—Help kids communicate versus slugging it out.
    "How did this happen?"
    "What do you want to tell her?"
    "How could you solve this problem?"
    "How could you use it without fighting?"

Step 4: Generate Alternative Solutions

—Give children the job of thinking and figuring it out.
—Suggestions may be offered by disputants or observers.
—Ask questions:
    "Who has an idea of how we could solve . . .?"
    "You could take turns."
    "You could both use it together."
    "You could both do something else."
    "No one could use it."
—Common mistake: rushing this stage; give it the time it deserves.

Step 5: Agree on Solution

—When both children accept a solution, rephrase it ("So, you both say that she will be the driver?").
—If any solution seems unsafe or grossly unfair, you must tell the children ("It is too dangerous for you both to stand up and ride downhill together. What is another way you can agree?").

(continued)

Table 3.5   (Continued)

Step 6: Follow-Through

—Monitor to make sure agreement is going according to plan: If the decision is turn-taking, you may need to be a clock-watcher.
—Tell the players and the group:
  "Looks like you solved your problem!"
—Use the power of language to:
  Reinforce the solvability of the problem
  Note the ability of the players to do so
  Point out the positive environment to be successful

From *Beginnings and Beyond: Foundations in Early Childhood Education* by Gordon & Browne, (Delmar 1996). Used with permission.

To become skilled in this process, children need experience in making decisions and listening to others. They need teachers who listen to them, who encourage them to think beyond normal boundaries and responses, who support their ideas, and who create new ways of looking at familiar things. Group gatherings provide an arena in which teachers can introduce the children to problem-solving strategies. Cooperative activities, group games, puppet play, and role-playing can be integrated into the curriculum to help children become aware of the complexities and potential in conflict resolution.

Prerequisites to problem-solving with children are a well-established climate of trust and teachers who make time for this process a priority in the daily schedule. To be successful, this approach calls for children and adults who are ready and willing to be engaged in social problem-solving, whose benefits include better communication skills, practice in analytical thinking, and an increase in self-esteem.

In conclusion, many techniques are available to deal with children's behavior in guiding rather than punishing ways. As a teacher, you must develop a discipline style of your own, one that takes into account who you are as a person with values and as a teacher with professional ethics and expertise. Which technique you choose in any situation also depends on the child and the circumstances.

No one can tell you what to do in every discipline situation. Teaching children does not conform to a formula; it is a dynamic, changing process and it is a teacher's job to learn about that process. You might think of learning how to guide and direct children's behavior as you would think about learning how to walk. What starts as a deliberate intention evolves into an innate process. The basic elements of walking are to lift a leg up, put one foot in front of the other, swing your arms, and watch where you are going. Adjust and change according to the conditions of the path—whether slippery, rocky, sandy, or smooth. Confidence comes with every step and by meeting each challenge as it presents itself. In this chapter we have given you some of the elements and processes of discipline, to be used according to what your children bring to you every day you teach.

Think It Over

Which discipline strategies would be the most difficult for you to use? Why? Discuss with your classmates why you believe that behavior modification may (or may not) be an unfair manipulation of children. Why do you believe children are capable of learning to solve their own problems?

It Begins with the Teacher

In the normal course of events, at home or at school, there are times when children's behavior does not conform to an adult's perception of what is good or desirable at that time. Much of what we term "misbehavior," however, can be seen as a sign that these are healthy children, exhibiting normal signs of growth. The teacher has the critical role to play, creating a climate in which the needs of children are met and the response of the adult is sensitive and appropriate.

Developing Your Own Style

As a teacher, you are finding your own personal discipline style and looking for effective alternatives that work well in the classroom. We know that all methods do not work with all children and that teachers need a good repertoire of techniques to meet the needs of the individual child. Some strategies may be more effective than others, depending upon the child, the situation, and your own experience. Remember the Triangle from Chapter 1? See page 25 for another way to look at the relationship among these three variables.

The techniques discussed in this chapter can be useful with the children we met at the beginning of the chapter, and in most classroom settings. They work well at critical times when immediate intervention is necessary (in the case of Eddie and Marco) as well as under less explosive circumstances (such as Reggie's plight).

Immediate and long-range goals are influenced by the teacher's choices of discipline methods as they, in turn, influence that choice. It works both ways: teachers choose strategies to support the goals they have set, and the goals dictate what those methods are. Learning various techniques and methods is valuable for teachers of young children, but it is also important to understand why these strategies are considered effective. Knowing the how and why of various methods, teachers can use the most timely strategy, basing their choice on a clear understanding of its impact on the child, the situation, and the overriding goals of the program. Cammy, Julian, Eddie, and Marco all used aggressive behavior that infringed on another child's feelings or activity, but the similarity ends there. A teacher's response to hitting undoubtedly differs from a response to name-calling or being disrespectful of another's property. A teacher's response takes into consideration the ages, personalities, and histories of each of the children.

A teacher's discipline style evolves over many years. Experience is the most important contributor to creating a personal and professional approach, which reflects a particular way of interacting with children. A first-year teacher or first-time parent lacks the confidence that comes from dealing with a number of children over a long period of time. We use those first-time experiences to build on, as opportunities to get to know children and how they react to our guidance style. We learn what works and what does not and come to appreciate that the more we do it, the more it becomes second nature and therefore easier.

There are ways to determine which methods might be the right one to use for a given situation. Guidelines, such as those in Table 3.6, help us make the right decision, one which supports Roxeanne and Julian's good work, yet confronts their rejection of Reggie, or honors Eddie's family advice, but prevents him from hurting others.

Establishing Trust

One of the first things any classroom teacher does is establish a trusting relationship with the children. It is one thing to work with children when things are going smoothly and they are actively and creatively involved in their work and play. It is quite another thing to interfere in their play, set limits to their behavior, or prevent them from doing harm to themselves or others. A teacher moves from one role to the other by creating a climate of trust. We want children to know they can learn to trust what happens to

Table 3.6

How to Choose the Best Guidance Method

You Should:	For Example:
Know the child: be well versed in child development theory so that the method will fit the age range and experience of the child.	Toddlers and Two's have a strong sense of ownership about their possessions; sharing them with others will lead to further upset.
Help children see the results of their own behavior so that they may come to accept responsibility for their actions.	"Yesterday when you threw sand you hurt Bennie. That is why he doesn't want to play with you today. How can we make sure that doesn't happen again?"
Be confident in your ability to control children's behavior; project an attitude that you are in charge as you gain experience and become more confident and skilled.	"It hurts when you kick me, Danny. You seem very angry, but I am not going to let you hurt anyone here at school. Do you want to tell me what made you angry and we can talk about it, if you like."
Use simple techniques that are generally successful and follow with more complex strategies.	First time: "As soon as I am finished helping Shiranda, I'll be able to look at your writing, Mike." Second time: "I don't want you to keep interrupting me while I am helping other children, Mike. I know it's hard for you to wait, but I have already come over to your desk three times. Can you think of a way to signal me that you are ready and I could signal back that I'll be there just as soon as I can?"
Each method should help children express feelings, listen to others, and learn to verbalize.	"I know you are feeling impatient, Rayna, but Elise isn't finished yet. You can ask her to give you that book when she is finished. Let's listen for her answer."
Know yourself: be aware of how you control yourself in order to set a positive example to children.	"Sometimes I get angry, too. So I take a deep breath and let it out very slowly. Then I am ready to talk about the problem. Try it with me, Keenan. Good. Now tell me about the fight."
Talk about how you want children to behave and model being the kind of adult you want to be with them.	"I saw a lot of people helping each other today. That makes me feel good when I see you taking care of each other. I also noticed how clean the patio looked after all the chalk painting was cleaned up. That took a lot of cooperation and working together."
Be more intentional and selective in interactions with children.	Stand back to see if you are really needed to intervene in an argument. Give children ample time to try to solve their problems. Hesitate before you get involved to see if you are really needed. "Emilio and Robbie, I was watching you work together on digging that hole today. You two kept

(continued)

Table 3.6   (Continued)

You Should:	*For Example:*
	from having a big argument when you decided to share the hose. That was good problem solving."
Find a colleague and talk over what strategies work best. Take advantage of the experience of others.	"Bonnie, I see that kids respond so well when you set limits. I don't feel confident when I have to help JanNell and Marilyn through transition times. Do you have any suggestions that would help me?"

trust. We want children to know they can learn to trust what happens to them at school. Teachers build trust by:

- Treating each child with respect.
- Allowing children to express their needs and feelings.
- Accepting the child's right to make mistakes.
- Engaging children in solving problems.
- Nurturing and supporting the growth of each individual.
- Being fair and just.
- Granting children the time to learn and grow at their own pace.

Trust begins with teachers who have confidence in the normal process of child growth and development. Good teachers of young children fully enjoy the early childhood years for what they should be: time when children move through stages of growth according to their inner timetable.

The foundation of guidance is a trusting relationship. Teachers who are warm and responsive to children and enjoy their company help children learn to trust and rely on adults.

They understand that love and acceptance are the cornerstones for creating a trusting bond on which guidance is based, and they delight in seeing each child as the fascinating, creative, and uniquely emotional being she is.

Stay in Touch

A busy classroom makes many demands on teachers, and it is often difficult to be aware of what is happening in all areas of the room or yard. Cammy, Roxeanne, and Marco's interactions (and hundreds like them) do not always take place in the immediate vicinity of an adult. Teachers need to stay in touch with what is happening through regular and systematic observation of the classroom scene.

Observations are a significant tool for understanding child behavior and selecting appropriate discipline methods. As children reveal themselves through their play and work, we learn more about their motivation, needs, abilities, and behavior. We gain insights into their relationships with others and learn what influences their behavior. Marco, for instance, has been bullied a lot by other children. His comment about self-defense is important. Observations may give us clues to a cultural or familial basis for behavior. We then have to work with it at school with sensitivity to the impact on Marco in his life outside of school. Observations give the vital information we need to assess a situation fairly and check our impressions against the facts. It seems as though Cammy has become more aggressive. Observations would also clarify how often Roxeanne and Julian exclude other children from their play. Concrete information is the first step toward a supportive guidance approach.

Teachers find that observation helps them make the critical link to developmental theory. Often, textbook examples come alive as teachers observe active, involved children at play. When "special friends" Roxeanne and Julian exclude others from their play, the teacher's response is tempered by her knowledge that children that age develop "in-group" friendships and often refuse to let others join their play. Therefore, a teacher's comments to Roxeanne and Julian will be sympathetic toward their new friendship while also considering Reggie's feelings.

Objective observations, free of bias and interpretation, are relatively easy to integrate into the teaching experience. Pocket notepads allow teachers to make notes while chil-

Try It Choose two children to observe, one who has good social relationships and one who seems to have difficulties with peers. Observe the adult's interactions with both children. What are the differences? How effective are the strategies teachers are using with both children? What would you change?

dren go about the daily business of school. Later, the observations can be discussed among the teaching staff in ways that have new meaning for both teachers and children.

"But I Helped . . ."

Two teachers and a group of children were on the patio. Both teachers were finishing art projects with some of the children when they announced it was clean-up time. Three boys began to put away the hollow blocks with which they had been playing. Ardith, the teacher closest to them, reminded the children that everyone must help clean up and those who did so without reminders would be congratulated during group time.

Taryn approached the boys, and said she wanted to help, but was told "no" by all of them. Hearing this, Ardith asked each boy in turn if Taryn could help. The first two said "no," but Piero said nothing. Ardith then said, "Taryn can help you, Piero," and turned back to the art table. As Taryn picked up the blocks and placed them against the wall, Piero took them out of her hands, saying, "That doesn't belong there." He placed them at another spot along the wall where he had stacked his blocks. This routine continued; each time Taryn placed a block down, Piero removed it and placed it elsewhere. After six such attempts, Taryn finally walked away and began to fit herself into a small opening created by the stacked blocks.

When Ardith saw that Taryn wasn't cleaning up, she told her to get busy but warned that since she had to remind her, Taryn wouldn't be congratulated at group time. Piero, who was busy working nearby, looked up at Ardith and grinned. She complimented him on his hard work.

During group time the teachers named the children who had cleaned up without being reminded. All the children cheered as each name was called. Piero strode toward the front of the group to receive his acknowledgment. Taryn, sitting near the teacher who was leading the group, spoke up in a soft voice, "But I helped." After she said this three times, Ardith called out, "But remember, Taryn, you stopped to play and I had to remind you to clean up." Taryn's eyes teared up, and she put her head down and remained quiet for the rest of group time.

This example points out the need for teachers to be fully aware of what is happening in the classroom: to be tuned in, visually and perceptually, to be most effective in their discipline approach. Ardith reinforced Piero for cleaning up, but was unaware of Taryn's efforts to help and ignorant about Piero's behavior toward Taryn. Developing good observation skills among the staff would eliminate the unfortunate impression Ardith had of Taryn's efforts and would help her better understand Piero's need for constant adult affirmation. Had she observed the entire interaction, Ardith could have strengthened both children in their efforts by any of the following verbalizations:

- "Look at the way you boys are cleaning up! Taryn's ready to help. At which end of the patio would you like her to start?"
- "What seems to be the matter, Piero? You look upset."
- "Piero, you have found a great place to stack the blocks. Taryn has found another good place for hers. Both of you are working hard."
- "Today I saw a lot of people cleaning up, inside and out. Taryn and Piero helped with the blocks on the patio. So did Calvin and Jeremy. Who else helped? Let's clap for everybody's hard work."

To be in tune with events throughout the day, teachers make themselves accessible to children. They always position themselves so that they can see the room or yard. Children have the opportunity to select from a number of activities, many of which they participate in without a teacher. Teachers, then, can be resources to any number of children and can be available to observe, intervene, and help problem solve at critical times.

One way teachers can use their own observational skills to help children look at a situation is to notice aloud and ask questions. Ardith did just this in the examples above as she called on children to become aware of what was happening. In this way, children can become engaged in observing a situation to help to resolve it.

Creating the Climate

As adults, we are responsible for creating a relaxed atmosphere that promotes feelings of trust and well-being, where children can feel safe and accepted, so that they can be free to play in caring and cooperative ways with others. We understand that children behave according to our expectations and they will be productive and purposeful if we communicate that expectation to them. We also know that adults who are generous, tolerant, and caring in their interactions with children foster those same characteristics in their students. Table 3.7 highlights ways to create a climate that supports good discipline practices.

A healthy, trusting climate is one in which children feel genuinely good about themselves, where they feel liked, and where they have a sense of their own competence. This kind of atmosphere encourages children to live up to our best expectations and reduces the negative behavior that happens when a child's self-esteem is damaged.

Table 3.7

The Guidance Continuum

Ideally, we start from the least intrusive, most hands-off approach and move to the most intervening, hands-on methods when guiding children. Adults are aware and involved throughout the process, but what they say and do varies. Children and adults share power in each of these steps, but in different measures: children are most in charge of what happens in the first steps and adults gradually increase their intervention in the later steps.

1	2	3	4	5	6	7	8	9	10

1. *Ignore.* Let children sort it out themselves.

2. *Listen and watch.* Make sure you hear what children are really saying. Become aware of the issues. Make sure children see you are watching and available.

3. *Act as reporter.* Say what you notice and hear. "It looks like there's a problem here." "I see two children fighting." "There are three children and one wagon." "I'm hearing shouting/whining/crying."

4. *Step in/set limits.* Protect physical or emotional security. "Hold it. Stop the hitting!" "In this school we use words, not our hands." "I can't let you hurt her feelings like that." "Running inside causes accidents. Wait until you go outside." "Leave other people's papers alone."

5. *Ask questions.* "Is there a problem?" "Are you all right about her choice?" "What is happening here?"

6. *Brainstorm.* Encourage the child to say what to do. "How could we solve this problem?" "Who has a good idea for figuring this out?" "What can you do so that you will both be happy?" "What could you do instead of grabbing/pushing?"

7. *Offer ideas.* "You could get another hammer and work on that together." "Would it work if you each made a plan?" "Maybe you need to play alone for a while." "Perhaps Tommy would help you settle this."

8. *Offer a choice.* "These are the three things that need to be done. You may choose which you will do first, second, and last." "You can put your things away now and hear our story, or you can put them away during story time and miss hearing it."

9. *Take action alongside.* "Here's what we'll do together." "Let's make a plan so that this won't happen to you tomorrow."

10. *Do it yourself.* Take command and tell children what to do. "It seems too difficult for you to be here; make another choice and play elsewhere for a while." "No closed games at school, so make room for another player." "You have to do something to make him feel better; go get some ice for his scraped arm."

A teacher builds a good interpersonal or affective environment by being flexible yet consistent. That is not as contradictory a statement as it might sound. Children need consistent limits and adults they can count on to act in predictable ways. Yet they also need teachers who are willing to go along with a new idea or suggestion, who are willing to try alternatives children suggest, and who do not always have to be right. If the children think that playground behavior will improve if no one uses the swings for a day, a teacher should be willing to try their approach and let the children experience the results when swings are declared off limits for a day. When they are invested in the solution, children are avid monitors of one another's behavior to see that their decision is given a fair chance. In this case, a follow-up discussion on the success of the "no swings" day continues to involve the children and the teacher in working together to make school a responsive and nurturing environment.

Think It Over

What are ways in which you might begin to build a trusting relationship with children in your care? How do you think Roxeanne and Julian's exclusive play affects the climate of the classroom? If a teacher had observed Eddie and Marco, what kinds of questions might be asked to resolve their conflict before they hit one another?

Summary

The practical techniques we use in guiding children's behavior are many and varied. Our goal is to strengthen children's self-esteem through positive action and communication so they will become confident, independent, and cooperative. Directly and indirectly, nurturing adults provide opportunities for children to learn the skills and knowledge they need to become self-directed, self-controlled, and socially competent.

Many factors influence the way children behave. We want to help children learn to behave appropriately, not just correct their behavior when they do not act as we wish. Wise teachers make judicious use of the physical environment to set out the expectations for children's behavior in the classroom and to prevent problems from arising. The amount of space, its layout, the choice of equipment and materials, the amount of time available for various activities, and the interpersonal climate are our tools. We consciously plan for the developing needs of the children in our classroom and match the environment to those known quantities. Nonverbal guidance, group size, developmentally challenging curriculum, and the opportunity to learn social skills through play help us create appropriate environments that foster positive child guidance.

Direct guidance involves adult interaction and, often, intervention to help children develop a sense of personal responsibility as they come to see the consequences of their own behavior. Fostering this independence and self-control is a primary goal as we assist children in learning active problem-solving and negotiating skills. Direct guidance techniques are effective if viewed in the context of an overall discipline philosophy and are changed as children grow and learn. Most effective methods use an inductive process, which, through reasoning or explaining, helps children see the consequences of their behavior. Active listening and working with children to learn conflict resolution strategies reinforce the concept that children are capable of helping to solve their own problems.

The teacher carries the key to successful guidance. Caring and nurturing teachers create a climate where children can trust what will happen to them because they feel safe and accepted. The affective environment includes appropriate limits, reasonable rules, and aware and sensitive teachers who are firm and positive, clear and consistent, and self-reflective and respectful in their relationships with the children in their care.

Observe and Apply

On one side of a piece of paper, create a list of the "I" messages you heard while observing a classroom. On the other side of the page, make a list of inappropriate, angry, or sarcastic messages you heard. What behavior resulted in each case? How do you see this observation affecting your interactions with children?

Review Questions

1. What are some ways the physical environment can be structured to enhance positive behavior? Give three examples of how the arrangement of equipment and types of materials hindered or helped children to behave in appropriate ways.

2. Describe how curriculum is related to behavior.

3. What is the difference between a *natural* consequence and a *logical* consequence? State five reasons why these are useful guidance techniques, citing examples for each.

4. When might "time out" be appropriate and effective? Describe three concerns about using "time out" with young children.

5. Describe the six-step approach to problem solving, giving examples from recent experiences.

6. Observe a classroom in which you believe a climate of trust exists between teachers and children. What specific teacher behaviors support your feelings? Give examples of how teachers encourage children's attitudes about their own competence, taking responsibility for their own actions, and solving their own problems. What rules or guidelines (stated and unstated) are operating in this setting?

Bibliography

Allen, K. Eileen. *The Exceptional Child. Mainstreaming in Early Childhood Education.* Albany, NY: Delmar. 1992 (2nd ed.).

Bailey, Donald B., & Wolery, Mark. *Teaching Infants and Preschoolers with Disabilities.* New York: Merrill, 1992.

Bredekamp, Sue (Ed.). *Developmentally Appropriate Practice in Early Childhood Programs Serving Children From Birth Through Age 8.* Washington, DC: National Association for the Education of Young Children, 1987.

Bredekamp, Sue, & Rosegrant, Teresa (Eds.). *Reaching Potentials: Appropriate Curriculum and Assessment for Young Children.* Vol. 1. Washington, DC: National Association for the Education of Young Children, 1992.

Collis, Mark, & Dalton, Joan. *Becoming Responsible Learners.* Portsmouth, NH: Heinemann Educational Books, 1990.

Crary, Elizabeth. *Kids Can Cooperate.* Seattle, WA: Parenting Press, 1984.

Crary, Elizabeth. *Without Spanking, Or Spoiling.* Seattle, WA: Parenting Press, 1993.

Faber, Adele, & Mazlish, Elaine. *How to Talk So Kids Will Listen and Listen So Kids Will Talk.* New York: Avon Books, 1980.

Gordon, Ann Miles, & Brown, Kathryn W. *Beginnings and Beyond: Foundations in Early Childhood Education.* Albany NY: Delmar, 1996 (4th ed.).

Gordon, Thomas. *Parent Effectiveness Training.* New York: Peter H. Wyden, 1970.

Hildebrand, Verna. *Guiding Young Children.* New York: Macmillan Publishing Co., 1980 (2nd ed.).

Hitz, Randy, & Driscoll, Amy. "Praise or Encouragement? New Insights Into Praise: Implications for Early Childhood Teachers." *Young Children,* July, 1988: 6–13.

Hoffman, M. L. Moral development. In M. H. Bornstein & M. E. Lamb (Eds.), *Developmental Psychology: An Advanced Textbook.* Hillsdale, NJ: Earlbaum, 1988 (2nd ed., pp. 497–548).

Maccoby, E. E. "Gender and Relationships: A Developmental Account." *American Psychologist,* 45 (1990): 513–520.

Miller, P. H., Danaher, D. L., & Forbes, D. "Sex-Related Strategies for Coping with Interpersonal Conflict in Children Aged Five to Seven." *Developmental Psychology,* 22 (1986): 543–548.

Mitchell, Anne, & David, Judy (Eds.). *Explorations with Young Children*. Mt. Rainier, MD: Gryphon House, 1992.

Nelsen, Jane. *Positive Discipline*. New York: Ballantine Books, 1987.

Nelsen, Jane, & Glenn, H. Stephen. *Time Out: Abuses and Effective Uses*. Fair Oaks, CA: Sunrise Press, 1992 (2nd ed.).

Prutzman, Priscilla, Stern, Lee, Burger, M. Leonard, & Bodenhamer, Gretchen. *The Friendly Classroom for a Small Planet*. Philadelphia, PA: New Society Publishers, 1988.

Wichert, Susanne. *Keeping the Peace*. Philadelphia, PA: New Society Publishers, 1989.

4

Issues of Diversity: Family, Culture, Gender, and Ability

Profiles

"You say you are having problems with our son," Bahraim's mother tells his child care teacher, "And we think it is because you are too easy on him, and that is not good for boys. Now he is hard on us, especially when we go to a store and he wants something. He won't take 'no' for an answer and starts throwing things and having tantrums. I know you tell us to explain to him why he can't have those things, but that is not our way. The more I explain, the more he keeps at me, and then it turns into an argument. It is so shameful having a disobedient child that I take him outside, but then he often hits me out there, which is forbidden for a child in our culture. Then I tell him no more cartoons, but he screams, 'I don't care!' This is a disgrace to our family. He's only a little child, but by the time children are three they must know not ever to hit or speak back. We feel it is time for punishment." Bahraim's teacher has spoken with his parents about his tantrums and aggression. The parents continue to urge the teachers to be tougher on him because he is a boy, and the teachers continue to explain why they will not spank or be physically aggressive with Bahraim. They are at a standstill.

Kailee has just turned five, and has a three-and-a-half-year-old brother. The teacher knows the family well. Kailee has been a difficult child, negative and withdrawn her first year at the center, and just beginning to trust by the second year. There was initial concern about her language development, with little improvement noted in two years. Kailee had a speech and hearing evaluation recently, which indicates that she has some learning difficulties. This is hard for the family to accept, because Kailee is their pride and joy. The problem seems worse to her parents, because they compare her to her younger brother. Tom has normal speech and hearing and surpasses Kailee in language ability. He is also becoming very competitive with her. They have many fights at home, and their parents are at their wits' end. Kailee is now sucking her thumb and withdrawing at school and the teachers seem unable to help her.

A small group of seven-year-old boys has begun to gang up on other children, primarily other boys, at recess. Each day they pick on a different child, teasing until the child cries. The seven-year-olds shout "Crybaby! Crybaby! Go home and get your diaper!" until the child flees from the schoolyard. Many times the group will include children who have been teased in this manner only a few days previously. Although their teacher has been aware of this behavior and has talked with the group about it, the teasing continues. Yesterday the group included racial taunts to the child who was being singled out, and his mother has informed the teacher that she wants something done about it.

Think It Over

What do you think you need to know to respect Bahraim's family's cultural values, yet follow good guidance principles? Are the conflicts between Kailee and her brother just a parent's issue? Should the teachers get involved? What is your response to the boys who tease and taunt other children? Were you ever teased in this way? How did you feel? What did you do?

Defining Diversity

Diversity, according to the dictionary, is a point or respect in which things differ, where they are separate and distinct, unlike each other. That definition could certainly describe the population of the United States at the brink of a new century. We are a nation of many different racial, cultural, ethnic, and religious peoples who represent a variety of social, economic, and linguistic experiences. In a special issue on multiculturalism, *Time* magazine (1993) hails the United States as "the first multicultural society . . . of unparalleled diversity . . . a great national pool" of peoples, cultures, languages, and attitudes. No longer a melting pot, or even a mosaic, but a "collection of intertwining subcultures each contributing its own character to the nation's life . . . while remaining distinct."

Four major variables—race/ethnicity, gender, social class, and ability (also known as exceptionality)—influence teachers and children both singly and in an interactive way. "Multicultural education" is the broad term used to suggest a type of education "concerned with creating educational environments in which students from a variety of microcultural groups such as race/ethnicity, gender, social class, regional groups, and people with disabilities experience educational equality" (Banks, 1994). Figure 4.1 on page 114 shows how these variables affect an individual and behavior.

Figure 4.1

A Kaleidoscope of Lenses

Dealing with diversity in a teaching and guidance setting means taking into account the complexity of the individual. Many variables influence children's behavior, and interact to create a dynamic situation. The kaleidoscope design has nineteen different interacting circles.

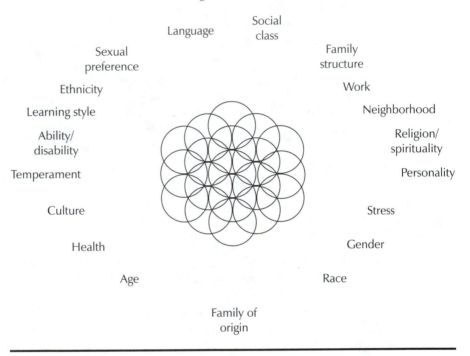

Language   Social class

Sexual preference   Family structure

Ethnicity   Work

Learning style   Neighborhood

Ability/ disability   Religion/ spirituality

Temperament   Personality

Culture   Stress

Health   Gender

Age   Race

Family of origin

Spitz, McLaughlin & Browne 1993, *Parents and Professionals: Adult Learners in Process,* National Association for Education of Young Children: Atlanta, 1994.

By the close of this century, we will be teaching children who are growing up in a country of unparalleled diversity. Cultures new to the American scene are converging, and people throughout the United States are redefining themselves to include their own cultural roots. With the passage of PL-142-147, children with disabilities are entering programs to gain an education in the least restrictive environment possible. Adding to this mix are religious and regional issues, as well as the overall problems of divergent social class and gender roles.

Children are more alike than they are different. The new century brings the challenge of mutual understanding and respect for different cultures.

The Teacher's Challenge: A Pluralistic Mindset

American children are experiencing population trends that affect their lives. The children we teach and the classrooms in which we teach do not greatly resemble the classrooms in which we learned. Children who were previously excluded by language, race, economics, and abilities are now sitting in classrooms together. What may be unfamiliar to us adults is now very familiar to our children, and the ability to adapt to the needs of a diversified group of students will be the challenge for the teacher of the 1990s and beyond.

Living with this challenge requires a pluralistic mindset and an ability to communicate across cultures and individual circumstances; it is exciting to many teachers and frustrating to others. The migration of so many cultures to the United States and the inclusion of so many divergent abilities and experiences cause feelings ranging from distrust, fear, and prejudice to eagerness, joy, and expectation. Discipline and guidance are deeply embedded within the values and beliefs of the family. Therefore, as teachers of the 1990s, we must examine our own values and learn about the beliefs held by the parents of the children we teach. We must make our own personal and professional journey through these remarkable times to prepare children to live in a diverse world.

This challenge has a twofold purpose. We want children to know and celebrate their own family and cultural heritage and take pride in who they are. At the same time, we want them to experience the diverse culture of people they meet, so they learn to understand and respect the cultural backgrounds and uniqueness of others. Both goals reinforce the belief that good discipline practices teach children behaviors and attitudes that help them live peacefully with other people.

It Begins with Me

As noted in previous chapters, the teacher has a particular and important role as a behavior model. Through self-understanding, teachers become aware of how their own attitudes and prejudices affect their approach to discipline. Just as with the children we teach, our own sense of self-worth derives from our family history and personal experiences, and we must be open to learning how that influences our work with children who come from many backgrounds. Accepting and understanding oneself is the first step toward accepting all children. For instance, a major pattern that emerges consistently in research studies on teacher-student interactions is that teachers give boys more attention, both positive and negative. Observe yourself teaching and see if you, too, fall into this category. A self-awareness campaign is described in this chapter and Table 4.1 offers some self-awareness exercises for teachers.

Our self-awareness affects the way we relate to children. Our personal histories reflect biases about how "other" people live, work, and play. We may not have experienced immigration to a foreign country, used food stamps at the grocery store, or tried to fit a wheelchair on a city bus. English may be the only language we have ever spoken, and we may never have questioned the salary scale differential between male and female employees where we work. Our own family culture shaped the way we feel about children who live differently than we do, and we may still buy into some of those prejudices without even being aware of them. Without firsthand knowledge or experience, we have probably developed strong feelings about children from backgrounds with which we are unfamiliar. In many subtle ways, we communicate this to the children in our classrooms.

The "anti-bias" approach (Derman-Sparks, 1989) to teaching young children is a program worthy of all teachers' attention. This important movement helps us confront our beliefs, attitudes, and actions that may harm children's self-identity and self-esteem and thereby create further behavior and discipline problems. When we learn some of the cultural norms and habits of the children in our classes, when we work with parents to promote the most acceptant atmosphere for their child who has a handicap, when we enrich the curriculum to reflect the diversity of humankind instead of gender stereotypes, we model a respect and concern for all. We operate from the premise that each child is valued as part of a family system, no matter its origins or definition, and that our role is to help reaffirm

---

Table 4.1

Self-Awareness Activities

One way teachers begin to know children better is to start by raising their own awareness of who they are. Self-awareness activities such as these can be done by a single teacher, a group of teachers, or parents and teachers together.

Racial/Ethnic Identity

Think about your racial/ethnic identity, then your gender identity, and about yourself in terms of ability/disability.

What is important and not important about you in these aspects of yourself? If it is important, why? If not, why not?

How do you feel about your racial/ethnic identity? Your gender identity? Your physical abilities and limitations?

How did you learn about each of these aspects of yourself? What are your earliest memories? What was fun or painful as you learned about them?

How do you agree or disagree with your parents' views about race, ethnicity, gender, and abledness? If you disagree, how did you develop your own ideas? What and who were significant influences on you? What do you teach your children?

Write a list of acceptable and unacceptable behaviors for girls and boys, men and women. Think about the range of sex-role behaviors you accept in the children you teach.

Make a list about what you want other people to know about and what you don't want people to say about your racial and ethnic identity. Repeat this for your gender identity and abledness. Think about how you want someone who knows very little about your group to learn.

Write down an incident in which you experienced prejudice or discrimination against yourself. What did you do? Next write about an incident in which you observed prejudice or discrimination directed at someone else by a third party. What did you do? Are you satisfied with what you did then? What do you wish you would have done? What might you do now?

(Adapted from Derman-Sparks 1989.)

the child's sense of security and personal identity within the family. Unconditional respect and the ability to grow with children in a greater understanding of diverse cultural issues creates a climate in which positive behavior and discipline can thrive.

You've Got to Be Carefully Taught

Children are not born with prejudices about differences in people; as the Rodgers' and Hammerstein song states, "You've got to be carefully taught." Children are aware of differences and will often comment on skin color, physical handicaps, gender roles, foreign accents, and material possessions in prejudicial ways (Derman-Sparks, 1989). Many children have strong feelings and attitudes about differences in people. Their comments often reinforce stereotypes and indicate a "pre-prejudice" attitude about people who are somehow different from them. Children begin to categorize and label what they see, just as they begin to see similarities and common interests and ally themselves to those. We need to notice their conclusions about what they notice, for they may be in error and begin to form mistaken attitudes and beliefs. The early childhood years are most appropriate for acquiring a variety of experiences and information so that children begin building positive attitudes about likenesses and differences among people, an appreciation of others, and the communication skills that promote positive interactions. Young children *can* be carefully taught about ethnic and cultural diversity.

Young children are primed for information and experiences that lay the foundation for multicultural appreciation. When children echo the hurtful biases and attitudes of adults, we know that although the children may not really understand the meaning, they are on the road to prejudiced behavior and attitudes. As teachers, our job is to help the children of the 1990s learn to live and work together. To prepare them to live in a world where cross-cultural interactions are common, we start by enriching their direct experiences. As adults, they need the ability to understand and appreciate different cultural views than the one in which they were raised.

The twenty-first century is shaping up as a multicultural global society, and we have an unprecedented opportunity to help our children learn about the rest of the world from the richness found in our classrooms. The ecology movement's phrase, "Think Globally, Act Locally" may well mean to early childhood teachers to keep in mind the world these children will live in and teach about tolerance and diversity by considering new ways to guide and discipline effectively.

Think It Over

When you were growing up, were there families in your neighborhood who came from other cultures or backgrounds? What were your family's attitudes toward them? Do you have the same attitudes? Have you ever been the target of discrimination? How did you respond?

How Diversity and Discipline Are Related

It Takes Two to Tango

Guidance and discipline are embedded in values. This makes the work of the early childhood professional interesting, intensely personal, and very complicated. More than any other aspect of teaching, guidance and discipline ask the most from the teacher. Good discipline practice calls upon the teacher to "Know thyself" and, at the same time, to know every one of the children as a unique human being, and to understand the family setting in which the child operates.

"Who am I?" is a universal human question that is a cornerstone of a child's early development and experience. To consider what the child brings to that question requires understanding children in two important aspects. First, each child has a unique *individuality*—temperament, age, race, gender, ability. Second, children bring the *context* in which they live—family, culture, ethnicity, religion, socioeconomic level, neighborhood community, and the like. When we consider these influences, we are better able to match the child with the most effective and learnable guidance and discipline.

A child does not come into our care from a vacuum, but possesses an individuality and a social identity. Because the art of guidance is also the teaching of values, it is especially important to understand both. We learn about children's individuality in many ways. We observe children in our care, and we interact with them daily. We notice how they respond to sensory input, how they react to new things, how they seem to take to others, how they deal with change and conflict. Some of these characteristics are similar to others. For instance, we know that all children are the same in certain universal ways: they have the same needs and rights, go through the same developmental stages, and have particular developmental goals. Bahraim, for instance, is similar to most young children in that he has strong wishes and feelings that sometimes get out of control when he is thwarted in getting what he wants immediately.

At the same time, children's family and cultural expectations will affect how they behave and what is considered appropriate behavior. The family's values, culture, and ethnicity determine their ideas about and techniques for discipline. Children in any one age group may have lots in common, but our learning and notions of how to behave are culture-bound. Teachers without appropriate knowledge of children's cultures and families risk misapplying what they know of development and teaching. Moreover, they may find themselves in opposition to rather than in alliance with the parents and families of the children in their care. To best guide young children, teachers must know each family's values and discipline techniques.

This is neither easy nor simple. It would take far less work simply to do what your own experience or training taught you, and be done with it. If we lived in a monoculture, this might work. Then, professionals could assume a certain belief system and family structure and teach from that one perspective. For instance, teasing among primary children is not new, but the racial taunts that accompany it are different now that we live in a more diverse society. Furthermore, it is no longer acceptable to allow children of the dominant culture to belittle those of minorities. For the teacher, *diversity and discipline are related and inseparable.*

A final note: If it takes two to tango, why can't these two simply be the child and teacher? Why does the parent have to be involved? As a crucial part of the socialization and education of the young child, teachers must look at the child in a family context. To the child, where and when you learn are not relevant: the childrearing that goes on at home and the education that goes on at school or in a child care setting are intimately tied. Teachers can set policies or procedures for classrooms that manage children's behavior there. To make a positive difference in children's lives in the long run, teachers must work with families to establish ways of guidance and discipline that make sense for both sets of adults. This way the child can experience the consistency necessary for healthy self-esteem and self-discipline. *An authentic blend of diversity and discipline connects family and teacher guidance practices in some meaningful way.*

A Portrait of America 2000

In truth, we don't live in a monoculture, in terms of culture, ethnicity, family structure, or socioeconomic status. The majority of families no longer fit a stereotypical model of father working and mother at home with children. The advent of the 1990s saw a majority (60 percent) of mothers with children under six in the work force, and the population of children under ten from single-parent households is approaching nine million (Edelman, 1990; Osborn, 1991).

The very definition of a family must be widened to include children who live with:

- A dual-career family, with two parents working outside the home;
- A single parent;
- Extended families, such as grandparents;
- A teen parent living with or without family support;

- A parent and other adult household members;
- A blended group of adults with children who have remarried to form a new family; and
- A kind of extended family, with another parent or parents and their children.

Families vary infinitely in their makeup, and in the ways they raise and socialize their children. The reality is that many children now live in a family setting different from the traditional, two-parent family that many call a "nuclear family." Many live in single-parent or blended families, need to learn flexibility and independence early on, and often experience poverty or economic uncertainty.

Families from such different groups and with such wide experiences vary tremendously in childrearing practices and in parent-child interactions. The values and attitudes about behavior, problems, expectations, even seeking help are bound to vary widely among parents of the children we teach. Often professionals have been trained by standards or have lived in primarily white, well-educated, middle class America. Inevitably, most work with families who have backgrounds, experiences, and value systems that are different from those of the teacher. Later in the chapter, Table 4.3 on page 133 illuminates the challenges of working with families from many cultural backgrounds.

D + D = S/E

What's a mathematical formula doing in a guidance text? It simply means that Diversity of children and families added to Discipline strategies equals Self-esteem! A primary goal of discipline is self-discipline for the child, and good discipline practices emphasize the process that helps children learn more about themselves and how to get along in the world. The basic tenets of child guidance (see Chapter 1) remind us that discipline is influenced by many factors, and the "Guidance Triangle" (see Figure 1.1) shows us that we must take into consideration *child, adult,* and *situation.* As teachers adapt their discipline practices to the children and families they teach, they provide the child with the basis of discipline: the development of a cohesive, successful self.

Self-esteem comes from a positive and realistic self-concept. Teachers who take individual diversity into consideration when guiding a child are reflecting to children both what they *need* to do and what they *can* do. When her playmates won't climb a fence with her, Kailee begins to taunt them, calling them "stupid babies." A shouting match ensues; what might be done next? The teacher knows that this name-calling is what Kailee hears from her little brother, and that her own limitations sensitize her to being called a baby. If the teacher can see Kailee's behavior in that light, there might be less overreacting to her words. The teacher can talk with Kailee about the hurtful words, but can also emphasize learning other ways to respond when her friends don't like her ideas. This is a guidance moment that preserves self-esteem by flexing with the individual child's life experiences.

What's a Teacher to Do?

Today's families may take many shapes and sizes, but their functions remain protection, communication, and provision for self-esteem. They also often offer financial support, housing, intellectual stimulation, traditions, and the like. For the purposes of guidance, however, the most essential function lies in the need to teach about social and intimate relationships (Gonzalez-Mena, 1993). Through early interactions and family relationships, an infant and toddler develop the capacity to form attachments. Preschoolers learn how to get along in a family setting, and primary children use the family as a touchstone and place for support and interpretation about the larger world.

Teachers need families in many ways. Encouraging a high degree of family enthusiasm for their children's schools and child care centers, "is one of the best ways in which teachers can attempt to build children's self-esteem and can reduce discipline problems and can boost children's regard for themselves as learners" Greenberg (1989). The family that endorses the child's school signals that they approve of what the child is doing. Whether through informal daily interactions, direct parent participation in the classroom, or overall parental influence in school affairs, the teacher who shows respect for the parent is more likely to have children who understand and respect the teacher and program.

What skills are needed to ensure that interactions between teachers and families are positive and facilitate consistent discipline practices for children? McGoldrick (1983) suggests that the primary skill required of professionals who work with diverse families is to be "open to understanding values that differ from our own and [to] no longer need to convince others of our values or give in to theirs." Teachers need to ask questions and get to know families in an individualized approach that reflects a respect for family diversity. By becoming familiar with a family as a unique, valued part of a child's life, teachers also avoid stereotyping. For instance, single-parent families are not a homogeneous group; assuming a particular parental discipline style based on that one fact would be erroneous.

As overwhelming as this might seem at first glance, this approach is, in fact, simply an extension of our work with children as unique individuals. Teachers blend their knowledge of children in general with what they learn about a child as an individual. Applying this strategy to families allows the teacher to incorporate such diversity into guidance techniques.

Galinsky (1987) has written about the changes that parents make as they live with their children. She has found that most parents experience stages of parenthood. The phases correspond roughly with the age of the child and the kinds of tasks that the child is engaged in at the time. The parent's own age and life experiences affect the stages of development, as do the age and number of children in the family. Knowledge of these three factors is useful for the teacher in building relationships with parents. Table 4.2 outlines the six stages of parenthood.

Table 4.2

Stages of Parenthood

Images of parenthood will affect how parents see themselves and their child, which, in turn, will influence how they respond to children's behavior and how they set expectations.

1 Image-making stage	During pregnancy	Form images of what will come, of birth and parenthood
2 Nurturing stage	Birth until child says "No."	Compare one's images with reality; become attached to child; set priorities
3 Authority stage	Two–four years	Decide what kind of authority to be, what rules there will be and how to enforce, what to do when they are broken
4 Interpretative stage	Preschool-kindergarten to adolescence	Review parenthood; interpret selves to child and the world to the child; how to answer child's questions, what to promote
5 Interdependent stage	Teenage years	Rework of Authority stage issues; form new relationship with child who no longer is one
6 Departure stage	Offspring leave home	Evaluate images and experiences as a parent; take stock

(*The Six Stages of Parenthood,* adapted from pp. 9–10, © 1987 by Ellen Galinsky. Reprinted by permission of Addison-Wesley Publishing Company, Inc.)

Teachers need to develop ways to communicate with family members respectfully and clearly. It is important to recognize that differences do, in fact, exist. How we understand each other's values and the discipline practices that evolve from them will measure our success in guiding children in our care.

A teacher's job is to be open-minded and untiring in the effort to work together with parents. Parents and teachers educate each other about their common interest: the child. Parents are gold mines of information and insights about their child, and need the listening ear of the teacher regarding the child, the family, and the lives they lead.

Teachers are gold mines, too, of facts and feelings. They can inform parents about child development, early childhood curriculum, and guidance techniques that can enlighten the parents about their own child and their ongoing role as a teacher in the child's life. In an open-minded exchange of helpful information, teachers can communicate their expectations and understandings.

The "us-versus-them" attitude that teachers and parents often have is counterproductive. Instead, the idea of parents and teachers as allies encourages both to find ways to share openly and effectively about the children. Think of the teacher as generalist, the parent as specialist. Teachers help parents learn about children in general, for they can share their knowledge of typical child development and what they have learned from their experience with children this age. Parents help teachers learn about this particular child, for no one knows the child like the parent. The intersection of these two lines of knowledge is the child.

Moreover, misconceptions about each other's cultural heritage or family style lead to many unnecessary conflicts. Trying to find out more about a family includes asking about their beliefs and ideas about how children should behave, and will prevent you from relying on a stereotyped idea of that family or its culture. "Cultural miseducation" (Lightfoot, 1978) often results in damaging parent-teacher relationships and creating distrust, a "worlds apart" attitude among people.

Effective strategies for learning about diversity include:

1. *Teachers acquiring accurate and proactive information on the values, characteristics, and attributes from cultures different from their own.* This often takes the form of continuing education, workshops, and in-service offerings. It also requires inviting meaningful interactions with parents; as Greenberg (1989) reminds us, "One-way communication isn't communication and doesn't work."

2. *Shared teacher-parent activities that bring them together in mutual support and to broaden each other's knowledge.* A parent work-afternoon to rebuild and fill a sandbox can often bring parents together to talk about their children and life at home in a way that lets teachers learn comfortably. A parent evening on a timely topic can stimulate new thoughts, and a discussion after the speaker leaves often brings out parents' opinions and teachers' lives in a new way. Asking parents to participate only by silent attendance or on your "turf" may result in resentment and apathy. Develop plans that invite participation and shared activities.

3. *Parent involvement in planning and carrying out classroom activities that capitalize on children's diversity.* Programs must have ways for parents to contribute that important part of themselves which represents their background and heritage. You may invite parents to share their way of celebrating a holiday, to help the children label their classroom in a language other than English, to teach the group a song from another culture, to rearrange and enrich a dress-up corner with cultural dress and jewelry, or to put together a counting book in everyone's native language. Parents were children once; those who felt frustrated or left out as children may need many genuine invitations and ways to be in a classroom without failure.

4. *Family–school events that integrate cultural learning.* A breadmaking morning, with as many recipes from individual families as possible, makes a Saturday at school fun for children and offers a safe environment to share much about each other. Children who feel that they have to reject their family to succeed at school are often discipline problems. Conversely, children for whom school is an extension of their family do not find themselves in two separate worlds; rather, they learn that one way to get family approval is to do their best at school. When families and schools integrate, the adults who care for children become more united in their expectations.

Think It Over

How would you explain to a "culture-bound" teacher that diversity and discipline are closely related and have an affect on one another? How many definitions of family do you see in the classrooms where you observe? What examples do you see of teacher's developing communication links with families from cultures other than their own?

Understanding Culture without Stereotyping

Teacher, Know Thyself

Why should teachers pay attention to differences among people, or children in particular? Derman-Sparks (1989) suggests an answer: "Children are aware very young that color, language, gender, and physical ability differences are connected with privilege and power. They learn by observing the differences and similarities among people and by absorbing the spoken and unspoken messages about those differences. Racism, sexism, and handicappism have a profound influence on their developing sense of self and others." Remembering that "Diversity + Discipline = Self-Esteem," we know how children's early guidance experiences will affect their attitudes about themselves and other people. Phillips (1992) reminds us that "it has been said that actions more often than not speak louder than words. And if this is so in the case of child-rearing, then we must be especially vigilant in our actions to shape the values children will attach as they learn about the people in their world." This is particularly true for young children, and of heightened importance in the area of parent-teacher overlap: that of guidance and discipline. Children who experience contrasting strategies of discipline and tension-filled interactions about guidance between two of the most important influences in their lives will feel the discomfort of dissonance and likely behave accordingly.

Taking into account a child's diversity and family culture in our teaching and guidance calls for teachers to engage in a self-awareness campaign. As mentioned earlier in this chapter, "it begins with me." This process has two steps: (1) developing an understanding of your own culture and family background, and (2) conducting a "needs assessment" about your own knowledge and attitudes, recognizing your own biases and identifying areas of ignorance. Derman-Sparks (1989) and others have developed materials to help the early childhood teacher gain awareness of familial and cultural diversity, and of the biased and ignorant behaviors that society, adults, and children display. Teachers can get started by educating themselves. Figure 4.1 outlines more specific self-awareness activities.

Second, teachers look at what they already know and what attitudes they may have about various racial/ethnic groups, about boys and girls and their behavior by gender, and about physical abilities and limitations. For a teacher to guide children well, accurate information about all these areas is essential. Teacher knowledge, attitudes, and skills work together to provide responsive and effective guidance. The bibliography for this chapter offers several resources to engage in this process.

Who Are the Families I Will Meet?

The 1980s saw a wave of immigration not experienced since the great immigration nearly a century ago. This time, people are coming from Asia and the various Hispanic cultures, not just from Europe. The following statistics tell the story:

- The Anglo population in the United States has decreased to 80 percent, while the African-American population rose to 12 percent and Hispanics climbed to 9 percent (Armstrong, 1991).
- In the last decade, the number of Asian-Americans more than doubled: they now make up approximately 3 percent of the total population (Armstrong, 1991).
- In the last decade, the Hispanic population grew more than 50 percent (Armstrong, 1991).
- In 1992, 37 percent of U.S. immigrants came from Asia (U.S. Census Bureau).
- In 1992, 44 percent of U.S. immigrants came from Latin America and the Caribbean Islands (U.S. Census Bureau).
- Thirteen percent of Americans speak a language other than English at home (U.S. Census Bureau).
- Between 1985–1991, enrollment in public school increased by just over 4 percent, yet the number of students with little or no English language skills increased by 50 percent (Gray, 1993).
- Over 127 languages and dialects are spoken by students in the Washington, D.C., school system (Gray, 1993).
- One out of six children in California public schools is born outside the United States and one-third of them speak a language other than English at home (Gray, 1993).

By 2050, the population, according to the Census Bureau, is predicted to be 52 percent Anglo, 16 percent Black, 22 percent Latino, and 10 percent Asian, with Hispanics (who can be of any race) the largest minority population. Teachers who have information about and experience with children of these diverse racial and ethnic groups will be better able to deal with issues of guidance with their families.

We may react to a given situation based on not only our own cultural background but also on our experiences with a particular ethnic group. Ong (1994) suggests a helpful metaphor: "Think of an iceberg. What we know is what we can see. But two-thirds of an iceberg is under the surface and it is that two-thirds that we must be conscious of if we want to stay out

Each family has its own values and beliefs about raising children. For the most effective approach to guidance, teachers learn to understand the interests and concerns of parents from many backgrounds.

of trouble. Culture is like the iceberg, Some of it you can see. Most of it you cannot see." A previous experience with one child from El Salvador does not mean the next Latino child will be the same. To find out more, we need to look deeper.

Return to the definition of family and its main functions: protection, communication, provision for self-esteem, learning about social and intimate relationships. A child's experience of guidance and discipline comes from the family, so it behooves teachers to know those families well. It helps to know that Bahraim's parents expect the children in a family to share space and possessions, and that they value cooperation over individualism. The ideas of independence that the center teaches may be acceptable for self-care, but may feel uncomfortable when a preschooler asserts herself about "I want it!" or "You're not my boss!" Bahraim's experiences about personal relationships are based on the pattern of interactions in his family. His response to authority or about closeness is based on what he knows from home. When the "discipline moment" arises, the teacher who knows what Bahraim hears and responds to from home is better able to help him.

A teacher uses several strategies to find out about families and their value systems. One way is to ask directly, either with an interview or in writing. It may elicit some useful information, but it is incomplete and out of context. A home visit is a friendly way to get acquainted with a child and family on their turf, as long as the teacher can give the time, and has an easygoing manner to dispel any discomfort the family may feel about a school official seeing their home. Programs that invite family members to participate and visit their child regularly will be able to observe firsthand those relationships and discipline techniques. Inviting parents to bring artifacts and other expressions of their own culture is also useful.

Learning about individual families usually happens in two very different ways. The first is a pleasant one. Slowly and frequently, over time, families and teachers get acquainted. Through conversation and shared experiences, they build a trusting relationship. They begin to feel safe in exchanging opinions and anecdotes that show what they feel is important. The teacher, for instance, makes a point to talk to Kailee's grandmother at pick-up time. The grandmother doesn't live with the family, but is an integral part of her upbringing. Through conversation, the teacher shares important events in Kailee's school day, learns what her grandmother is thinking, and may gain insights into Kailee's relationship with her brother. The teacher gains valuable information about Kailee's behavior, and the grandmother finds out more about child development. Both learn something useful, and perhaps more importantly, form a bond about working together to help Kailee grow in self-discipline and self-expression.

The second way teachers learn about families and their values is less pleasant but no less important. Often abruptly but usually unavoidably, a teacher and parent find something they disagree about and are in conflict. Conflicts are inevitable, and conflicts about children and their behavior often occur between teacher and family.

What is particularly tricky is that any discussion about a child's misbehavior or some other negative issue brings with it a natural tension on the part of both parties. Both Bahraim's teacher and his parents feel uncomfortable about his temper tantrums. Their approaches differ: the teacher wants Bahraim to use reasoning and other strategies, but the parents feel a spanking is called for. Because most people have difficulties talking through their differences, both parent and teacher may feel uneasy. Parents usually have heightened feelings of worry or inadequacy regarding their own parenting skills and a protectiveness toward their child. Teachers may feel defensive about their own techniques, or anger at their inability to fix the problem themselves.

If these discussions are also about cultural conflicts, the problem may become more emotional, and can end with increased tension, without a solution, and with a breakdown of trust. Teachers can follow some guidelines with all families when discussing issues about children, their behavior, and guidance.

- *Be clear.* Know what you believe in and be aware of your own values.
- *Be willing.* Bring differences out in the open and discuss them in as candid and open a manner as possible.
- *Become an effective cross-cultural communicator.* Find out more about different styles of communication and the cultural messages such styles may convey.
- *Be a problem-solver.* Learn to use a conflict resolution method that engages you and the parents in a dialogue about your common interest, their child.
- *Commit yourself to becoming educated.* Specifically, commit yourself to continuing education about your families and other cultures.
- *Be a critical thinker.* Reflect on what you see and read as well as avoiding stereotypes. (Adapted from Gonzalez-Mena, 1993.)

Try It   Many holidays and celebrations reinforce cultural, religious, or ethnic stereotypes. Survey the teachers and parents in a classroom about their preferences and expectations. Find out what celebrations they have at home and what celebrations they believe should or shouldn't be celebrated at school. From this information, have discussions with other students and teachers about the following:

- What to do if a parent takes exception to celebrating certain religious holidays at school, including ways to find out more about their beliefs and how to respect their position.
- Cancelling all holiday celebrations at school and replacing them with ones that children create.
- Developing a school policy regarding holidays and celebrations.
- What "age-appropriate" means in relation to holidays and celebrations.
- Generating a list of civic and community celebrations for families.

A Sampling of Culturally Diverse Childrearing and Discipline Techniques

As we educate ourselves about culturally and socially diverse children and their families, we need information about childrearing that affects how families discipline their young children. The following points can form a basis for our own understanding of others:

- *The characteristics of an ethnic or cultural group are an integral part of a person's social reality.* An ethnic group is a special kind of cultural group that has an ancestral tradition with certain values, behavioral patterns, and interests that influence the lives of its members. Factors such as region, social class, gender, and race may also affect how individuals see themselves as ethnic or cultural members. Cultural groups identify themselves by ideas and the values attached to them, rather than objects. "It is their values, perspectives, and ways of viewing reality that distinguish cultural groups, from one another in the United States, not their clothing, foods, or other tangible aspects of group life" (Banks, 1994).

- *Cultural learning starts at birth and is largely nonverbal and unconscious.* We often don't notice this part of our lives until we find something that is different. Working with young children is lively and confrontative because they often simply say aloud what we have forgotten or about which we feel uncomfortable. Yet it is this directness and sensitivity about what they see, hear, and feel that makes children's cultural learning and individual feelings so important for the teacher to notice.

- *Culture determines our values, and values drive guidance and discipline.* Culture may seem invisible, or simply an integrated part of our make-up, but we have to address it openly if we are to be effective with children and families. This is sometimes less apparent when working with a young child than with a parent. Nonetheless, we need to take culture into consideration to avoid putting children in the emotionally stressful situation of having to compartmentalize their two worlds of home and school because they are "too different."

- *Be careful about making generalizations about families from their structure or culture.* Simply knowing someone's race, family structure, religion, or neighborhood does not tell you everything you need to know. Be cautious about generalizing from one family to the next; for instance, just because some of the boys who teased and bullied other children are of divorced parents does not mean that *every* single parent will have an alienated or troubled relationship, or that this is the cause of the bullying. Thinking that Kailee is deficient because of learning difficulties would have disastrous negative effects. The same kind of thinking might turn Bahraim's family of Iranian origin into a vision of passivity that simply doesn't exist in that household. We belong to many microcultural groups—of race, ethnicity, social class, gender, religion, exceptionality—that will interface in a young child or individual family in such a way that overgeneralizing will result in serious mistakes.

This section informs teachers about childrearing and discipline techniques beyond the traditional white middle-class view. Each teacher must use this information carefully. These ideas allow you to begin a dialogue with your own families and the children you teach about this essential area of discipline and guidance. Three issues that have direct application for the teacher and for discipline strategies in early childhood programs follow. Table 4.3 describes some of the patterns and kinds of discipline that might parallel such childrearing styles.

Attachment and Separation

"The world may be seen as divided into two halves: those cultures who cut the apron strings and those who do not" (Hall, 1981). Those who encourage independence from parents and an ability to make a child a separate individual are from cultures that cut the apron strings. These cultures usually encourage a primary attachment, usually to the mother, at the same time that they have the longer goal of producing children who can stand on their own.

Those who encourage a more permanent connection, whose membership in the extended family remains as they mature and stay interconnected, rather than separate, are from cultures where growing up does not involve cutting the apron strings. Often these cultures involve multiple caregivers and less exclusionary or primary attachments.

These two halves illustrate a set of priorities, rather than absolutes, a difference of degree. In both kinds of cultures, children are encouraged to feel close to others and to succeed both inside and outside of the family. Both want them to attain a measure of individuality and achievement. But there is a difference in the degree of separateness, both with very young children and also in children as a matter of course throughout childhood. And it is this difference of degree that makes it important to look at a family through its cultural eyes.

With high infant mortality and economic insecurity, these care practices make abundant sense. However, even when external conditions change, such habits are already ingrained in the childrearing practices passed on

Table 4.3		

Sample of Culturally Diverse Family Patterns That Affect Guidance and Discipline

Knowledge of culturally diverse family patterns and guidance strategies to parallel these childrearing styles can allow you to begin a dialogue with the children you teach.

Cultural Patterns	Child's Behavior	Guidance Strategy
Reside in extended family household	High level of cooperation and responsibility; children do not like being separated	Provide activities that build on cooperation and sharing; have mixed age groupings
Family members share in decision making	Learns to negotiate, compromise	Give choices; use problem-solving techniques
One family member makes all the decisions	Expected to be obedient, follow commands, respect authority	Support child in making choices; do not force eye contact
Child considered an infant for first twelve months	Cries when told "no" and slapped on hand; allowed to cry it out	Use simple, short commands at end of first year
Child is considered an infant until two years old	Relies on constant contact with mother; has not learned self-help skills	Touch, hold, and carry child often; play near/with other children, not alone
Child is considered an infant until five years old	Has not been disciplined until now; may still drink from bottle; parents unconcerned about development milestones	Allow for separation anxiety; support this with transitional objects from home
Family life includes discrimination, violence, lack of opportunities	Used to being ignored or ridiculed; learns to tolerate inequality	Firm but delay responses to child; respect parents' need to keep child safe
Strong, closely knit family	Learns that family, not individual, comes first	Understand that school demands will take second place to family needs
Independence	Held infrequently, has own space/toys at home	Allow solitary play with little pressure to share; needs to move around independently
Pride and dignity	Upholds family honor; used to being disciplined for rude behavior and poor manners	Tell parents of child's accomplishments; be sensitive to their pride when discussing discipline problems
Family comes from strong oral tradition	Behavior has been guided by stories with morals	Use songs and stories to model acceptable behavior
Family expresses feelings readily	Crying, screaming, and temper tantrums are common	Support with your presence while gently setting limits

(continued)

Table 4.3   (Continued)

Cultural Patterns	Child's Behavior	Guidance Strategy
Family does not show feelings	Has been told not to cry; showing of feelings are discouraged	Comfort as soon as child cries; remove from group while expressing feelings
Discipline is harsh: spanking, threats, humiliation	Understands authority	Begin with firm statements; model desired behavior; praise appropriate behavior
Foster harmony and avoid conflict	Scolded and shamed when misbehaves	Find ways to encourage/praise cooperation; teach problem-solving techniques

(Adapted from *Roots and Wings: Affirming Culture in Early Childhood Programs,* by Stacey York. St. Paul, MN: Redleaf Press, 1991)

from family to family. It is hard to separate these survival practices from cultural values and patterns of attachment and separation.

Further, the attachment patterns of the two different orientations show a difference in the degree of independence and interdependence, not in competence and dysfunctionality. The outcome of the "string-cutters" is individuals who stand alone; the outcome of the "string-savers" is individuals with lifelong attachments to the group. In America we have cultural groups of both kinds.

Potential areas of cultural conflict may arise in whether parents are comfortable with their babies left on the floor, or children allowed to cry on separation. Indeed, some parents may wish to leave their children as soon as they arrive whereas others may insist on staying for days or weeks in your program along with the child. Other issues that may arise concern appropriate guidance and discipline for the very young child. Is it all right to let a child cry unattended when the parent leaves? Some would say that any crying child should be picked up and held by any available adult, and distracted or cajoled out of crying. Others might claim that a child should be allowed to "cry it out," and that an adult nearby for the child to call is sufficient.

A third example of such cultural differences occurs in care-taking routines:

- Napping/sleeping: Does the adult lie down with the child? Is the child rocked until asleep? Must the child stay in the bed or the crib?

- Dressing: Are they expected to feed or dress themselves (and when)?
- Toileting: How early to begin? Six months? Eighteen months? Three years? Do they wear diapers, training pants, or no pants? Is both bowel and bladder control to be achieved at once?

What do adults do when a child screams to get something? Do they redirect the child, or keep repeating "no"? Teachers who work with children under three should consider the family patterns and try to establish some consistent and appropriate expectations.

There is quite a difference between cultural differences and actual dysfunction, and the teacher has to look carefully to determine this. See the family through its eyes instead of only yours. Try not to see "dysfunction" just because it's different from your own. The family who asks you to feed their four-year-old at lunch may be just as healthy as the one who insists their two-year-old can pedal a trike across the neighborhood to your center alone. They may not be either as "overprotective" or as "abandoning" as you see it. You will need more information about the particular family and their childrearing patterns before you decide.

At the same time, the sensitive teacher needs to look closely to avoid making the reverse mistake. You may look at a family with difficulties and see only cultural or familial differences where there are deeper problems. A male-dominated family can be the cultural norm; a family in which the father threatens and emotionally bruises the children is not psychologically healthy.

Socialization and Power

Socialization is the process through which children learn to get along with others. A lifelong process, it is intensified in the preschool years, and is of primary importance in most programs for children two-and-a-half to five years of age. Discipline and guidance are most often needed in the important area of interacting with others. The socialization process is influenced by the situation in which it happens, and the people who are involved.

Once again, the two kinds of cultural orientation will cause people to see things differently and they will respond in different ways to children's behavior. The individualistic orientation has the cultural value of individual accomplishment. Thus, what is begun in the very early years as a move toward initial separation extends into the area of socialization in preschool and into competition with others in the primary years. In the white, European-based culture, a person is seen as a distinct human being, with rights and needs as a separate individual. Children are often told they are special, and their belongings and personal space are valued. Their achievements are touted, as is individual freedom. The expression of individual feelings is encouraged.

Alternative Approaches

Think back on Bahraim, the expressive two-and-a-half-year-old. His parents and teachers are in a dilemma that can only be resolved with cultural sensitivity. His mother feels that he needs to learn respect for the feelings of his elders, and so he needs to suppress his anger. His teacher has been educated (and, perhaps, raised) to believe that it is important for these young preschoolers to be allowed to work out their anger, and that not allowing complete expression will be unhealthy for a child's self-esteem.

But who is right? It is a question of balance and of value. Perhaps Bahraim's teacher will be able to work out a middle ground by blending the educator's experiences about self-expression and normal two-year-old behavior with the family's priorities and vision of the child as a growing person. They may not agree, but they will understand each other's views better if each adult's wishes and positions are respected. If Bahraim's mother is overridden by the teacher who strongly believes, "This is what all children are like and need," she will most likely get quiet and not tell or ask again. If, however, his mother is listened to and her ideas about respect for elders are taken into account, she will be more likely to incorporate the teacher's notions about "developmentally appropriate" tantrum behavior and allow more feelings to be expressed than she ordinarily might. Which outcome helps Bahraim more?

They could start by finding some common areas of agreement: perhaps that Bahraim will be withdrawn from the group if he throws a tantrum. They should also agree that neither will imply to Bahraim that the other is in the wrong. Inviting Bahraim's mother to class to tell a story about the country where she was born or to share a special piece of music will help teacher and parent get to know each other on subjects other than Bahraim's behavior. Sharing some examples of Bahraim's positive behavior with each other will move the focus from his misbehavior as the point of conversation. Continued conversation about parental expectations, cultural differences, and school discipline policies will keep the dialogue going until solutions are found that respect the two points of view.

In the cultures with a collective orientation, such as in many Asian and Latin American cultures, the group, not the individual, is of primary importance. Making a fuss about what belongs to whom may look to them like teaching selfishness to children. Children are encouraged to help each other, and there is less of an urge toward achievement than encouragement toward being part of something larger than themselves. Comparison is seen as meaning that someone is better than another, putting the individual in an uncomfortable spotlight. In cultures that value group harmony over individual expression of feelings, the idea of encouraging full expression runs counter to the underlying value of contributing to a shared feeling. The control of these strong feelings is seen as more likely to result in maintaining harmonious social relationships than the full expression of one's feelings or opinions.

Conflict Resolution and Cooperative Learning

Two areas of guidance, conflict resolution and cooperative learning, have particular application to the older end of the early childhood spectrum. As in the other issues, there are culturally diverse responses to these two strategies. How children learn to resolve conflicts and learn with others is influenced not only by their cultural and family background, but also by their personal experiences.

By the time children enter formal schooling, most of them have a pretty strong idea of who they are (or aren't) and some fundamental attitudes about adults, authority, and school. Furthermore, although most of them have developed attitudes about race, ethnicity, gender, and ability, "few children have extensive positive experiences with racially, culturally, economically, or otherwise different children" (McCracken, 1993). They are still curious, and may ask direct questions as they did in preschool. Now, however, they need more response—not a lecture, but more information. Primary children are more self-conscious as a group than their younger counterparts. Their prior attitudes may affect their behavior, but they may be less open about acknowledging their own attitudes or beliefs and less willing to change them.

Children's diversity is always present in a classroom, but individual diversity may be tolerated less by primary-age children. Some differences, such as the ways boys and girls talk and relate to each other (see Gender Issues in this chapter), have important implications for teaching and guidance. Teachers may be called on to take a strong, if also more subtle, role in promoting individual diversity. Authentic self-esteem (McCracken, 1993) is critical in the primary years as the child becomes more independent of the family in school and so must stand alone more often. Children need practical ways to feel pride and encouragement in their efforts more than ever; respect for each family's culture and knowledge of the family's goals is essential for children to feel pride in themselves, in their cultural heritage, and in their ability to make their way in a world with so many different people.

At the same time, the cultural heritage that the child brings is still mostly unconscious, and it is beyond children's ability to logically shift or open up to scrutiny their own beliefs or attitudes on an intellectual level. What they can do, however, is articulate in their primary language a great deal about their wants, opinions, and ideas. This is why the strategies of democratic conflict resolution and cooperative learning can be so useful. Still, a child's own culture and family experiences influence how these two strategies work.

Think back to the group of seven-year-old boys. Our knowledge of children's language and behavior tells us that it is not unusual for children this age to be working on issues of inclusion and exclusion. Children this age are also constructing ideas about appropriate gender roles. If teasing and forming a group (or "gang") is a cultural or gender role for boys, it is not surprising that these boys are bringing their behavior into line with such ideas. When teachers know what forces are driving the children's behavior, they can better fit the intervention to the situation. In the case of the seven-year-old boys, the teacher realized that children tend to copy same-sex adult role models at this age (Grossman & Grossman, 1994). She called in some of the fathers and a male teacher to communicate some gender-specific expectations; that is, what it means to be a strong boy without being mean. These adults had an impact in eliminating both the "ganging up" and racial epithets; they helped the boys find other ways of being part of a group.

Conflict resolution techniques, as explained in Chapter 3, are particularly relevant to the four- to eight-year-old, because of their overall language proficiency and emotional impulse control. Developmentally, rules are considered the creation of an all-powerful authority figure and are not to be changed (see Erikson and Kohlberg in Chapter 2), so primary children are ready to follow rules but are also sensitive to issues of fairness. This conflict resolution helps develop self-discipline, the goal of most early childhood guidance principles and one of the tenets of this book. It also encourages a blending of the individual and group cultural orientations. Individual contributions to identifying a problem and posing solutions encourages individuals to feel a sense of personal achievement. At the same time, cooperation and helping each other is encouraged, an important component to many collective cultures.

Not all cultural conflict is avoided with this strategy, however. For instance, not all cultures work toward such inner control at this age. Hale (1986) and Snowden (1984) both note that adults in many African-American communities play the social control role. Rather than expecting children to conform to rules on their own, they make a network of adults throughout the community who "correct undesirable behavior whenever it occurs and report such behavior to the parent" (Hale, 1986). Sandoval and De La Rosa (1986) comment that in the Hispanic community the extended family also plays a role in providing external control over children. Other parents thus serve as a kind of "consensus protection."

Cooperative learning is the other strategy that is often encouraged in the early childhood classroom and school-age center, but tends to drop out in elementary school. This is an example of what is often labeled "institutional bias": that is, that the structure or system has an in-house bias against certain kinds of behaviors or attitudes. Because most elementary schools are developed from systems promoted by the dominant, Eurocentric, and individualistic cultural orientation, teachers are usually trained to offer activities that promote skill development, individual achievement, and, indirectly, competition. Classrooms that value collaboration, cooperation, and group skills are those from more of a group cultural orientation. These classrooms offer activities that have children work in pairs, on teams, and in committees. Children negotiate as individuals, but also accommodate to each other's

Cooperative learning extends from the classroom to the playground. Children learn to appreciate teamwork as well as individual achievements and to accommodate for each others skill and knowledge.

diverse languages, knowledge levels, and thinking styles. This teaching technique is usually thought of in terms of curriculum development or academic learning. However, the wise teacher prepares the environment, considers the interpersonal tone of a program, and devises indirect methods for guiding and encouraging behavior.

As before, cultural conflict may arise from using cooperative learning as a strategy for guidance. Parents of primary children are becoming concerned about their children's academic achievement, and their memories of school, however difficult, may greatly affect their opinions about how learning should proceed. Those from an individualistic orientation may see this as a step backwards from the "natural" progression begun in the very early years as initial separation and a valuing of the individual. Competition with others in the primary years is seen by this group as a healthy component of becoming task-oriented and persistent, and of developing a drive to succeed and achieve. Without the competitive spirit, such a culture would argue, children cannot develop a will to do well and to keep fighting against difficulties. These parents may need lots of evidence that demonstrates their children's learning with less rigorous and more group-oriented guidance.

Think It Over

What do you know about your own racial and cultural identity? Where did your ancestors come from? Were you from apron string-cutters or not? When do you first remember learning about people from a different race or ethnic background? When were you first aware that gender mattered? How did you first experience a person with a handicap? How has this knowledge and experience defined your values, affected your sense of competition, and influenced your attitudes about cooperative learning?

Individual Variations on a Theme

As we described in the opening part of this chapter, children bring to our programs both the context in which they live and their individuality. Certainly, each child's response to our guidance techniques is affected by their temperament and their age (see Chapter 1). Two other areas of individuality that affect how we discipline are gender and ability/disability.

Gender Issues

Gender Research

"While generalizations about gender differences can be misleading, it is important to recognize that some gender differences cut across class, ethnic, and geographic boundaries . . . Such generalizations can be helpful because they can sensitize educators to the possibility that their students behave in certain gender-specific ways" (Grossman & Grossman, 1994). Of course, it is important not to assume that children always behave in gender-stereotypic patterns, but it is helpful to know about gender differences and what teachers often do in relationship to girls and boys.

In describing gender differences and their origins, Grossman and Grossman (1994) analyzed over seven hundred studies from a variety of sources. Their conclusions are as follows:

- *Gender differences do not appear all at once.* Only a few differences emerge during the infant and toddler stages, and cluster around levels of excitement and intensity of emotion. By eighteen months, girls' outbursts are decreasing and they seem quieter and calmer than boys, but boys' intensity and excitement levels do not drop off. Some sex-stereotypical toy preference is also seen.

- *During preschool, there are marked differences in what children play with and where they play, as well as how preschoolers relate to each other.* Boys are more rough-and-tumble than girls: girls tend to be more polite and helpful, and less aggressive than boys. Particularly relevant to guidance are these observations: "When faced with potential conflicts, girls tend to attempt to preserve the existing harmony by compromise and avoidance, while boys are more likely to confront them head on. Boys get their way with others by physical means, pushing, posturing, and demanding. Girls are more likely to use verbal manipulation . . . while boys may demand and order others." Also significant is the differential response to teachers: girls appear responsive to teachers and peers of either sex, boys are less responsive to teachers and ignore feedback from girls. Girls often become more passive in the presence of boys, but boys tend to interrupt girls. This pattern of male unresponsiveness to female peers and even female adults extends into middle childhood.

- *As children advance into elementary school, the gender differences in preschool continue, and additional differences emerge.* The emotional differences persist: girls are often more willing to express fears, but when boys express emotions it is done more intensely. Boys are angry more often than girls; girls are more likely to see themselves as sad. In general, boys continue to be more assertive, aggressive, and concerned about dominance, whereas girls tend to avoid conflicts with others, rather than dealing with them openly. Boys continue to exercise a dominant role in mixed-sex groups, initiating and receiving more of the interaction and doing more of the talking; girls seem equally responsive to both sexes, whereas boys continue to be responsive mostly to other boys. In communication style, most of the research has been done among European-Americans only. Girls tend to "avoid conflict, preserve harmony, and organize their relationships with others in nonhierarchical egalitarian ways. . . . In comparison to boys they speak politely, with few four-letter and forceful words. They tend to suggest and hint rather than command, and they express themselves less directly."

These gender differences are often mitigated by other circumstances. For instance, culture can play a role: African-American females do not appear to act so passively and are less likely than their European-American counterparts to allow boys to dominate mixed groups. Economic factors also make their mark: a social class with lower income and higher marital disruption might well result in the necessity of female independence; this could result in different models for children of that class and therefore different gender behaviors.

Living as a Girl and Boy: A Cultural Perspective

Gender differences have important ramifications for girls and boys as they live in families, communities, and educational programs. Just as with race/ethnicity, children's gender makes a difference in how they see themselves and how they relate to others. Children's school-related experiences are flavored by the gender differences.

For instance, many children, and particularly girls, probably learn more efficiently in cooperative learning environments. Boys tend to maintain their ideas in spite of what others think or feel, so they may do well in a more competitive atmosphere. However, because girls are more likely to conform to others, they might get overpowered in mixed-sex groups.

Girls are more adult-oriented than boys, and their self-esteem seems more dependent on feedback from others. Although they do ask for help from teachers, boys are more responsive to their peers (especially other boys) and seem to prefer to function independently.

Implications for Teachers

Teachers play a critical role in the gender differences we see in educational settings. As mentioned previously in this chapter, research shows convincingly that adults model gender-specific behaviors for children and that children tend to copy these models. School plays a major role in how children see themselves and develop.

More importantly, teachers exert a major influence in how children learn to behave. They reward the behavior they wish to see increased and punish behavior of which they disapprove. Because their encouragement and discipline interaction is so important, it serves us to find out what is actually happening. Table 4.4 illustrates teacher differences in respect to gender.

There are several problems with differential treatment of boys and girls in guidance and discipline. First, the comparative lack of guidance and encouraging attention to girls may convey the idea to girls, however subtle, that what they do matters less to teachers than what boys do. Although one's gender identity is important, it is problematic for children to conclude that a particular gender role closes them off from certain activities,

---

Table 4.4

Gender Research on How Teachers Guide Girls and Boys Differently

Gender research reveals some interesting ways that teachers respond differentially to boys and girls. Teachers play a critical role in the gender differences seen in educational settings. Watch yourself for the next week and see what you do.

Attention
1. Teachers give more attention to boys.
2. Teachers give girls and boys different kinds of attention.
3. Teachers give boys more positive feedback.
4. Teachers give boys more praise and attention for achievement.
5. Teachers give boys more praise for creative behavior.
6. Teachers call on girls less than on boys.
7. Teachers praise girls more for conforming behavior.
8. Teachers spend more time disciplining boys than girls.

Response to Inappropriate Behavior
1. Aggression is tolerated more in boys than in girls.
2. Disruptive talking is tolerated more in girls than in boys.
3. Boys are reprimanded more than girls.
4. Teachers use more physical means of discipline (poke, grab, push, squeeze) on boys than on girls.
5. Teachers use more negative comments or disapproving gestures with girls than with boys.

(Research findings from Grossman & Grossman, 1994 and Maccoby & Jacklin, 1974)

skill development, or overall growth and achievement. Finally, public and harsh reprimands are devastating to self-esteem, particularly in young children, and can cause hostility and rebellion in older children.

Try It   Gender stereotyping can lead to discipline problems. Often boys and girls feel excluded or exclude themselves from play in certain activities. Over a period of time, try the following suggestions in a classroom setting. Record the children's reactions and listen for responses from parents and other teachers.

- Declare a "girls only" day in the block corner.
- Place "boys only" garments in the dramatic play area.
- Omit all comments to girls about their clothing; admire what boys are wearing.
- Add scissors, paper, tape, and string to the block area; observe how children react and respond.
- Call for "strong bodies" and "good muscles" to help move furniture. See if girls as well as boys respond.

Evaluate the responses and consider repeating or enlarging these intentional efforts throughout the school year. What guidance situations arose that you did not expect? How were any discipline problems solved by these or similar ideas?

There is no one position on gender differences and educational practices, nor is there a single prescription for accommodating to existing differences while ensuring fair treatment for both girls and boys. In the area of discipline, however, the recommendations are clearer:

1. Pay equal attention to all children, calling on both girls and boys, providing the same kind and amount of help, and praising both boys and girls for achievement and creativity.
2. Be equally attentive to misbehavior in both girls and boys. Establish general guidelines of behavior that take into account developmental, cultural, and gender information. Then, encourage *all* children to behave within the same standards of behavior.

Sex role stereotypes begin to affect children's behavior at an early age. What are some of the ways we reinforce rigid role definitions for boys and girls?

3. Avoid excessively harsh punishments with both boys and girls.
4. Discourage dependent, helpless, and excessively conforming behavior in both girls and boys.

In a related subject, teachers of both genders in early childhood programs can learn something from the data available on teaching differences between male and female teachers. Although an individual's teaching style cannot be predicted on gender alone, research does indicate that men and women tend to use somewhat different classroom discipline techniques. Besides learning more about teaching styles in general, teachers can then consider widening their own teaching approaches toward discipline.

In comparison with their female counterparts, male teachers tend to be more direct and subject-oriented. They tend to be more tolerant of boys' aggressive and disruptive behavior, but also reprimand children more often and publicly than do female teachers. Male teachers seem to allow more assertive, active behaviors than female teachers. In general, European-American male teachers tend toward a teaching-discipline style that has a stronger authority figure and stresses independence, whereas many European, African-American, and Hispanic females who conform to the typical female teaching style tend to demonstrate warmth and approval, stress cooperation and group work, and encourage positive behavior through modeling rather than reprimand or punishment (Grossman & Grossman, 1994).

There is little research regarding the actual effects on behavior of male teachers, particularly in the early childhood years. Some studies at the elementary school age indicate that boys may form a more positive attitude about school with a male teacher even though there is no significant difference in their learning from male or female teachers (Vroegh, 1976).

More importantly, teachers need to know their own gender biases and discipline style, and understand that often their own style may be more effective with one gender or the other. In that case, it may be advisable to seek a teaching staff for a group of young children that is diverse in all areas discussed in this chapter.

Special Needs Issues

Integrating children with special needs has been a priority for many early childhood programs over the years. More recently, legislation required the inclusion of children with handicaps from ages three to twenty-one. The passage of PL-99-457 mandates that children are entitled to a free and appropriate education and related services in the "least restrictive" environment. As more and more children with special needs are enrolled in a greater number of early childhood programs, this raises questions about the nature of discipline and guidance measures.

All children behave in ways that challenge teachers and parents. Children with special needs have many of the same behaviors we see in children without disabilities: tantrums, hitting others, refusing to comply, taking anger out on property, and so on. Just as this behavior is unacceptable in children without disabilities, teachers must maintain the same limits to behavior with children who are disabled. The language and means of communication may differ, but the situation must be dealt with equitably. We must be demanding of and responsible to each child's capabilities, disabilities notwithstanding, and model our belief that all children have the potential for growth. At the same time, teachers may have to learn new ways to communicate expectations and provide follow-through and appropriate consequences in flexible ways that respond to children's special needs.

Children Are More Alike
Than They Are Different

The most important thing to remember is that children with handicapping conditions and children who do not have special needs are more alike than they are different. First and foremost, they are all children who grow and develop in the same sequence, if not at the same pace. Children with disabilities are like other children in their needs, feelings, and interests, and their expression of frustration, fear, and anger is as appropriate as it is for their nondisabled peers. The means of expression may differ but the emotion is the same.

It is especially important to treat each child with a disability as an individual, recognizing the child's unique personality and characteristics. Adults who work with children with special needs draw upon their knowledge of child development and assess each child's social, emotional, physical, intellectual, and language skills. In doing so, they round out their picture of the child's many attributes and avoid having the disability become the defining characteristic.

One way to point out the significance of children's similarities rather than their differences can be found in descriptions of children with special needs. Note that "children" was placed *first* and the condition followed. Follow the general rule of *children are children first* when talking about disabilities. A description of a "handicapped baby" or "deaf girl" emphasizes the disability rather than the child, whereas "a baby with cerebral palsy" or "a girl who wears hearing aids" helps us remember the common elements of child or infant, boy or girl.

Implications for the Classroom

Universally accepted principles that help children gain confidence, learn social skills, participate in groups, and increase their ability to control their own behavior are applicable as well for children with disabilities. As we have noted, behavior problems emerge as children become more comfortable in group settings, and as more demands are made upon them to understand and appreciate the rights of others. Self-esteem and self-confidence are critical to the process. Children who have special needs require that we support their self-worth in order for them to achieve the same level of behaviors expected of their nondisabled peers. There are many ways to help children with special needs achieve a sense of self-worth and learn desirable social behaviors such as sharing, cooperating, and helping:

- Children with disabilities should be allowed to do as much for themselves as they can manage. This is true in personal care routines as well as in negotiating the classroom or the yard. "Kailee wants to tell you something, Jonah. I know you sometimes have trouble understanding some of her words but I cannot always be around to help you figure it out. Ask Kailee to tell it to you very slowly."
- Invite others to assist, but let each child decide how much help she or he wants. "I know you want to help Kailee with her story, but you should ask her first if she wants to read it by herself."
- Encourage children to ask for help when needed. "If you don't understand how to pronounce Joaquin's name, Kailee, I'll be glad to help you figure out how to say it clearly."
- Build on their strengths and skills. "I see you were listening very carefully to my story and I know you have a good memory, Kailee. Perhaps later you can tell me the story in your own words."
- Guard against pitying and overprotecting children with disabilities or patronizing their efforts. "Yes, Vaughn, Kailee does sometimes have trouble pronouncing words correctly because she doesn't hear words as clearly as you do. What can you do so that you might understand her better?"
- Promote activities in which they can enter as fully as other children. "Everybody plays 'Looby-Loo' today! Let's all join in and do it together. Come on, Kailee, take Vita's hand."
- Provide open-ended materials and activities in which all children can explore and be manipulative with varying degrees of skill, such as blocks, Lego's™, and art materials.
- Communicate expectations that all children must learn to respect other's feelings and belongings, obey class rules, and learn problem-solving skills. "You hurt Kailee's feelings when you call her a baby. In this class it is not okay to make fun of someone who doesn't speak like you do. I'd like for you to find a place for Kailee in your group. I know she is a big sister like you, Dora; perhaps she could be the new babysitter."

It is critical for children to see themselves reflected throughout the school environment in order to feel accepted and valued. Photos, posters, books of people wearing glasses, using wheelchairs, hearing aids, and leg braces help the children with disabilities see their place in the world as well as in their classroom. A sense of belonging and being understood fosters positive interactions and appropriate behavior (see Chapter 2 on Dreikurs).

Talking about Differences and Similarities

The greatest need children with disabilities have is to be accepted by other children and treated in a similar fashion (Chandler, 1994). One of the most common behavior situations is a child's rejection of another child or adult, based on a fear or misconception of a disability.

> *Deon is a husky five-year-old who matches the physical skills and energy level of his classmates. When he was born, Deon was diagnosed with spina bifida, a spinal cord injury, which left him with no bladder or bowel control. As a result, Deon wears diapers. Craig, a newcomer to the class, observed Deon changing his diapers and later refused to join Deon and two other children in planting a garden. Craig proclaimed: "I don't like him. He's a baby cuz he still wears diapers. He can't play here. I'm not gonna play with no babies." The other children looked puzzled; Deon looked surprised.*
>
> *Christine is a teacher who is blind. She is a college student who has been placed in a kindergarten classroom for her practice teaching. Malia was assigned to Christine's special small group but did not participate during the first week. At recess one day, Malia asked the regular teacher if she could move to her friend Jenny's group because she didn't like Christine. When pressed for a reason, Malia finally blurted out that Christine scared her.*

Young children are very forthright with their emotions and their fears. They notice differences among people and ask questions about what they see. They also may be confused and anxious about the nature of the disability and its effect on them. All of this is within the normal range of curiosity and emotion for this age group. Yet we cannot allow rejection on the basis of a person's disabilities. According to Derman-Sparks (1989), young children need:

- To have rejection handled immediately, with support and assurance given to the child who was rejected that this type of behavior is not permitted.

> *The teacher put her arm around Deon, squatted down to eye level, and said, "Craig, what you said about Deon is very hurtful. Tell me more about it." Craig mumbled something and then admitted that*

Deon looked funny in diapers because he was so big. The teacher asked Deon if he would like to tell Craig why he wore diapers. Deon responded: "When I was born, there was something wrong with my spine so I don't feel it when I have to go to the bathroom. I wear diapers so that I don't wet my pants." "Does it ever hurt?" asked Craig. "No way, no," said Deon. "I just have to remember to change so I don't get a rash." Teacher: "It is okay for you to ask questions about why Deon wears diapers, but you can't say 'you can't play here.' In our class, everybody gets to play and work together."

- To help recognize how they are different and how they are alike.

"Craig, you and Deon both have to go to the bathroom during the day. Your body tells you when it is time to go and because Deon's doesn't, he has to wear protection. You are both good diggers in the garden, too."

- To have their fears about disabilities taken seriously and have adults understand that children often worry that they can somehow get the same disability.

Malia's teacher asked her if Christine had done anything to frighten her. When Malia responded no, she then asked her, "What do you think will happen to you if you stay in Christine's group?" "I won't be able to see," responded Malia. The teacher then explained that what happened to Christine's eyes was the result of an accident many years before and reassured her that her own sight was not in jeopardy. "Christine's seeing-eye dog is just like the kind of dog you have at home. You might ask her to bring the dog to class some day. You can see and Christine can't, but you both have dogs."

- To have their questions answered promptly, truthfully, and simply. Use the children's own natural curiosity to talk about disabilities as demonstrated in the examples. Use correct terminology for equipment and devices, and names of diseases or disabilities. Ask questions to clarify misconceptions and allow children with disabilities the opportunity to answer for themselves whenever possible.

By following these guidelines, a teacher can remove the potential for hurt feelings, disruptive behavior, and subtle tension that create discipline problems in the classroom. All children benefit from an environment that supports open discussion and dialogue.

Adapting the Classroom

Effective guidance is based on what we know about individual children and how they fit what we know about the age group in general. The same holds true for children with special needs. Teachers of children with special needs may have to make a few changes to best serve each child who has a disability. Depending on the range of disabilities, teachers may have to:

- Speak slowly and more clearly.
- Learn sign language or other forms of communication to match the child's level of understanding.
- Communicate nonverbally with some children—with gestures, pointing, signs, computers.
- Provide outlets of expression suitable to varying handicapping conditions.
- Rearrange the room to reduce obstacles for walkers, wheelchairs, and children moving about with crutches and leg braces.
- Learn to allow longer for a child to process and respond.
- Model ways for children with special needs and children without disabilities to interact with one another.
- Provide more structure for children who need it.
- Provide greater supervision to areas where needed.
- Show children how to play with toys and materials, by pounding, shaking, hammering, pushing, or pulling, if required.
- Encourage and extend their play by your presence and involvement.

Developmental Alerts

The first issue is deciding that the child's behavior is atypical, beyond the normal variations in children under ordinary circumstances. Atypical behavior describes "children with developmental problems—children whose development appears to be incomplete or inconsistent with normal patterns and sequences. These children are often said to be either delayed or different in their development" (Allen & Marotz, 1994). The child with developmental delays may be functioning at a less mature level, more like a normal but younger child. Whether a developmental deviation is disabling depends on the aspect of behavior that is affected. Atypical behavior also applies to those child behaviors that may be caused by environmental rather than developmental conditions, such as emotional disturbances or extremely aggressive or withdrawn behavior. The teacher needs to know child development well enough to perceive the extraordinary and must have enough experience with many children to be able to rule out the behavior as simply a manifestation of individual differences.

Knowing both child development and young children helps the teacher be alert to a child's unusual behavior. To be effective and helpful, the teacher must be aware of community resources and share this information with the family in need. How does the teacher assess the family concerns as well as evaluate the child's behavior?

When parents bring up the problem, the teacher's best course of action is to listen to their concerns. Parents are usually the first to suspect a problem, although they are not always the first to act on the thought. A teacher can best help the family by putting their child's behavior into perspective. Making some comparisons with most children this age will help the family and reassure them that great variations exist in children of the same age. However, the teacher should take seriously the parents' concerns, and observe the child carefully for the next few weeks. Observing the child and taking time to reflect can prevent immediate overreaction. Teachers must take care not to become too involved, or assume an expertise they do not possess. Too often, in their desire to be supportive, teachers take on the role of a specialist, child therapist, or family counselor.

Teachers who have cause for concern are ethically obliged to communicate their concerns to the child's family, however uncomfortable it may be to do so. Parents who hear that their child may not be developing normally may react strongly and not be ready to seek help for a number of reasons:

- Denial of the problem: "It's nothing to worry about."
- Reluctance to acknowledge the problem: "Everyone in our family is like this."
- A different value system/culture/religion: "It's God's will."
- Uncertainty about what to do: "We don't know where to get help. Who do we go to?"
- Uneasiness about seeking help: "But what will we say is wrong?"
- Timidness about themselves or cultural pride: "What will others think? What if it is my fault?"

Teachers help families by learning to express concern and give advice. It is critical that teachers come prepared to these talks with specific incidents that demonstrate why they think there is a problem. Careful record keeping provides objective documentation for parents and teachers to look at together. Teachers must also understand that a parent's reaction and fears may mean several conferences before they are ready to act. Still, at each exchange, the teacher is prepared with suggestions of what to do next, from contacting other parents who have faced the same issues, to seeking outside consultation. The teacher is prepared to help the parents proceed.

About Behavior Modification

The use of behavior modification strategies can be particularly helpful with children with special needs. Learning through modeling is particularly effective in an integrated classroom where children can learn by observing their more skilled peers. Positive reinforcement is a useful tool, readily available in any given interaction between teacher and child. Blending developmental and behavioral practices can help teachers meet the challenging demands of classrooms which include children with special needs. Review Chapters 2 and 3 for ways to implement behavioral and developmental strategies.

Parents of Children with Special Needs

Surely parents of children with disabilities have some special needs themselves related to attaining the appropriate programs and support for their special needs child. Teachers provide this through frequent contact, developmental conferences, help in assessing growth and development, and referrals to appropriate support agencies.

Legislation has mandated that parents are actively involved in the educational programs designed for their child with special needs. A team of experts assesses the progress of each child and classroom teachers can avail themselves of their advice and counsel. This type of multidisciplinary approach benefits all involved: the child, the parents, and the school. Working with parents this way fosters a sense of partnership that bodes well for solving discipline problems. Both teachers and parents have access to other professional insights where effective strategies and appropriate behavioral standards are balanced against the overall goals for the child.

The universal needs of parents are the same: understanding and support. Teachers should be aware, just as they are with parents whose children have typical needs, that family stress from raising a child with a disability may be manifested in the classroom through a child's behavior. The support system of the parents, the child's other professional advocates, and the teacher can be the avenue for solving these problems as they arise.

Federal law now gives children with a variety of disabilities and children who are not disabled the opportunity to work and play together. The teacher's challenge is to support the autonomy, confidence, and growth of all children, taking care that stereotypic attitudes and prejudices do not hinder anyone's potential but foster respect, compassion, and empathy.

Think It Over

When you were in school do you remember times when boys or girls got special treatment? Do you think gender has anything to do with liking or not liking certain children you have met? How do you know whether your teaching style favors one gender over the other? Have you ever had someone observe you for gender bias? Have you ever been uncomfortable with someone who was disabled? If so, how might you act differently today?

Summary

We value children first as individuals, not as members of a group, in order to instill a concern for the dignity of each person. We focus on the individual, not the culture, not the gender, not the handicap. It is when we lump people in a group that we lose sight of the individual nature of every child and begin to stereotype them. Children should come to know schools as places large enough and diverse enough to hold an infinite variety of people whose rich backgrounds of culture and experience are not rejected or taken away. When we foster respect and understanding of one another, no matter our differences, we create a climate where positive social interaction can thrive and prevent many discipline problems from arising.

Our children are growing up in a world in which people of many different cultures work, play, and live together. The early childhood years provide a prime opportunity for children to learn positive aspects to differences in people. They learn to appreciate themselves—their particular skills and abilities—and come to know how they are similar to and how they are different from their friends. They learn that different means "other than" not "less than." This fosters a genuine appreciation of self, which is the first step toward understanding others. Anything we do to help children make sense of who they are and what their world is like ultimately affects their behavior.

Observe and Apply

What do you know about cultures other than your own? On a continuum from low to high, rate yourself on:

- How well I understand culture
- How well I teach culture to children
- How sensitive I am to culture
- How sensitively I teach culture

In your work with children, how do you apply this self-awareness? Often? Rarely? Do you work in an integrated program? Do you display multiethnic pictures in your classroom, play music from other cultures, read folktales? Do you know anyone of another race or ethnicity well? Do you speak a second language? Have you traveled to other countries? Do you have friends and relatives from other parts of the world? What do you do in your teaching setting to bring in the understanding you have from these experiences?

Review Questions

1. Why is cultural diversity an issue for teaching in the twenty-first century? Why is it important to know about children's family backgrounds? How can this information affect discipline and guidance in the home? At school?

2. What are some ways teachers can make a classroom inclusive for all ages, gender, abilities, and cultures? How will this likely affect children's behavior?

3. Different cultures have different childrearing patterns. Give an example of how that affects behavior as an individual or as a member of a group.

4. Describe the gender differences in the way preschoolers behave. Compare that with their behavior in the early elementary grades. What problem behaviors are created? How can you ensure equitable treatment for boys and girls?

5. How can teachers help children with special needs learn prosocial, positive behaviors?

Bibliography

Allen, K. Eileen. *The Exceptional Child: Mainstreaming in Early Childhood Education.* Albany, NY: Delmar, 1992.

Allen, K. Eileen, & Marotz, Lynn. *Developmental Profiles: Pre-birth through Eight.* Albany, NY: Delmar, 1994.

Armstrong, Liz Schevtchuck. "Census Confirms Remarkable Shifts in Ethnic Makeup." *Education Week,* March 20, 1991, p. 1.

Bailey, Donald B., Jr., & Wolery, Mark. *Teaching Infants and Preschoolers with Disabilities.* New York: Merrill, 1992.

Banks, James A. *Multiethnic Education: Theory and Practice.* Boston: Allyn & Bacon, 1994 (3rd ed.).

Berns, Roberta M. *Child, Family, Community.* New York: Holt, Rinehart & Winston, 1985.

Byrnes, Deborah A., & Kiger, Gary (Eds.). *Common Bonds: Anti-Bias Teaching in a Diverse Society.* Wheaton, MD: Association for Childhood Education International, 1992.

Chandler, Phyllis A. *A Place for Me.* Washington, DC: National Association for the Education of Young Children, 1994.

Derman-Sparks, Louise. *Anti-Bias Curriculum: Tools for Empowering Young Children.* Washington, DC: National Association for the Education of Young Children,1989.

Edelman, Marian Wright. "Economic Issues Related to Child Care and Early Childhood Education." *Teachers College Record,* 90, No. 3, Spring, 1989.

Galinsky, Ellen. *The Six Stages of Parenthood.* Reading, MA: Addison-Wesley, 1987.

Gonzalez-Mena, Janet. *Multicultural Issues in Child Care.* Mountain View, CA: Mayfield, 1993.

Gonzalez-Mena, Janet. *The Child in the Family and the Community.* New York: MacMillan, 1993.

Gray, Paul. "Teach Your Children Well," *Time,* Special Issue, Fall, 1993.

Greenberg, Polly. "Parents as Partners in Young Children's Development and Education: A New American Fad? Why Does It Matter." *Young Children,* May, 1989.

Grossman, Herbert, & Grossman, Suzanne H. *Gender Issues in Education.* Boston: Allyn & Bacon, 1994.

Hale, Janice. *Black Children: Their Roots, Culture, and Learning Styles.* Baltimore, MD: The Johns Hopkins University Press, 1986.

Hall, Edward T. *Beyond Culture.* Garden City, NJ: Anchor Press/Doubleday, 1981.

Hoyenga, Katharine B., & Hoyenga, Kermit T. *Gender-Related Differences: Origins and Outcomes.* Boston: Allyn & Bacon, 1993.

Lee, Dorothy. *Freedom and Culture.* Englewood Cliffs, NJ: Prentice-Hall, 1959.

Lightfoot, Sara L. *Worlds Apart: Relationships Between Families and School.* New York: Basic Books, 1978.

Lubeck, Sally. *Sandbox Society: Early Education in Black and White America.* Philadelphia, PA: Falmer Press, 1985.

Maccoby, E. E., & Jacklin, C. N. *The Psychology of Sex Differences.* Stanford, CA: Stanford University Press,1974.

Matthiessen, Neba. *The Hmong: A Multicultural Study.* Fairfield, CA: Fairfield-Suisum Unified School District, 1987.

McCracken, Janet Brown. *Valuing Diversity: The Primary Years.* Washington, DC: National Association for the Education of Young Children, 1993.

McGoldrick, M. Ethnicity and family therapy: an overview. In M. McGoldrick, J. K. Pierce, & J. Geoidano (Eds.), *Ethnicity and Family Therapy.* New York: Guilford Press,1983.

McLaughlin, Karen, & Spitz, Gay, *Parents and Professionals in the Life Cycle,* Workship presented at National Association for Education of Young Children Conference, November, 1993.

Ndoc Dung, Trinh. "Understanding Asian Families: A Vietnamese Perspective." *Children Today,* March-April,1984.

Neugebauer, Bonnie (Ed.). "Beginnings Workshop: Considering Ethnic Culture." Redmond, WA: Exchange Press, March, 1993.

Neugebauer, Bonnie. Going one step further: no traditional holidays. In *Beginnings Workshop: Rethinking Celebrations.* Redmond, WA: Exchange Press, November, 1994.

Ong, Norma Quan. "Listening to Our Stories: A Place at the Table." Workshop presentation. Santa Clara, CA: California Association for the Education of Young Children, March,1994.

Osborn, D. Keith. *Early Childhood Education in Historical Perspective.* Athens, GA: Daye Press, 1991 (3rd ed.).

Phillips, Carol Brunson. Foreword. In Bonnie Neugebauer (Ed.), *Alike and Different: Exploring Our Humanity with Young Children.* Redmond, WA: Exchange Press, 1992 (2nd ed.).

Sandoval, M., & De La Rosa, M. A cultural perspective for serving the Hispanic client. In Harriet Lefley & Paul Pedersen (Eds.), *Cross-Cultural Training for Mental Health Professionals.* Springfield, IL: Charles C. Thomas, 1986.

Snowden, Lonnie. "Toward evaluation of black psycho-social competence." In Stanley Sue and Thom Moore (Eds.), *The Pluralistic Society.* New York: Human Sciences Press, 1984.

Thanh Binh, Duong. *A Handbook for Teachers of Vietnamese Students: Dealing with Cultural Differences in Schools.* Arlington, VA: Center for Applied Linguistics, 1975.

Time Magazine. "The Numbers Game." *Time,* Special Issue, Fall, 1993.

Tobin, Joseph, Wu, David Y. H., & Davidson, Dana H. *Preschool in Three Cultures.* New Haven, CT: Yale University Press,1989.

United States Census Bureau, "Racial Makeup of Population" U.S. Government Printing Office, Washington, DC 1990.

Vroegh, K. "Sex of teacher and academic achievement: A review of research" *Elementary School Journal* 76, No. 7, 1976.

Wardle, Francis. Celebrations, festivals, holidays: what should we be doing? In *Beginnings Workshop: Rethinking Celebrations.* Redmond, WA: Exchange Press, November, 1994.

Wolery, Mark, & Wilbers, Jan (Eds.). *Including Children with Special Needs in Early Childhood Programs.* Washington, DC: Research Monograph of the National Association for the Education of Young Children, Vol. 6, 1994.

York, Stacey. *Roots and Wings.* 1991; *Developing Roots and Wings: Affirming Culture in Early Childhood Programs.* St. Paul, MN: Redleaf Press, 1992.

Cultural Resources for Adults

African American: Hale-Benson, Janice E. *Black Children: Their Roots, Culture, and Learning Styles.* Baltimore, MD: The Johns Hopkins University Press, 1982.

American Indian: Levine, Francine. *Beyond Bows and Arrows: Resources for Teaching Young Children About Native Americans.* Lake Hughes, CA: The Olive Press, 1987.

Chinese-American: Sung, Betty Lee. *An Album of Chinese Americans.* Franklin Watts, New York: 1977.

Japanese-American: Aoki, Michiko Y., & Dardess, Margaret B. *As the Japanese See It.* Honolulu, HA: University of Hawaii, 1981.

Mexican-American: Catalano, Julie. *The Mexican Americans.* New York: Chelsea House, 1988; Hall, Suzane, & Peck, Carleen. *Integral Education: A Response to the Hispanic Presence.* Washington, DC: National Catholic Education Association, 1987.

Southeast Asian-American: Caplan, Nathan. *The Boat People and Achievement in America: A Study of Family Life, Hard Work, and Cultural Values.* Ann Arbor, MI: University of Michigan, 1989; and *Children of the Boat People: A Study of Educational Success.* Ann Arbor, MI: University of Michigan Press (1991). Knoll, Tricia. *Becoming Americans: Asian Sojourners, Immigrants, and Refugees in the Western United States.* Portland, OR: Coast to Coast Books, 1982.

5

The Very Young Child
Infancy through Two Years

Profiles

Meet Vanessa, a nine-month-old infant at the Good Times Child Care Center. Vanessa lives in a metropolitan neighborhood with her parents and three older brothers. Her parents both work full-time jobs in the city, and her older brother goes to the same child care center, although he is in the preschool room. Her two other brothers, seven and nine, attend the neighborhood elementary school. As the youngest of four, Vanessa has had her share of family attention, although it often comes in the form of being carted around by her brothers. Already she is struggling to catch up with them. Having crawled at five months, she is pulling herself up on everything and trying to "cruise along." She seems to crave attention, and screams when she is left alone for any length of time. It is hard for her to get to sleep, and she is easily awakened. She seems irritable and chews on her hands often. Although she has been at the center since she was eight weeks old, she has now developed a fear of some of the caregivers, and thrashes around when left off in the morning. She grabs others' toys regularly, both at the center and at home, and almost seems to do it deliberately. She won't leave the TV buttons alone, nor will she stop banging on a closed door if she wants in or out.

Here comes Jessie! She is sixteen months, and raring to go. You can see the meaning of the word "toddler" as she lurches forward, her fat-diapered bottom with two sturdy legs plopping down straight from the hip; she waddles to and fro with great energy and greater enthusiasm. "Mah," seems to be her name for Mom, their cat Mariah, and "More." She goes to a family child care home during the day. Sometimes her mom or dad can pick her up after naps, though it's usually Dad because Mom works late at the office and takes classes at night. Jessie loves going to Jackie's family daycare home, and seems to save her negativism for her parents. This is especially hard on her mother, who wishes she could work less and enjoy life more. But the bills are high, now that Jessie's grandfather is so ill, and the house payments on their fixer-upper keep the family from doing anything else. They would like, at least, to do something about the yard. That's why they bought the place, so their child could have a place to play. Mom wonders if having this baby was such a great idea.

Across town lives Matthew. An older toddler, this two-and-a-half-year-old has definitely learned the meaning of "no" and uses it often. He is the older of two, his younger sister being just four months today. His mom, in her early twenties, was unprepared for her husband's leaving when the baby

*was born. The three of them live in a two-story house that they share with
her parents. Matthew's family has the upstairs two bedrooms and bathroom, and he has been reprimanded about not playing on the stairs for
more than a year. His mother has kept her half-time job to help out with ex-
penses. Grandma watches the children, but the newborn is so cute, and
Matthew is so exhausting! Why he refuses to be toilet-trained is beyond her;
he's so stubborn. He seems to bounce between being overly active and withdrawn. This same pattern is creeping into his parent-child playgroup,
which he and his mom attend twice a week.*

These three children, so different in many ways, are all part of the early
childhood years we describe as Infancy and Toddlerhood. As we explore
these early years we will learn more about Vanessa, Jessie, and Matthew,
their family and care settings, their development, behavior problems, and
how to guide them.

Think It Over

Do you know children like Vanessa, Jessie, or Matthew? If you were
Vanessa's caregiver would you be concerned about her? As Jessie's
dad, what would you want to ask Jackie about? Is Matthew's behavior a sign of stress or indicative of a deeper problem?

Who Is the Very Young Child?

Developmental Profiles

The youngest children in the early childhood years are those from birth to
roughly two-and-a-half or three years of age. These children are often divided into three groups. Those from newborn to walking are called *infants.*
Children who are walking (from about one year old) to two years are called
younger toddlers. And those from two to two-and-a-half or three are known
as *older toddlers.*

In early childhood education, teachers learn to think about children
from both an individual and general viewpoint. "Development" encompasses
many areas of growth, which interrelate and overlap. We have separated development into three areas: physical and motor; intellectual (or cognitive)
and language; and affective (emotional, social, and creative). Because any

effective guidance practices stem from a knowledge of child development (see Chapter 1), we present developmental profiles as a springboard for learning about effective discipline for the young child.

Growth and Motor Skills

From the moment of birth, infants are plunged into a world of sight, sound, smell, taste, and touch. They immediately begin absorbing this input, constantly gathering information through their physical senses, and begin to organize and make sense of it. Then they move around and explore.

Perceptual Development

Taking in the information is an important part of infants' and toddlers' lives. Two other aspects of development are physical growth and motor skills. Physical and motor growth have less impact on guidance and discipline than do the intellectual or affective areas. Therefore, we simply summarize this aspect of child growth in Table 5.1.

In guiding the very young child, teachers pay particular attention to how the child responds with the senses to the world, and attempts to handle the

Table 5.1

Perceptual Development and Guidance Tips

Perceptual development of the very young child starts early; teachers need to understand how the various senses work to communicate and guide the child under three.

	Points to Note	Guidance Tip
Vision	Eyes function, vision blurry at birth	Early visual experience important to eye development.
	Faces recognize by four months	Use eye contact to make communication bids
	Visual dominance by six months	
Hearing	Infants especially attuned to sounds of human speech	Talk to preverbal children often
	Infants use hearing to locate	Use your voice to help children find you
Smell/Taste	Both functioning at birth	Respect children's likes/dislikes
Skin Senses	Sensitivity to pressure, pain, heat/cold present at birth	Swaddling/holding may soothe child
		Respect temperamental differences in sensitivity to touch and being held in discipline moments.

child with that knowledge. The link between vision and hearing is such that infants as young as three months use their hearing to locate an object or person. The parent and caregiver can help the young child keep track of them by *talking them through* what is happening, such as in diapering and feeding.

The senses of smell and taste, fully developed at birth, bring with them clear likes and dislikes. Just ask Vanessa's brothers about her ideas about food. Ever since she began to eat solids at around six months, she has turned up her nose at peaches and apricots. In fact, they love to give her a piece of their favorite fruit and see her wrinkle her nose in distaste! Teachers are wise to respond to young children's signals, and avoid unnecessary feeding problems.

Sensitivity to pressure can be seen even in utero, and babies show by movement or swipes that they can tell where they are being touched. Swaddling or holding and patting an infant to soothe her indicates this sensitivity.

Physical Growth and Motor Skills

During the first year physical growth is rapid. In fact, physical growth and motor skills are at their peak in the early years. Such dramatic changes in size and shape do not occur again until puberty. It is striking how few motor skills newborns possess. They flail, they cannot coordinate arm or leg movements, and they are unable even to lift their heads. Above the neck, their senses are already well developed; below the neck, they have a long way to go.

In planning for guidance, teachers remember that when babies and toddlers try a movement, or when older toddlers are asked to respond to a request, they are usually rather uncoordinated and diffuse. They need to

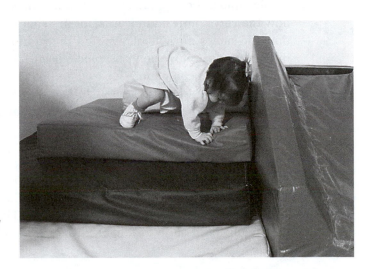

In planning for guidance, teachers recognize that the very young child is rather uncoordinated, and will need to repeat movements to learn.

repeat movements over and over again to learn them. Eye-hand coordination needs practice as much as motor skills: as the eyes develop, the body can be better coordinated. At the same time, motor development seems to progress in its own way, with maturation determining the sequence and accuracy of motor movements. Children do not need special training to move; as long as the child has a safe environment in which to try and repeat the movements, little intervention is required. Vanessa's "cruising" is one example of typical infant motor development that occurs between crawling and walking.

Infants' small size make them vulnerable. Parents and caregivers, in these early years, should take special care to provide for their safety. Knowing about their perceptual and motor skills can help in providing the environments that care for and challenge infant and toddler development. In particular, parents and caregivers must provide for the young child's physical needs to establish the trust on which discipline is based.

Intellectual and Language Understandings

Intellectual growth refers to the development of thinking and language skills. These mental skills develop in a combination of maturation and experience; that is, the child learns to gather information, organize her thoughts, and use information. The child learns both from getting older and from doing things. Naturally active and interactive, very young children are well-suited for the task of learning. Coming to an understanding of their world is a busy endeavor.

Cognitive Development

As described in Chapter 2, Piaget's cognitive theory describes the very young child as being in the "sensorimotor stage." It is an apt description of how the very young child learns, for in using and combining sense perception and motor movements we find the rudiments of thinking. Gradually, infants' random movements become repeated actions. These manipulations combine and become more focused and coordinated, as the infant experiments and tries to cause actions to happen. This evolves into more organized and planned thinking behaviors, which are practiced and form the basis of new actions.

This understanding of the world and how their bodies can make things happen is remarkable to the baby, and is a giant step in thinking and doing. At about one year of age, infants begin to use objects as tools, and start to get around by crawling or toddling. They manipulate the environment more deliberately, and on a wider scale. The toddler can use a stick to get at something out of reach, or pull on a leaf to get the whole plant onto the floor. By using their senses and muscles together, they can now think of new and more complex ways to behave. They can think of new ways to act, even think it out in their heads before they do it. Toward the end of the toddler years, children are using imaginary toys and playing pretend games. One of Matthew's favorite games, for instance, is to use one of Grandma's big pan lids as a steering wheel. He runs through the house, making car noises and steering the wheel like a race car driver.

In guiding the very young child, teachers and caregivers are challenged to remember that very young children do not think logically, nor are they deliberately trying to anger us when they do something we don't like. In fact, they can rarely be counted on to remember something as complex as "rules," so teachers need to repeat themselves regularly and try to get the environment, not small children's memories, to tell the children how to behave. Still, by the time children are two years of age, teaching basic guidance (such as how to touch gently or lie down to sleep) can be done through pretend play with puppets or stuffed animals.

Language Development

Very young children are developing ways to communicate what they want and what they know. Language development in the very young child can be divided into two phases. The first year of life is called the prelinguistic or prelanguage stage. Infants must use methods other than speech to communicate. One way, of course, is crying. Infants' cries begin to differentiate to communicate their various needs (hunger, fear, pain, etc.). Toddlers continue to use the cry to express negative feelings and to get others' attention or to get someone to do something. Another way to connect is by looking, or gazing. Making eye contact helps the baby connect first with mother or caregiver and later with others. Finally, children use the smile.

Nonverbal communication evolves into babbling and initial words toward the end of infancy and into toddlerhood and the preschool years. This is the second phase of language development, the *linguistic or language stage.* Toddlers play with sounds, then start using single words. One- and two-word phrases come next, followed by elaboration of language. Jessie seems to be in transition into this stage, and her parents find it delightful. Her dad loves the way she sits on his lap, facing him, with her hand tickling his mustache, and tries to repeat simple words such as "ball" and "dad." The "chatterbox" stage of the later toddler and early preschool years is just ahead.

In guiding children under three, it helps to remember that children understand what is said before they use words themselves. Adults must take care in both how they talk and what they say, as children now begin to pick up both voice tone and the actual words said. There is a wide range of individual differences in the age of onset of talking, but the receptivity and understanding of others' talk occurs before verbalization. Because receptive language precedes expressive language, children can respond to the names of objects, short commands, and simple concepts before they say or even have the words to describe or explain. Jessie, for instance, will toddle to the door when asked if she wants to go out, although she does not say "Door" or "Go out" yet. And she understands well the word "No" about pulling hair or "Hot" about touching the stove.

Teachers and parents help children learn and then use language when they pair their speech with action. We cannot expect a very young child to understand a long lecture about safety and the streets, but when we insist on "holding hands" with both words and gesture, we know they are learning the power of words and the importance of cooperation.

Affective Development

The development of emotions and feelings, of social skills, and of creativity is known as affective growth. How children feel, how they see themselves, their relationships to others, and their creative expression are important to guidance and discipline. Affective development is the critical link to positive growth in children. A secure attachment to an important adult is a prerequisite for cognitive growth. Children with high self-esteem are more likely to engage in risk-taking; those with emotional insecurities may find it more difficult to try new tasks.

Emotional Development

The development of feelings and their expression begins early, but with little refinement initially. Often, newborns and young infants seem to have only two emotional states—either agitated or not—like an on-off switch. Humans seem to possess a small set of emotions. Our "basic" emotions include enjoyment, excitement, fear, interest, sadness, disgust, and anger; the facial expressions corresponding to each of these emotions are present in newborns or very young infants, and have been observed in many cultural and ethnic groups (Fogel, 1980; Charlesworth & Kreutz, 1973; Eibl-Eibesfeldt, 1971). Therefore, although Vanessa, Jessie, and Matthew are different ages and in varied stages of development, they have the same basic set of emotions.

Emotional states differentiate and become more specific as the infant matures. This refinement continues into the second year, and by the time toddlers are two, a variety of emotions can be expressed. Added to the pleasure, fear, and anger that emerged in infancy are such feelings as willful-ness, pride, embarrassment, doubt, shame, and empathy.

Children's unique temperaments also come into play in emotional de-velopment. Some children are more sensitive to the environment or have a stronger response to their surroundings than others. The "feisty" or difficult baby tends to exhibit one or more of the following characteristics: irregular and unpredictable eating and sleeping patterns; an overall mood of unhap-piness or crankiness; negative reactions that are strong in intensity; and dif-ficulty in adapting, either to new stimuli or simply ongoing situations (Turecki & Tonner, 1985). Babies seem to be cuddlers (or noncuddlers) from birth, regardless of the way their parents act toward them (Schaefer & Emer-son, 1964). For example, Vanessa seems to have a feisty temperament; she has been very active physically since before birth and has strong reactions to foods and changes. She is an irregular and light sleeper, very easily roused and "riled up" but difficult to calm. Jessie, however, seems more flexible; although she is an autonomous, sometimes oppositional, younger toddler, she still is fairly predictable in her sleeping and elimination, and easygoing about changes in routines.

In guiding the young child, caregivers remember that children's feelings are strong, and changeable. Young children have little impulse control, so much of their expression of feelings is strong because it is not yet filtered by self-control or the development of judgment. If teachers react to children's

Emotional states become more specific as the infant matures, and by age two, a variety of emotions can be expressed.

high feelings with similar intensity, the situation is likely to get over-whelming. Adult acceptance and expectation of children's emotionality can help children to calm themselves.

Try It You're in the "Toddlers and Twos" class and the children just will not go to sleep at naptime! There are three of you for the fourteen children, but there is such chaos and crying, only a few end up napping. What can you do?

As individuals, children vary widely in their "tiredness" as well as their ability to get to sleep at all. As a group, young children have difficulty doing much together, so the notion that an entire group could actually sleep all at once is unrealistic. Sleeping calls for a child to trust and relax enough in a place away from home.

Don't try to get them all to sleep at the same time. Create your space so that a small group of children can nap anytime, and then know the children enough to spot when fatigue is setting in. This individuality allows you to respond to children's temperaments and self-set pace, and to help one child at a time make the transition from wakefulness to sleep.

Create a "napping environment." At this young age the environment speaks stronger than words, so make the environment speak loudly: a darker space, a quieter place, a softer spot, and with whispers, soft music, backrubs or rocking, familiar blankets, and "lovey" toys. Your words and gestures all need to say "sleepy."

Be sure to program enough active, physical movement. Young children who have been relatively sedentary indoors may be intellectually tired but physically not fatigued enough to nap.

Teach "getting to nap" skills. Use your own attachment and emotional bonds with a child to establish a trusting relationship and work toward cooperation. Don't ask questions that will elicit a "no" answer; instead, tell them of the upcoming change so that they can anticipate and prepare themselves for it. Acknowledge their feelings if they don't want to nap, even while you move them gently in the "nap direction." Redirect their attention on how to get ready. "Show and Tell" applies to teachers of toddlers: pair your words with a demonstration ("Where is your blankie? Let's hold hands and find it together.").

Understand that the struggle around nap is also about normal development. Toddlers and twos are working on "me" instead of doing it someone else's way. The drive toward autonomy is strong and healthy. The wise teacher uses this to move toward "me do it" in getting ready for a nap.

Teachers can guide children more effectively if they know their individual temperaments. The fearful child needs encouragement in taking small steps, the feisty one may need a firmer hand in changing out-of-bounds behavior, and the flexible child may simply need to be noticed more often.

The social world of the child influences the expression of emotion, and must be respected. Children's experiences with parents and caregivers directly influence how they learn to express themselves emotionally. Children with strong and positive attachments can develop a more open, relaxed, and expressive manner than those whose connections with adults is inconsistent, shaky, or abusive. Teachers work to develop trusting relationships with young children, and take into consideration the child's experiences elsewhere. Individual families begin to shape a child's behavior early on, and children's emotionality is tolerated very differently from one family to another. The culture that allows toddlers to have a tantrum or two-year-olds to loudly express their fears and wants is likely to have a different emotional set of young children on their hands than one that consistently discourages such expressive behavior. For instance, consider Matthew. By living in a house with stairs, he encounters a place he is regularly forbidden to use. At the same time, his grandparents do not believe he should be allowed to cry about it; "It just doesn't do," says Grandma, "to coddle a child or let a boy get into the habit of crying." Matthew learns to curb his outbursts at an early age, and the teacher understands such familial influences while working with him.

Social Development

Social development for children under three years of age is concerned primarily with their first social relationship: the one between the child and parent(s). This connection, which may include caregivers as well, is of central importance during infancy and toddlerhood. Therefore, social development in the very early years is about attachment and, for the toddler, autonomy.

Attachment   Attachment is the emotional connection between two people. An affectional bond, this relationship serves as a starting point for the baby, as a safe base in which the child gets essential needs met and begins to develop mutuality, and as a connective dance between the baby and parent. It appears that human infants are programmed to make such attachments; the mutual gazing of adult and infant, accompanied by smiling and cooing, mean that social interactions have begun. Babies who are responded to consistently and sensitively to trust their world; those whose cries or bids for attention go unanswered may come to distrust the world.

The universal tendency for humans to become attached (usually to mother) and remain close makes sense; it increases the chances of survival.

By six to eight months, the child begins to show distress when the attached person leaves or the child is left in an unfamiliar place. "Stranger anxiety" (fear of an unfamiliar person) often occurs as well, as it has now in Vanessa. As they approach one year, infants start looking toward their parents' faces for information about how to respond to something. This "social referencing" helps the infant decide whether to respond with distress, relaxation, or joy. An infant has only a few ways to keep these important grown-ups around. Toddlers are at their most dangerous (with increased mobility but no judgment or impulse control) just at the time when clinginess is at its peak (thirteen to fourteen months).

It appears that a secure attachment plays a very important part in children's later socialization, for when toddlers do not learn to form attachments, "they tend to follow and cling to any available adult. As preschoolers they are likely to be overly friendly toward strangers and very demanding of attention. By middle childhood they are often restless and disobedient, and they tend to get on poorly with adults and other children. Few appear to form lasting relationships with anyone" (Rutter, 1979). Matthew's mother is wise in keeping herself available to him, even though shifting to a full-time position would help financially.

In guiding the very young child, keep in mind the normality of stranger anxiety and clinginess. Very young children take direction from those they know. Build the relationship as much as possible before trying to discipline. When trying to change a child's initial behavior, expect a strong reaction if you are not familiar. With children who have not known significant attachments, understand that the relationship-building time may need to be much longer, the reluctance to trust or comply may be stronger, and the need to be both firm and kind may be more intense than with those whose early social experiences are more bonded.

Autonomy   After forming attachments, the child's next challenge is to act apart from those people. From the second year of life until around age two and a half, toddlers are engaged in a struggle for identity. The big issue in their lives is the development of an independent self. "Me do it!" and "No!" are the watchwords of this age. Now mobile, they are moving out in the world, wanting to move, touch, get into, and control just about everything and everyone around. During this time, these children need to learn to flex their muscles (of body and of mind) as well as begin learning the rules of their society. This socialization, learning the behaviors, attitudes, and knowledge of the family, culture, and society, is a process that extends throughout early childhood and into adolescence and adult life.

In guiding very young children, limit-setting begins with safety for younger toddlers. These children are into everything, and adults must keep the child safe and healthy. Bugs or small stones cannot be eaten, the rocking chair or closed toilet is not for climbing, electric cords cannot be pulled or gnawed. As the toddler matures, limit-setting moves into the basics of dealing with objects and other people. Blocks are for building, not throwing or clubbing. Gentle touching is better than hitting, and biting is for food and chewies, not others. Parents and teachers find this kind of limit-setting especially difficult, but it is an essential part of helping the child become autonomous, self-directed, and socialized.

It may help the beleaguered teacher of toddlers to know that a number of factors affect toddlers' compliance with these rules. Gender plays a part. Girls seem to comply somewhat more than boys, although this is not a strong tendency. Neither Jessie nor Vanessa seems particularly compliant. Boys seem to ignore requests more than girls, but there are no particular gender differences in refusing, defying, or negotiating (Hoyenga & Hoyenga, 1993).

There may be an age difference in compliance: older children are less likely to ignore and more likely to negotiate a command, and seem to have more self-control and cooperate more as they become preschoolers (Kuczynski, 1987; Howes & Olenick, 1986). It appears easier to get Matthew's cooperation about the stairs now that he is two than earlier, although he still doesn't like it. Securely attached infants were found to be more obedient toddlers (Londerville & Main, 1981). Parents who fight seem to have less obedient toddlers, especially boys (Jouriles, 1988).

A final note about social development and guidance. Very young children have social experiences with people other than their parents and caregivers. Infants and toddlers often develop close relationships with older siblings, grandparents or other extended family members, and many connect with a wide range of peers in child care settings. Social development for the very young child, then, can include learning to deal with other children. However, because of the intense nature of early attachment and autonomy, we concentrate on these in the infant and toddler. For the purposes of this book, we have included friendships as part of the social development of preschoolers.

Creative Development

Children are naturally curious and creative. Give an infant a piece of cloth, and who knows where it will end up. Show a toddler a push toy and it will find its way into unknown territory. Put a cookie in a two-year-old's sight but out of reach, and see how many ways there are to get it. Children love to play games, with objects, sounds, words, and people. What adults think is messy, destructive, or naughty may more likely be an act of creativity. The creative urge seems to be innate; like a seedling, it needs only the preparation of the soil and the right conditions to flourish.

In guiding children under three, remember that very young children are not trying to be creative, or to impress others with their skills. They simply are actively engaged in "doing." This implies that adults who care for these young children have to provide plenty of materials and experiences that are rich in sensory input. They provide a schedule and expectations that allow for flexibility and novelty. They give choices within clear safety boundaries. They enjoy the unexpected!

Typical Behavior Patterns

Given all this developmental information, it would seem easy to describe the "typical" infant, toddler, or two-year-old. However, there are so many differences! Babies are not all alike; temperaments differ and the unique combination of traits makes each child one of a kind. There are substantial group differences; cross-cultural research reveals observable cultural and national differences. Such differences could be related to genetics; also, cultural differences in childrearing are prevalent. Many American babies in the suburbs are used to "baby-proofed" homes; such environments are un-heard of in many tribal cultures (Howrigan, 1988).

Additionally, all parents are not alike. There are substantial gender differences in parenting styles. In mainstream American society, mothers spend much more time with their babies and perform a much larger pro-portion of the child care chores than do fathers, even when both parents are employed. Fathers tend to be less available to their young children, engag-ing in doing something else while minding the baby. A father's play is less carefully tuned into the child's response or ability, and his speech is usu-ally less adjusted to the baby's level of development (LaRossa, 1988; Ninio and Rinott, 1988). As more mothers are employed outside the home, chil-dren may well be under a father's care more. Also, children may have a wider variety of adult care, which may affect in some way how the child ex-periences the world.

Parents with problems can be neglectful or abusive. Parents who are unresponsive are less likely to encourage a warm attachment so essential to a child's affective development. These individual differences in children's first social relationships make outlining the typical very young child a dif-ficult task.

Still, children's development does follow a somewhat predictable se-quence, and teachers of very young children can expect to encounter cer-tain general behavior patterns. There are some important implications for guidance in each developmental area. Taking into consideration what we know about perceptual, physical, and motor growth, we find several clear ideas. Table 5.2 summarizes these points.

Table 5.2	

Applying Child Development to Guidance

By applying knowledge of child development to how we guide children, teachers use the predictable sequence of child growth to establish effective ways of dealing with children's sometimes unpredictable behavior.

Developmental Area	Tips for Teachers
Physical and Motor Growth	
Children need to use all their senses to learn about the world	Make the environment safe; free from ingestible and fragile materials. Infants should be in positions most free and least helpless. Toddlers have to be allowed to get into a place and out of it by themselves as much as possible.
Promoting motor development does not mean pushing it	Wandering, carrying, and dumping are skills to be practiced, not stopped. The children need close supervision, but not a particularly structured program. The place will be messy!
Intellectual and Language Understandings	
For cognitive growth to occur, children must have a secure attachment and have their basic needs met	Attend to crying, clinging rather than ignore it. Be sure children are not hungry, fatigued, overly soiled. Don't tell a story *before* snack!
For children to learn, they must interact	Let children get themselves in and out of places and situations with each other. Talk to children; describe and label what is happening.
Children learn through actions and words together	Telling a toddler what to do is not enough; pair your words with actions. Have toddlers *show* you what they want, or don't like, and then give them the words.
What a child wants is translated immediately into action	Children explore each other readily; grabbing what they want without thinking about how this feels to some one else. Your words help them focus on what is happening, but it will not stop them from doing it. Show them how to do it "right."
Toddlers need time to explore, try it on, and communicate about it	Allow "all by myself" opportunities. Try not to rush or interrupt; this will create confusion and tension, not accomplishment.
Thinking and language skills develop over a long time, and in unique ways	Ask parents about their children's idiosyncrasies. Invite parents to interpret their children's ways of communicating.

(continued)

Table 5.2   (Continued)

Developmental Area	Tips for Teachers
Affective Development	
Feelings are real, and belong to the person experiencing them	Acknowledge and accept the feelings, even when you need to redirect the behavior.
	Help children to recognize and cope with their feelings; it adds to their inner sense of self-direction and competence.
Children are capable of strong feelings	Help children put words on their feelings.
Positive attachments are crucial to the development of the self	Help babies form positive attachments, and toddlers to keep them.
	Support parents' close ties with their children, rather than encouraging withdrawing or avoiding, especially at separation/reunion times.
	Give parents tips on how to interact in positive ways with their children.
Toddlers have a drive for autonomy	Make a place that says "Yes" to children.
	Make a few, necessary limits about safety and constructiveness; they are more likely to cooperate if there are not too many rules.
	Allow a child to say "NO!" and give them a few minutes to "decide" to comply.
	Consider letting toddlers say "Mine!" and keep a prized possession; until they gain a sense of mineness they cannot truly share.
	Help children stay within appropriate limits by paddling with the current, not against it.

Think It Over

What kind of a toddler were you? Were you flexible, fearful, or feisty in temperament? What were the early messages you received in your family about the expression of emotions? How do you think this might affect how you treat a child who says "NO!" to you?

Guiding the Infant, Toddler, and Two-Year-Old

Environmental Tips

The total environment of the very young child includes health and safety factors, physical and time considerations, and the play/learning opportunities. We consider the interpersonal environment as well; these will be dealt with in the sections in this chapter entitled Developmentally Appropriate Discipline Techniques and Working with Parents and Families of Very Young Children.

A Safe Place

Safety is a primary consideration when caring for infants and toddlers. A safe environment is one in which every space a child can get to is evaluated and checked for hazards, and in which the supervising adults are well-trained and appropriately prepared. In terms of guidance, adults must supervise the children constantly and appropriately. A toddler can transform a safe setting to a dangerous one unless supervised. Children are allowed to play freely without being overcontrolled, but are not ignored or left unattended.

A Healthy Situation

Handwashing is an essential element of every program. Adults wash their hands often: after every diapering, accident, nose-wipe, cough, and sneeze, and before food preparation. Children's hands are washed, and, despite their occasional protest, older toddlers are taught how to wash after toileting and before eating. As for eating, the experienced teacher knows that battles over eating are best avoided: in educational settings, very young children may be fed, or may be taught to feed themselves, but are not forced to eat at certain times or eat foods they refuse. Toddlers can enjoy finger foods and eat similar foods as others their age. Avoid foods that might cause choking (such as popcorn or nuts), and try to keep to the "lowness quotient": low in sugar, salt, fat, additives, or chemicals.

Health, safety, and nutrition are mentioned here in light of very young children's particular vulnerabilities, yet they are important aspects of the "preventive medicine" of guidance. Preparing a proper learning environment is another.

The Learning Environment

To plan an appropriate learning environment, the indoor and outdoor space should be designed with the children's physical, intellectual, and affective development in mind. The environment is a powerful regulator of behavior, especially for the very young. They take their cues about where to go and what to do from how the space is laid out. Chapter 3 discusses how to use the environment to aid in guidance.

A good learning environment has age-appropriate equipment and experiences for the group. The program may have both infants and toddlers; thus, flexibility is called for. To respond to the needs of each group, keep in mind that the younger the child, the smaller the groups and space should be. Infants can feel overwhelmed and may cry with an overlarge or too-busy place. Toddlers need a larger space; to avoid the aggression and crankiness that comes with restrictions on their drive for independence, provide more places for movement and toys to manipulate.

Developmentally Appropriate Discipline Techniques

Generally speaking, the teacher of very young children can be more effective by *staying flexible* and *individualizing* the program. Issues of temperament are at their height in the earliest years; parents are at their most inexperienced and most vulnerable, and what both need from a teacher and group care is primarily support and understanding.

Gonzalez-Mena and Eyer (1993) have interpreted the works of Pikler and Gerber in a succinct and helpful way. They emphasize that relationships in infant and toddler caregiving are the most important aspect of teaching. The "three Rs" of the interactions that build relationships are *Re*spectful, *Re*sponsive, and *Re*ciprocal. To develop these relationships, ten principles of caregiving are followed:

1. Involve infants and toddlers in things that concern them.
2. Invest in quality time.
3. Learn each child's unique ways of communicating and teach them yours.
4. Invest time and energy to build a total person.
5. Respect infants and toddlers as worthy people.
6. Be honest about your feelings.
7. Model the behavior you want to teach.
8. Recognize problems as learning opportunities and let infants and toddlers try to solve their own.
9. Build security by teaching trust.
10. Be concerned about the quality of development at each stage.

As this section describes specific discipline techniques, notice how guidance practices follow these ten essential principles.

Working with Infants

Conflicts with infants usually arise around routine situations and in some play situations. The two call for different strategies, as they involve different players. Hast and Hollyfield (1993) describe strategies around routines and play, noting that problems in routines are usually between the infant and teacher, but those in infant play situations are with other children.

The routines of infant caregiving surround bodily functions. Feeding/eating, sleeping, diapering, and transitions can all cause problems. Experienced as a conflict between adult and child, it is often really an inner conflict within the adult about how to do things. When Vanessa eats a banana, it gets very messy because she tries to eat, finger, push around, and smear over the fruit. Her parents or caregivers may find this annoying: it causes a lot of clean-up work and takes longer than they would like. The strategy here is *anticipation* (for routines). Think about how the infant might behave; set up the environment so it works for both adult and child. No bananas in the living room, and put a sheet under the feeding chair. With sleeping, the rest area needs to be quiet and relatively unstimulating. To be ready to rest, infants need to be tired and need to be soothed into relaxation. Babies' individual patterns are observed and followed; a teacher anticipates a nose-wipe for the child by telling the child what is about to happen; for example, say, "I have a tissue and I'm going to wipe your nose. You have a cold and it might feel scratchy. I'll rub gently." Verbalizing is important; also helpful is showing him the tissue, letting him grab one, and gently finishing the task with his help.

In play situations, conflicts are usually between children. The strategies here are *modeling* and *intervention*. The environment is also key; providing different areas for mobile and nonmobile infants and multiples of similar toys prevents many problems. Adults model the kind of gentle interactions they wish to promote. Smiles and talking with babies gives them the idea that people are there to be connected with. When the problem is about safety or well-being, intervention is needed. As in routines, the adult is responsive, not reactive, in play situations. That is, the caregiver is alert and available, but doesn't jump in too quickly or overpower unnecessarily. For instance, hair-pulling and biting require a quick, but not harsh, response. An adult is like an island for the children to launch from for adventuring, and like a safe port when the seas get too rough. When Vanessa grabs a toy from another infant, the teachers watch the children. If the other child is not upset, they may let it go. If there is crying, the teacher can offer another toy or help Vanessa find something to "trade." Verbalization of feelings and situations is helpful, even though infants do not fully understand language yet. They see that as problems arise they are safe and cared for.

Remembering that infancy is a time to learn basic trust and gather a foundation of sensorimotor information, teachers help them learn that it is safe to venture out even when something difficult happens.

Toddlers and Conflicts

Toddlers and conflicts go hand in hand. They are actively involved in their environment and in becoming autonomous. The one- and two-year-old engage in many forms of testing behavior; with help, they learn, over time, to change that into appropriate reactions. Respecting their autonomy and still providing a safe place and appropriate limits is quite a challenge.

In routine situations, two effective strategies are *preventing unnecessary conflict* and *engaging the toddler's cooperation*. Try to give the child a say in it somehow; this supports the child's drive for autonomy and your wish to get cooperation. "In two minutes I need to change your diaper," or "Do you want to walk to the car or be carried?" are two ways to prevent conflicts around diapering and transitions. Hast and Hollyfield (1993) recommend using "The Four As":

1. *A*nticipation: "In two minutes I need to change you."
2. *A*cknowledging feelings: "That must have hurt when you bumped."
3. *A*lternatives: "Do you want to walk or be carried?"
4. *A*rticulation: "You might be hungry. Can you feel it in your tummy?" or "I'd like to play with that truck when you are finished." or "My turn next, please."

These work well in play situations as well. Instead of rescuing someone when their toy is taken away, use words to signal your availability, but have them try to find out what to do. When Jessie wants the wheel toy that her buddy Tomas is riding, she cries. Jackie, her caregiver, notices her predicament by saying, "Jessie, you want the trike and Tomas has it. You wish you could get on it right now." By articulating Jessie's situation and acknowledging her feelings, Jackie engages Jessie. As Jessie listens, Jackie says to Tomás, "Jessie would like that when you're done" or "Tomas, would you trade this wagon for the trike?" By the time Jessie is two, she will have witnessed some ways to solve these problems. By giving her the scripts for resolution, Jackie continues to encourage autonomy while decreasing discipline problems.

Another strategy for toddler discipline is: "For every no, give two yesses." Being positive is important for living the toddler years, for both adult and child. Biting, the "preverbal frustrates" (Hast & Hollyfield, 1993),

Using the 4 As of anticipation, acknowledging feelings, alternatives, and articulation, a teacher helps a toddler deal with conflicts.

is a common toddler behavior that cannot be allowed. The teacher gives a No—"Biting is not for people; it's not OK"—and then two Yesses—"You can bite this yellow or this blue teether." The toddler has a choice of appropriate actions. Two-year-olds can learn to ask for a teether instead of biting a friend.

Finally, older toddlers' quest for autonomy and independence often confronts adults with their own need for power. Toddler-adult struggles are often an issue of who's in charge. If the adult decides that the conflict must be resolved in an "I Win—You Lose" manner, both parties end up losing: the child loses a chance to become more independent and the adult loses the opportunity to be the teacher instead of the bigger force. Become aware of why the behavior bothers you, or notice if the conflict is arising again and again. Is it about you wanting power, or is the issue really important? As mentioned in Chapter 1, guidance asks for teachers to be aware of both the child and themselves, and to be prepared to change their own behavior. Redirection, positive rule-setting, or distraction may work better than needless confrontation. Instead of forbidding a child from climbing on the furniture, try redirecting the behavior: "I can't let you climb on the tables, but would you like to come outside and use the climber?" Or, try positive rule-setting: "Feet go on the floor." Distracting the child by changing the focus of attention might also work: "Instead of climbing on the table, let's put our new Playdough on it—can you carry it over?"

Infancy and toddlerhood are times for tremendous growth. Maintaining their trust and respecting the child's emerging autonomy can be done with developmentally appropriate techniques for discipline in the very young years.

The Teacher's Challenges

Infants and toddlers pose challenges for the early childhood educator. Attachment and separation, autonomy and independence, and perpetual motion require the teacher to be alert, available, and flexible. Consistent limit-setting needs to be paired with communication to promote a curious and competent young child.

Three issues in particular are hallmarks of the toddler teacher's challenges: temper tantrums, a contest of will, and sibling rivalry. Often, as in Matthew's case, they all seem to happen at once. Each requires some specific actions, and family support.

Temper Tantrums   Tantrums serve many purposes: discharging pent-up energies, expressing conflicting emotions, and testing a toddler's own con-

---

Try It   If you are in an Infant-Toddler program and someone bites, here are some things you can do:

When it happens
- Stop the aggressive behavior swiftly and calmly.
- Try *not* to shriek or shout, but say firmly, "Stop. No biting people."
- Comfort the victim. This may mean getting another adult to help, taking the child to get ice or a cold cloth, fetching tissues, holding or rocking to calm the one bitten.
- Show the biter the hurt (child and mark) and have them help you "fix it." This could mean any of the above measures.
- Try not to lecture or punish the biter in retaliation. Do tell them firmly that it is "not OK" because it hurts. To allay fears and set a clear limit, you might say, "I can't let you bite and I won't let anyone else bite you. It hurts; NO biting people."

Afterwards
- You may decide to find out more, once the situation is taken care of and emotions have calmed.
- Ask each child what they wanted, or didn't like. Use this to give other ideas: "When you want something, use your words. Say, 'I want that.' " "When they do something you don't like, say NO!"

trol. Remember, power struggles arise with toddlers; check your own place in them first. They also indicate a struggle within the child, as they tip up and down on an emotional seesaw of anxiety/fear and control/frustration. Once again, Erikson's model of psychosocial development is helpful: the toddler is struggling to learn a new layer of self-identity, and is in constant movement between autonomy and self-doubt. Children's own feelings are powerful, overwhelming them with their intensity and, sometimes, duration. They cannot control themselves, yet have all these emotions and situations to cope with. On the one hand, they are declaring independence, stepping out of the absolute control parents and caregivers had over them previously. Yet the shout of "Me do it!" shifts in a moment to a torrent of tears and clinging, crying "Don't go!" Whereas in the first moment they saw themselves as practically adults, suddenly now they are babies, needing continual protection and care. Toddlers are often ambivalent, independent one minute and helpless the next. They are in transition between being a baby and being a child, and it's often an uneasy and frustrating time.

- Give children a substitute for biting a person. Keep teethers in your pocket, and show all the children. Tell them, "When you feel like biting, bite this instead. I'll always have one in my pocket for you."
- Practice what else to do. Practice with puppets, role play with another adult in front of the children, make up stories about "children just like you who have big feelings and want to stop biting."

That same day
- Talk to the parents of both the biter and the one bitten. Stay calm, avoid judging or blaming, but be sympathetic to their upset, and try to keep the situation in developmental terms. Parents may be alarmed, but they must be informed: you do everyone a favor by explaining the "bigger picture" of how children behave and learn.
- Stay close and involved; the biter has as much to learn as the one bitten has to be reassured.

For a few days/weeks
- Observe; watch to see if the incident is repeated and if there is a pattern that can be anticipated, prevented, or redirected.
- Keep in touch with the parents; all parties may be anxious and want to know whether anything else (or nothing else) has happened.

Temper tantrums are the result of too much frustration, and are quite common. Dr. Penelope Leach (1984) reminds us of several important facts:

> More than half of all two year olds will have tantrums at least once or twice a week while very few children will have reached their third birthday without every having one. Toddlers who have a lot of tantrums are usually lively children who may be highly intelligent. They know what they want to do; they want to do a great many things and they mind a great deal when someone or something prevents them.

Think of a tantrum as an emotional fuse that is blowing. The child is out of control, and not responsive to words or lectures. Dr. Leach continues:

> While the tantrum lasts, the toddler is lost to the world, overwhelmed by his own internal rage and terrified by the violent feelings he cannot control. However unpleasant your toddler's tantrums are for you, they are much worse for him.

Toddler behavior may vary during a tantrum, from screaming to running around or throwing whatever is within reach, even breath-holding. If the toddler lets you hold her through the tantrum, your arms may be comforting when the rage is over, but often she cannot bear you to try to control her. Prevent the child from hurting herself and others, stay nearby, and be ready to offer gentle comfort when she is ready. Do not try to argue, scream back, or shake the child into stopping; trying to overpower the child while she is out of control can be terrifying to an already frightened child. Try not to reward or punish the child for the tantrum. You want her to see that a temper tantrum is awful for her and useless anyway. It won't get her what she wants, but she isn't a "bad girl" who needs to be punished for it, either.

Tantrums are a normal part of development, and taper off over time as the child learns language and becomes more competent. When tantrums occur frequently and increase in number and duration, that may be a sign that other parts of the child's life are not working, or that the child is in crisis and needs attention. Observe carefully the child's day, consult with parents, and you may find a source of tension that can be alleviated.

A Contest of Wills   Sometime between the child's second year of life and two-and-a-half years of age, most children engage adults in a "contest of wills." The struggle for autonomy (see Erikson in Chapter 2 and the earlier section on Emotional Development) and independence requires children to pull themselves up and assert themselves. This relates to the development of the self; having a strong will has long-term benefits in knowing who you are and feeling confident enough to grow and try new things. They push out the boundaries and push on anyone who gets in their way. This includes parents and caregivers as well as other children.

It is a frustrating time for both adult and child. On the toddlers' part, their reach exceeds their grasp. They want to do everything, they do not want to be thwarted by anyone, and they have little or no patience to wait, to try it someone else's way, or to stop themselves at all. On the adult's part, the placid or happy baby who's thrilled to see you, and kicked its legs in excited anticipation of a spoon of food or a ball or even your face, has turned into someone almost unrecognizable. Most everything you say or do seems to be greeted with "NO!" or running away, squirming out of your grasp, or shrieking with anger or delight as the wayward child they seem to have become overnight.

Parents are having a particularly difficult time as well. Home routines, cultural or ethnic etiquette, and parental expectations are all upended. Sleeping and eating are big issues for parents. The infant who went down easily at eight P.M. turns into the toddler who refuses to stay in the crib. The older toddler may even decide that an afternoon nap is just not necessary anymore. A predictable eater may turn into a finicky one. Mashed carrots have been Jessie's favorite food for months; now she turns her head away, or simply slops the mess all over the high chair.

During this time, many parents try to teach their children toileting skills. As much as we would like to believe that toileting is a matter-of-fact

Having a strong sense of self sets up a contest of wills for toddlers, who push out the boundaries . . . and push on anyone who gets in their way.

motor skill, it is a complex issue, especially in modern American society, that involves adults both emotionally and physically. There is cross-cultural as well as cross-generational variation about toilet training. Add an oppositional toddler, and teachers know that parents are frustrated and concerned.

Teachers also know that a "toddler versus adult" stance is neither effective nor helpful. The basic functions—sleeping, eating, and toileting—should not become a battleground between adult and child; punitive or unnecessarily harsh or humiliating methods only discourage the child and create hostility and tension. Teachers may need to explain these issues to parents, helping them to relax. Once again, the issues of control and power emerge between toddler and adult. The "Terrible Twos" can also be the "Terrific and Tender Twos." Knowing what you do about this age, realize that a willful toddler can be an opportunity or a predicament.

Siblings   For the child who is born into a family with other children, having siblings is a preexisting condition. Vanessa has never known a home without brothers. She may not like her brothers trying to make her eat a peach, but she scurries like mad to be in the same room with them. In fact, Vanessa's aversion to being alone may be due, in part, from her experience as a child with siblings.

Matthew, however, has spent two years being a single child. Life has been difficult enough with the changes he has made; the arrival of his baby sister is another change, and not an altogether welcome one. This is the experience of many children under three: the advent of another baby and the adjustments everyone learns to make are a big part of many older toddler's lives.

An amusing way to put the toddler's reaction to a new baby is to imagine you are married, and your spouse announces an exciting surprise: a new spouse is coming soon! "I love you so much that I've decided to get another one," you are told. "This new one will be our spouse, and we'll both take care of it together. I'll really need you to be a big spouse now, to help me look after the new one. You really don't mind, do you?" (Leach, 1984)

The fact that parents want and bring in another child makes the first child feel jealous and pushed out. Teachers can expect negative reactions to both the news and, more importantly, the reality. Not all toddlers exhibit all of these behaviors, but all of them are common:

- Increased clinginess to parent upon separation
- Increased temper tantrums and low frustration tolerance
- More "babyish" behavior
- Less interest in toileting; if started, some regression
- Defiance of parent and caregiver, sulkiness or withdrawal

Teachers can help toddlers and their parents through this time by offering a few practical ideas for the homefront and doing a few extra things at school. Table 5.3 gives suggestions of what parents and teachers can do.

Table 5.3

Adjusting to a New Sibling

Helping a young child with a new sibling is hard work, for the child's behavior and feelings are complicated. But it is worth the effort.

Matthew's grandmother hustles him into the class excitedly. "We have a new baby!" she beams. Matthew looks about sullenly. After his Mema leaves, having told everyone twice about the birth, the beautiful newborn, and her pleasure and pride, Matthew is aimlessly wandering around the room. What's a teacher to do?

Teachers

- Be a rock for the child, available and steady, someone to count on.
- Be the consistent part of the toddler's day and life.
- Without overdoing it, allow the child to express feelings of jealousy or loneliness.
- Have some books available that encourage a sharing of such feelings. (*I Want to Tell You About My Baby* [Banish]; *New Baby* [Berenstain]; *Just Like Me* [Ormorod]; *Baby and I Can Play* [Henrickson])
- Be accepting of common reactions without letting the child become aggressive or violent. Young children may withdraw, become hostile or moody, throw the doll babies around.
- Remember that gentle, cooperative behavior is a tremendous challenge for ALL toddlers, and will be especially so for the stressed sibling of a new baby.
- Above all, respect the child's dignity. Life goes on; sometimes the baby is special, and sometimes not. The toddler can survive and is always special to you.

Parents

- Encourage parents to help do everything possible to get the child's independence on the rise and working well before the baby arrives. This means learning to climb into their own car seats, pull on their own pants and shoes, feed themselves, etc.
- Help them find ways to continue doing with the toddler as many as possible of the things they like. Reading a story while nursing or watching the toddler do a puzzle while rocking reduces the child's sense of displacement.
- Enlist the help of fathers and other relatives and friends.
- Try to get the parent(s) to accept any offers of help from the child, but not to make it a requirement or otherwise making too much of "you're the big sister/brother now."
- Encourage parents to allow the child to behave in babyish ways and accept jealous feelings without letting the baby get hurt.
- Consider developing a feeling of "benign superiority" in the toddler and parent. "She just can't do much, huh?" Mom and toddler smile together.

Think It Over

Do you remember having a temper tantrum? What happened in your family when you said "no"? What is your family composition (single child, oldest, younger, etc.) and how has this affected how you feel about a child who is negative about a sibling?

Working with Parents and Families of Very Young Children

How to Learn the Family Components

Getting Acquainted

Teacher-parent relationships are built slowly, over time, and with many small steps. As parents entrust their children to other adults, they need information, reassurance, and support. Teachers help the process of developing trust and establishing a relationship by sharing as much information as possible about the program and about the child. "Even before a child has started school, many steps have been taken to assure parents that their child will have a safe, nurturing, interesting time there" (Stone, 1987). Teachers who know the child and the family have a better idea of how to integrate both into the program.

There are many ways to make these connections. The teacher may make a home visit before the child begins in the program, or soon after. The parents can bring the child to visit before formally starting the group. A teacher can talk to the parents at length about the child and family practices. A developmental history can be done in writing, although a personal interview allows the parent(s) to elaborate and to ask questions.

Separation

Once the child is ready to start, teachers and parents need to work together on separation. Separation from family is a lifelong process, one that involves both child and parents. It is almost always hard, and everyone feels uneasy at best. The teacher helps by befriending the child and reassuring both parent and child that their special attachment is honored. Teachers motivate parents and children to make the separation by being available.

Some tried and true techniques help when the parent has to leave a clinging child. Parents who stay awhile the first day or so help invest the program with a kind of safety; the child feels the parents' trust of the people and place because they are there for awhile. Some schools require parents to stay the first day, yet a few do not allow parents to stay at all. Most

To Go or Not To Go . . . That Is the Question!

Saying goodbye may be a lifelong process, so the first separation of child and parent is almost always difficult. Two teachers express their views. Which do you think is best?

Leave Soon

I expect children to cry when their parents leave. Of course, it's a new place, and they aren't used to it yet. But the longer the parents stay, the harder it is for the child to say goodbye. We establish a regular routine: the parent comes in for five minutes, helping the child settle. I come up and greet them, and we may have a brief conversation. But not long at all, because then I either take the child by the hand or carry them to the window. We say goodbye, and the parent leaves. We wave at them as they get into the car, and that's that. The child often cries for the first few days, but after that, it's no big deal. There is a difference between saying goodbye and being alone without your parent. Children never want their parents to leave, because they'd rather have their cake and eat it too. But they do fine once the departure is over; why drag it out?

Stay Awhile

Children have a special attachment to their parents, and it is important that they know I am not trying to break in on that. Also, both the child and the parents need some time to get acquainted with me and the place. Until a parent is reassured that I can be trusted with their child, they need to stay around. And unless the parent is confident and happy, the child probably won't be, either. Besides, the parents move all over, investing each nook and cranny with a kind of "familiarity magic" that the child feels and remembers. First, I have the parents follow their child everywhere. Once the child is moving through the environment on his own, I ask the parent to sit in one spot, coming over to the child only on his request, but watching and smiling all the time. The next stage is bringing a magazine or book; still staying in one spot, but being less available. Next, the parent might leave for a few minutes—to get coffee or use the bathroom—five minutes, to give the child the experience of "go and come back." This can take a few days or even months; we gauge what is happening with the child and parent each time. I've never had a child "regress" if we don't hurry them; in fact, some even say, "Mommy, you can go now!"

programs fall in the middle, trying to be flexible to parents' needs and ac-commodating to children's feelings. A teacher can help a family through separation by working with the parent to establish a regular routine or time to say goodbye, and helping the parent come across as steady and firm. The teacher then stays with the child in saying goodbye, offering ideas for the child to wave, look out the window, blow a kiss. And teachers stay with children as they cry or become upset, understanding that the point of sepa-ration is often more difficult than being apart.

Children vary. Sometimes separation proceeds easily, goes well for a week or two and then falters, or seems hard for a long time. Children can cry for a few minutes or an hour. Children need consoling, and then some other things to do. Children under three often need a lap (the reassurance of a friendly grown-up) and then having materials and interesting things to watch and do. Given plenty of time and space for free play, a young child can "cast off" the preoccupation of being separated and away from home and get into the environment and people of the new place. The section on Alternative Approaches elaborates on the various ways to guide the separa-tion process.

Keeping in Touch

Building relationships with parents involves keeping in contact and shar-ing what happens with the child. Often, the little touches count the most. At pick-up time, try to tell the parent about something positive or fun that happened with their child. Notice for them how the child is progressing ("She tried pulling up her own pants this afternoon" or "It's the first time I've seen him reach out to another child!"). With concerns or difficult inci-dents, be sure to communicate the issue briefly when it happens, then fol-low up as soon as possible. For instance, when Jessie bit a playmate, her parents needed to hear about it that day. But the details and Mom's feelings about such behavior are better dealt with in private, not at the door in front of everyone else or at a transition time when everyone is tired and ready to go. A telephone call after the child's bedtime is appropriate and effective.

Understanding the family situation makes a difference in working with children and parents. For instance, knowing Matthew's mother is liv-ing with her own parents helps his teacher understand the generational dif-ferences in childrearing that Matthew encounters. By keeping in touch with Mom about it, the teacher can be supportive about the frustrations inherent in this living situation, and may be able to involve the grandmother in the program. Knowing the stages of parenthood (see Chapter 4), a teacher may be able to help parents on issues of guidance. For instance, the parents of Vanessa and Jessie are raising very young children, putting them in the

Nurturing stage. Therefore, both are involved in the attachment process and need to establish priorities about where the baby fits in their lives. As the more experienced ones with three older children, Vanessa's parents may be more comfortable with how to hold on and let go. Because Jessie's parents have only one child, are just establishing themselves financially, and are more than a decade younger, the issues may differ. All these factors affect how these two sets of parents interact with the teacher and the program, as well as how they raise their children.

Communicating Your Expectations and Understandings

What parents need from teachers changes over time. For instance, parents of infants want to know "What's normal? What's next?" When children become toddlers, the questions seem to move toward "What should I do? When will it end?" As children move from one to two years, parents are usually tackling "What kind of authority am I? How do I make and enforce the rules?" Teachers guide parents by being prepared to answer these questions, and by offering ideas that work in the program. In this way, teachers make their own "wisdom" accessible to parents without presuming that the teacher always knows best or that parents don't.

Whether in informal conversations in the classroom, talks by telephone, or more formal conferences, teachers need to talk with parents regularly about problems with children's behavior. These times are often tense, and nearly always difficult, but there are ways to make these encounters more effective. When teachers communicate about development and share effective techniques for guiding children, they increase the likelihood that problems can be resolved.

For instance, Jessie's parents are very anxious about her upcoming conference. As the parents of a single child, they have no other reference points about childrearing. Financial and time burdens add to an overall tension. The teacher helps by:

- *Giving purpose and structure to the conference:* "My goal for this conference is to talk about Jessie's development overall and to look closely at her interactions with the other children, including the biting, which concerns us both."
- *Setting a social tone to put parents at ease:* "Can I offer you some tea? Let me tell you what a delight Jessie was today at lunch."
- *Outlining progress in specific areas of development:* "I've seen Jessie grow so much these last two months in feeding herself and saying goodbye without upset."

- *Asking questions:* "I've been doing all the talking! Tell me about how Jessie has been at home lately. What does she do when you are together?"
- *Looking for both parents' participation.*
- *Letting parents bring up their issues.*
- *Introducing areas of concern.* "It would help me work with Jessie if you would tell me more about what seems to happen when she's sad or frustrated."
- *Allowing differences to arise and letting the parent talk without interruption before presenting your educator's viewpoint:* "I'm listening carefully to what you are saying, and it seems clear that our thinking differs on this. I hear you saying you want Jessie to be spanked when she keeps fussing. Legally, I cannot, and as an educator I do not spank."
- *Providing everyone time to reflect:* "Let's both think it over and watch Jessie for the next two weeks, then talk again."
- *Being more firm if needed:* "I have to be frank with you and say I think she needs extra help from us now. From my experience, spanking makes a child more fearful or hostile, not more understanding."
- *Influencing parents without overcorrecting or undermining:* As the conference concludes, Bob was heard to say, "You know, maybe we don't *have* to spank her . . ."

Developmental Alerts

When behavior becomes atypical, the scenario becomes more difficult and complex. The child's behavior is of such concern to the teacher that more serious measures may be required. When this happens, parents need to be consulted and a health care provider or early childhood specialists should be consulted. It is often a perplexing problem to determine if a child is developing normally, and teachers often feel that difficult behavior just needs to be tolerated or stopped. However, when problems persist or escalate uncontrollably, the question must be answered quickly, because early identification and intervention can often lessen the seriousness of a problem. Table 5.4 illustrates some developmental alerts for children under three years of age.

Let's return to Matthew. At two-and-a-half, he has become very oppositional. His grandmother sees it in his refusal to engage in toileting, his mother finds it in his jumping about on the stairs in spite of repeated warnings about falling, and his teacher sees it in his adamant refusal to participate in activities with any adult direction. Taking a larger view of this child, his teacher notices that his family is recently divorced, he has a new sibling, is living in a new house, and has two primary caregivers (mother and

---

Table 5.4

When Behavior Becomes Atypical

The age at which early childhood skills are acquired shows great variation. At the same time, children whose development appears to be incomplete or inconsistent with the normal range of behavior need closer observation or intervention. *See an early childhood or child health care provider if the child does **not** demonstrate these skills by the intended age:*

Infant

1–4 months	Continue to grow steadily and measurably
	Smile in response to the smile of others
	Follow a moving object with eyes
	Turn head to locate sounds
	Reach for objects or familiar persons
4–8 months	Show even, steady growth
	Explore own hands and objects placed in hands
	Smile, babble, laugh aloud
	Search for hidden objects
	Play games such as peek-a-boo, pat-a-cake
	Appear interested in new sounds, objects
8–12 months	Imitate simple sounds
	Follow simple verbal requests (come, no, bye-bye)
	Show anxiety towards strangers
	Interact playfully with parents, caregivers, siblings

Toddler

12–18 months	Attempt to talk or repeat words
	Understand some new words
	Respond to simple questions with yes/no
	Exhibit a variety of emotions
	Show interest in pictures
	Recognize self in mirror
18–24 months	Verbalize needs and desires
	Speak in two- to three-word phrases
	Follow a series of two simple commands
	Avoid bumping into objects
	Chew food; self-feed and some self-undress
24–30+ months	Express needs and desires clearly
	Speak in short sentences
	Recognize own, familiar names
	Show interest in other children

(Adapted from Allen & Marotz, 1989)

grandmother) who have different styles and priorities. In the classroom, Matthew seems to move rapidly from withdrawn to almost out of control: he can refuse to do anything one moment, and be racing around shouting and pushing the next. He does not verbalize his needs or desires to the teacher, so a language analysis is difficult to do informally. His mother reports that he seems helpless at home, not even helping to take off his own clothes or shoes and socks.

Matthew's behavior is worsening, not improving. The teacher thinks he (as well as the family and school) need extra help. What can teachers do?

1. *Respond to concerns by observing and keeping a record of the difficult behaviors.* The teacher listens to both Matthew's mother and grandmother, watches Matthew carefully, and continues informal conversations.

2. *Offer the child's perspective.* The teacher tells the family how much Matthew is needing to cope with, and casually suggests ways to help a child adjust.

3. *If the behavior doesn't improve, call for a conference.* The teacher observes Matthew carefully to document specific details.

4. *Be prepared to offer specific suggestions and an appropriate referral.* The teacher may say something such as, "We've talked together many times about Matthew in the last two months, and we've both tried to give him time and space to relax and adjust. We've tried to use your ideas about letting him be, but the truth is that things aren't getting better for him. I am still concerned with his emotional well-being and his lack of language development, and think that he may need some special help and would benefit from a complete evaluation. I'd suggest we start with his doctor and go from there. It's not so unusual for children to be looked at, to find out why he is having trouble and how best to help him at this time. Would you be willing for me to talk with your doctor and call an early childhood consultant to observe him in class? I know three specialists that have worked with us before; and I trust their observations, about children's speech and language development and emotional issues. Would you like to think this over and give me a call by the end of the week? I know it's a big step, and I want you to have time to think about what I've said and feel OK about what to do. We need to plan together about what to do next."

5. *Remain sensitive to the parent's feelings.* Try not to sound bossy or judgmental. At the same time, the teacher has legitimate reasons for concerns and must stand firm in these professional conclusions.

We believe that parents and teachers are both invaluable sources of knowledge about children. We also believe that, particularly for the very young child, working with the family is critical to effective work with children. Given these two beliefs, we must look for ways to build respectful relationships. Guiding the infant and toddler includes consulting regularly with the parent of the child. This includes not only the difficulties but also the celebrations of the miraculous beginnings of these very young children.

Think It Over

Do you remember being bitten as a child, or biting someone else? How do you feel when you see one child bite another? What can you say to the parent of the "biter" at pick-up time? And to the one whose child was bitten? What can you say if the parent denies that the child ever bites, or blames you for not having prevented it?

Summary

The very young child is considered someone from birth until about two-and-a-half years of age. Infants, Toddlers, and Twos have unique developmental needs and strengths, and the sheer amount that they grow and learn is phenomenal. With this growth comes significant challenges, both in motor, intellectual, and affective domains. These translate into issues around attachment, separation, temper tantrums, biting, willfulness, and aggression. Additionally, the environment plays a powerful role in the behavior of the very young child. Finally, it is critical that the teacher involve the parents and family as much as possible in the mutual childrearing and education of the very young child.

Observe and Apply

Observe a child under three having a temper tantrum. If you are not currently working or living with a young child, try going to a local park when children are told it is time to leave, or to a supermarket near the checkout/candy stand. See if you can pinpoint:

1. What caused the tantrum?
2. What did the child do and say during the tantrum?
3. How did the adult respond? Were they effective? Humane?
4. What was the outcome of the tantrum? How did the child feel? How did the adult feel?
5. What do you think the child "learned"? About tantrums? Having strong feelings? Their self-esteem? How to express himself?
6. What triggers tantrums? How might you "tame the fury"? What can be done to prevent them? Why do children stop having tantrums?

Review Questions

1. Teachers of very young children are often told "Paddle with the current, not against it." Give an example of how to do this in the following cases:

   A toddler is stuck between chairs under a table.

   A two-year-old grabs a toy from another child.

   A nine-month old cries when her dad leaves her.

   A two-and-a-half-year-old shrieks "Not you" when you offer to change diapers.

   A toddler says "Mine" to nearly everything he wants.

2. Using the information from the chapter, interpret and give an example of the following statements from educators Nancy Balaban and Annye Rothenberg:

   "Toddlers want mutually exclusive things" (NB).

   "Children forget easily and therefore need many repetitions or answers" (AR).

   "Toddlers often don't know what they want—or they want everything at the same time" (NB).

   "When you impose limits, try not to allow yourself to become trapped in a battle of wills" (AR).

3. Review the "Four As" concerning toddlers and conflicts. Apply them to a child refusing to eat; now apply them to a child not wanting to be changed.

4. Here are four common guidance problems in the very young years. Give at least two solutions from the chapter for each:

"NO!"

Hitting/pulling hair

"Mommy, don't go!"

Grabbing toys

Bibliography

Allen, K. Eileen, & Marotz, Lynn. *Developmental Profiles: Birth to Six.* Albany, NY: Delmar, 1989.

Ames, Louise Bates, & Ilg, Frances L. *Your One Year Old, Your Two Year Old.* New York: Dell, 1982 (rev. ed.).

Balaban, Nancy. *Learning to Say Goodbye: Starting School and Other Early Childhood Separations.* New York: New American Library, 1987 (2nd ed.).

Brazelton, T. Berry. *Infants and Mothers, Toddlers and Parents.* New York: Bantam Doubleday Dell, 1989 (rev. ed.).

Brazelton, T. Berry. "Implications of infant development among the Mayan indians of Mexico." In P. H. Liederman, S. R. Tulkin, & A. Rosenfeld (Eds.), *Culture and Infancy: Variations in the Human Experience.* New York: Academic Press, 1977.

Charlesworth, W., & Kreutzer, M. Facial expressions of infants and toddlers. In P. Eckman (Ed.), *Darwin and Facial Expression.* New York: Academic Press, 1973.

Crary, Elizabeth. *Without Spanking or Spoiling: A Practical Approach to Toddler and Preschool Guidance.* Seattle, WA: Parenting Press, 1992 (rev. ed.).

Eibl-Eibesfeldt, I. *Love and Hate: The Natural History of Behavior Patterns.* New York: Holt, Rinehart & Winston, 1971.

Fogel, A. The role of emotion in early childhood education. In Katx, L. B. (Ed.), *Current Topics in Early Childhood Education,* Vol. 3, Norwood, NJ: Ablex Publishing, 1980.

Galnisky, Ellen. *The Six Stages of Parenthood.* Menlo Park, CA: Addison-Wesley, 1987.

Gonzalez-Mena, Janet, & Eyer, Dianne Widmeyer. *Infants, Toddlers and Caregivers.* Mountain View, CA: Mayfield Press, 1993 (3rd ed.).

Harris, Judith Rich, & Liebert, Robert M. *Infant and Child.* New Jersey: Prentice-Hall, 1992.

Hast, Fran, & Hollyfield, Ann. "Experiences for Infants and Toddlers Last a Lifetime: Promoting Curiosity, Conflict Resolution and Competence." Paper given at California Association for the Education of Young Children, Anaheim, CA, March, 1993.

Howes, Carolee, & Olenick, Michael. "Family and child care influence on toddlers' compliance." *Child Development,* Vol. 57, p. 202–16, 1986.

Howrigan, G. A. Fertility, infant feeding and change in Yucatan. *New Directions for Child Development,* Vol. 40, p. 37–50, 1988.

Hoyenga, K. B., & Hoyenga, K. T. *Gender-Related Differences.* Boston, MA: Allyn & Bacon, 1993.

Jouriles, E. N., Pfiffner, L. J., & O'Leary, S. G. "Marital conflict, parenting, and toddler conduct problems." *Journal of Abnormal Child Psychology,* 16, 1988.

Kuczynski, L., Kochanska, G., Radke-Yarrow, M., & Girnius-Brown. "A developmental interpretation of young children's noncompliance." *Developmental Psychology,* 23, 1987.

La Rossa, Ralph. "Fatherhood and Social Change," *Family Relations,* Vol. 37, p. 451–57, Oct., 1988.

Leach, Penelope. *Your Baby and Child: From Birth to Age Five.* New York: Alfred A. Knopf, 1984.

Londerville, S., & Main, M. "Security of attachment, compliance, and maternal training methods in the second year of life." *Developmental Psychology,* 17, 1981.

Mack, Alison. *Toilet Learning.* Boston, MA: Little, Brown, 1978.

Miyake, K., Chen S-J., & Campos, J.J. Infant Temperament, mother's mode of interaction, and attachment in Japan. In I. Bretherton & E. Waters (Eds.), *Growing Points of Attachment Theory and Research. Monographs of the Society for Research in Child Development,* 50, 1985.

Ninio, Anat, & Rinott, Nurith. "Fathers' Involvement in the Care of Their Infants," *Child Development,* Vol. 59, p. 652–63, June, 1988.

Rothenberg, B. Annye. *Parentmaking.* Menlo Park, CA: The Banster Press, 1981.

Rutter, M. "Maternal deprivation, 1972–78: new findings, new concepts, new approaches." *Child Development,* Vol. 50, pp. 283–305, 1979.

Schaefer, H. R., & Emerson, P. E. "Patterns of response to physical contact in early human development." *Journal of Child Psychology and Psychiatry,* Vol. 5, 1964.

Stone, Jeannette G. *Teacher-Parent Relationships.* Washington, D.C.: National Association for the Education of Young Children, 1987.

Turecki, Stanley, & Tonner, Leslie. *The Difficult Child.* New York: Bantam, 1985.

6

Guiding the Preschool Child:
Three to Five Years

Profiles

Rosie, a busy three-and-a-half-year-old, in the housekeeping area with her friend, Tess. Kendra enters and picks up one of the dolls.
>   Kendra: *"I'm a mommy, too."*
>   Rosie: *"No, you're not. I am. Only me."*
>   Kendra (insistent): *I can be too!"*
>   Rosie: *"You can't play here. Get out."* More firmly: *"You can't play here. We don't want you."*
A teacher observing nearby walks toward the girls.
>   Rosie (glancing up at the teacher): *"Come on, Tess. We're going to the store. Hurry up. We have to go to the store."* She grabs a big purse and one of the dolls and clumps away in her high-heeled shoes with Tess following. Kendra watches them go.

Frankie is an exuberant four-year-old, popular with his peers and generally compliant with adults. Lately, he has begun to resist even the most basic requests. At home he will eat only peanut butter sandwiches. At school he often yells at teachers, "You can't make me! You aren't my boss!" His greatest resistance comes at nap time as he dawdles on his way in from the yard, and is the last to prepare his cot and to find a book. When he has prolonged the process as long as he can, he states firmly, "No, I won't take a nap." He creates enough of a disturbance to upset other children.

Pushing, shoving, and grabbing are Claire's claim to fame in the group of five-year-olds. She does everything aggressively: slaps paint on the easel, drops blocks on top of one another, forces puzzle pieces together, punches clay into awkward shapes as she barrels around the classroom. Claire uses her husky body to push her way to the front of the group so that she can be first to claim a favored wagon. She grabs toys and materials away from others, and at snack time, will scoop up large portions of food. When other children tell her she has taken too much, Claire makes a silly noise and gets the other children laughing with her. Children like being invited to Claire's house because she has good play ideas and her behavior is not as intense outside of school.

Although these children exhibit typical preschool behaviors, there is more to their stories than what one can observe in a school setting. Rosie's new baby brother is only four months old. Her dad works two jobs and her mother just started babysitting for her sister's two children after school. Rosie's grandmother, who lives with them, now brings Rosie to school. Rosie has started wetting the bed at night and has nightmares about the monster in her closet. She sometimes cries when she has to go to school.

Frankie's weekends alternate between his divorced parents' homes. His mother has worked full-time since he started at the child care center and has a high-pressure job as a supermarket manager. She often works late at night and is a strict disciplinarian. His father is more lax in setting limits and feels "boys should be boys" by being active and feisty. Frankie's brothers, ages ten and twelve, help care for him when their mother has to work late. Frankie looks up to his brothers and tries to keep up with them.

Claire is an only child, the daughter of an older couple. Her father has teenage children by a previous marriage, and he has a large extended family. Claire's parents are both gregarious and social; they dote on Claire and find her boisterous ways delightful. There is a lot of activity in the house with the teenagers visiting regularly, the parents entertaining large groups, and many family gatherings. As the youngest, Claire suffers a lot of teasing and her demands and aggressive behaviors are considered "cute" by the rest of the family.

In meeting Rosie, Frankie, and Claire we get a look at the life and times of the preschool child. They have characteristics and behaviors typical of three-to-five-year-olds. The problems they present to their families and teachers are quite common to all who deal with active, energetic preschoolers.

Think It Over

When you were small, do you think you behaved like Rosie, Frankie, and Claire? What do you remember? How did your parents handle your behavior?

The Dynamic, Developing Preschooler

The preschool years generally refer to the two or three years before entering a formal, primary school setting. Many early childhood programs include infants and some may offer kindergarten for the five-year-old as well. For our discussion, we define the preschool years as those including children who are three, four, and five years old.

Overlap is inevitable when creating arbitrary age ranges. Some of the material about "older toddlers" in Chapter 5 is relevant to this chapter's discussion about three-year-olds. We include fives in this chapter because many children turn five during their final preschool year, and because many early childhood settings include programs for fives as well. As we move on to Chapter 7 on the school-age child, five-year-olds are also a part of the discussion of kindergarten as part of the elementary school setting.

An overview of the preschool child's growth and development enhances any discussion of techniques, methods, and approaches that work well with this age group. Table 6.1 indicates some of the most significant changes that occur during the preschool years, with implications for guiding behavior. This table underscores the interrelated nature of the child's growth and suggests ways to encourage positive behavior through the preschooler's emerging physical skills.

The Years of Energy and Activity

As they move through the preschool years, children's body movements become more coordinated and controlled. Constant motion and activity marks these years, and it is a time for using and developing large motor

Preschoolers become problem solvers as their imagination and curiosity soars. A longer attention span encourages purposeful exploration of materials and ideas.

Table 6.1

Developmental Profiles: Physical Growth in the Preschool Years

Developmental Parameters	Implications for Guidance	What Children Need
Growth Pattern		

Growth shows significantly slower rate:
    Weight gain = 10 pounds
    Height gain = 7 inches
    Now stands erect
	Support children's physical growth by providing them with the challenge their bodies need, thus eliminating some of the frustration that causes behavioral problems.	Open space for full body movement. Time and space and ways to run off energy.

Do not require a great amount of food	Remember: growth has slowed—they don't need as much food.	Opportunities to select their food and the size of their portion.
Food fads emerge. Can become picky eaters.	Recognize this as a testing of limits and a cry for independence.	Give them the foods they like and ask for.
Motor Skills		
Increased speed and accuracy. Mastery of hand movements. Emerging skill in finger dexterity. Becoming more coordinated and controlled.	Children can now perform a wide variety of self-help routines. Desire for independence is supported by clothes, children can manipulate themselves without fears, frustrations. Fosters sense of self-control and self-worth—important ingredients in behavior management.	Time and space to explore materials and objects: opportunity to gain variety of experiences through greater mobility. Variety of materials to manipulate. Materials which challenge. Provide clothing with buttons, zippers, openings that children can grasp easily. Implements (spoons, toothbrushes) which fit children's hands.
Constant motion and activity. High level of energy. Tremendous physical drive. Intense physical activity.	Use and develop large motor skills by providing activities that require active physical play. Do not require children to sit for prolonged periods of time.	Avenues for active, vigorous play—places to run, jump—to use body freely. Balance with quiet times.
Perceptual Development		
Movement becomes intentional and voluntary, not reflex.	Foster children's inner clock that reassures them that Mom will be back after naps.	Experiences with space, direction, time.
Gains a sense of temporal awareness.	Reassures unhappy children. Gives warning that play will end and clean up begin. Helps children anticipate change.	Routines, daily schedule, predictable meals for growing awareness of time sequence.

skills. Preschoolers love to move fast and their motor abilities support a high level of energy. Claire exemplifies the physical drive common to this age, and some of her pushing and shoving is a desire to use her body and newly honed skills. Some of her behavior is out-of-bounds, but her tremendous physical energy is typical of five-year-olds.

It is often difficult for some children to settle down once they have begun to play. Frankie's resistance to taking naps is typical of the active-till-exhausted exuberance of the preschooler. We know that children expend a lot of energy and they need some rest or quiet time to balance their physical activity. Afternoons at home or school where naps or rests have been forfeited are often filled with crises and tears, creating discipline problems far beyond those of learning how to help children unwind from active play. Frankie's teachers might help him calm down before he comes in from outside by providing soothing water play, or by giving him a five-minute warning to give him time to wind down his activity. He might be encouraged to do some quiet activity before settling on his cot, recognizing that he may need a longer period of transition from active to quiet play than other children, and that he need not be forced to lie down immediately.

To channel the energy and enthusiasm of the preschooler, teachers and parents are wise to allow the preschooler open spaces and time in which they can explore with their full bodies, areas where they can run off their energy, and materials that challenge them. We want to support children's physical growth by providing them with the challenges their bodies need and in doing so, eliminate some of the frustration that causes behavior problems.

Try It   Identify some children who have high energy levels, such as Claire, and who require a lot of teacher attention. Invite them to help you set up an obstacle course on the playground. Help them plan and build it. What do Tables 6.1 and 6.4 suggest to you as you plan and work together?

The Years of Imagination and Curiosity

Preschoolers are alert, excited, and infinitely curious. A growing awareness of a world beyond home, family, and school causes them to constantly question "How?" or "Why?" and otherwise demonstrate a strong intellectual drive. Three-to-five-year-olds are fascinating as they come to a greater awareness of themselves and their impact on the world. They move, explore, talk, and play out what they see and what they learn. We see their cognitive development undergo remarkable changes in these years before formal schooling as

- They become problem solvers,
- Their attention span increases, and
- They learn to negotiate for their own wants and needs.

From a guidance point of view, we can appreciate the preschoolers' need to assume greater responsibility for their own daily care. Chapter 2 reminds us that in Erikson's terms, this is the stage of initiative versus guilt. Initiative is the ability to take action, to begin a task and follow through with it. Allowing preschoolers the opportunity to work down the row of buttons, to choose what they want for snacks, and to pick out the clothes they wear, can be viewed as tasks that support their emerging initiative and enhancing self-confidence, rather than as activities designed to test the patience of adults. Sometimes a guidance approach is merely a change in our own attitudes or perceptions of what children are doing, how they are learning, and what stage of development they are in.

The preschool years also encompass Piaget's preoperational period. Although it is a time of increasing use of representational thought—children use words and symbols in communicating thoughts and actions—their knowledge is still fragmented. They have pieces of knowledge, but no overall framework (Schickedanz et al., 1993).

Preschoolers' Logic and Thinking

Preschoolers' logic and thinking differs markedly from how adults think. Children use a process called *transductive reasoning*, based on their own sense of logic. It is an intuitive rather than a logical approach, and the child often draws incorrect conclusions. Cause and effect are mistakenly related as well. "It isn't my bedtime yet because I don't have my jammies on." This child is not being argumentative, just expressing the only kind of reasoning in her cognitive repertoire.

Preschoolers see the world in fairly rigid terms: black/white, good/bad. Once a faulty or incorrect decision has been drawn, it is difficult to sway a child from that position. Although children this age are able to do some problem solving, they cannot examine their thoughts, conclusions, or strategies (Bee, 1992).

We tend to use logic in our discussions with children. It would appear that until they reach the stage of concrete operations, in Piagetian terms, our efforts are futile. Instead, we can help children experience the world through their senses and give them opportunities to learn through a hands-on approach. We must also accept that children may form different conclusions than we might, and be mindful that we do not humiliate or diminish their efforts at reasoning.

Taking Another's Perspective

Taking another person's perspective is not characteristic of preschoolers. Although they may work out solutions to problems with their peers, they do not really understand their friend's point of view. When we ask a preschooler to "think about how Sammy feels when you hit him," we are asking a child to perform a task more suited to an older child. We can help children by asking them to recall how *they* felt when they were hit. It is a beginning toward taking another person's view into consideration. Between the ages of three and five, children come to realize that thoughts are changeable, that one can correct misperceptions, and that ideas may change and evolve (Schickedanz et al., 1993). The late preschooler is just beginning to accept that other people may have different thoughts about the same thing they do; this concept is more complete in the school-age child.

Imagination

This is an age when children's *imagination* flourishes. It is a time when dramatic play reigns, when fact and fiction are often confused, when superheroes and monsters command attention, and when children will tell tall tales, frequently embellished with gory details. Our role is to provide avenues for imaginative thought, to be clear with children about what is real and what is not, and to understand the meaning of and need for figures who are larger than life.

Is it *lying or wishful thinking?* Embellishing stories is a common occurrence, and adults must be careful not to overreact when children do not tell the truth. Four-year-olds are notorious for denying wrongdoing to the point of what adults might call "lying." In fact, what appears to adults to be a lie is, to a preschooler, "magical thinking" so typical of the age and an aspect of the *transductive thinking* (Elkind, 1994) common to this stage of development. Wishes and fantasy are an important part of the child's imaginative life and reality is sometimes blurred. If you wish something to be true, it just may happen. The distortion of reality is not intentional but an outcome of imperfect logic and a confusion over what is real and unreal.

Children this age are not morally aware of lying, so we must be prepared to help them learn to tell the truth without focusing on the fabrication. If Conrad said his little sister broke the vase, yet we see evidence of flowers and spilled water in Conrad's room and we know his sister was napping at the time, we talk to Conrad in a straightforward way, without accusing him of lying.

"Looks like you broke the vase right here. Better get a sponge and clean up the water. You can put the flowers in another vase." This opens the possibility of talking with Conrad about what he was thinking or feeling when the accident happened, how it happened, and the fear or anxiety that may have led him to fabricate the story. In this way, we demonstrate that we understand the child's perspective by speaking the truth without belaboring the untruth. This avoids guilt and models a way for Conrad to deal with the situation where his wishes are not the same as reality.

Learning the Power of Words

Cognition and language are intertwined in ways not yet completely understood. Much of the preschooler's intellectual growth is demonstrated by their language development, and their language development is affected by their intellectual skills. Their behavior is influenced by both their ability to understand a situation (cognition) and their experience and use of words (language).

Uses of Language

Preschoolers have a lot to say, and now understand and use language well. They have mastered most grammatical structures and enjoy one-to-one conversations with adults. During this period, they learn to use language to:

- Communicate with other children
- Ask for turns
- Express anger
- Invite other children to play
- Stop aggressive acts directed toward themselves
- Call attention to themselves
- Provide an outlet for silliness and fun
- Invent words and sounds
- Play with words
- Exaggerate with words
- Shock adults with profanity and bathroom words

Private Speech

As you observe young children, you will notice that they often talk without concern for who is listening:

- Jamie (aloud, as he paints alone at the easel): "Red, red, red. Put on yellow, yellow. Oooooooh! I made a mess. Clean it up with the brush. Good. It's gone."

- Naomi (playing alone with her doll): "Bad girl. Bad girl. You'll have to be punished. Now don't cry when I spank you."

- Francie (muttering): "Don't touch. Don't touch." as she walks by the glass figurine on the coffee table at home.

One theory suggests that preschoolers talk aloud to themselves to help regulate their behavior and solve problems. *"Private speech,"* a phenomenon common to preschoolers, was first noted by Piaget, who called it "egocentric speech." He dismissed these utterances as another example of preschooler's egocentrism. Not so Lev Vygotsky, a Russian psychologist, who believes that private speech is young children's way of monitoring their own behavior. It serves the function of

- Helping children think out loud,
- Putting their thoughts into words,
- Focusing their attention on what they are doing, and
- Directing their actions.

In later years, private speech diminishes and becomes verbal thought (Harris & Liebert, 1992). Some of the research supporting Vygotsky's view (Berk, 1986) indicates that children who talk out loud to themselves are possibly better problem solvers than children who do not talk aloud, and that they stay more focused on the task at hand and begin to regulate their own behavior (Becker, 1988). Private speech affects children's sociability as well. Children who talked more to other children were the ones who also talked aloud to themselves (Berk, 1986). Adults who work with young children might want to consider how to enhance children's private speech as a way to help children learn to foster self-control.

For instance, the teacher hearing Jamie might say, "I hear you thinking out loud, Jamie, and you've found a way to take care of that runny paint!" To Naomi, "Sounds like you are pretending to do what some mommies and daddies do. Tell me, what do you think will happen when you spank the doll?" Francie's parents can reinforce her awareness of the rules: "That's right, Francie. It sounds like you are remembering what I told you about touching the statue." Reinforce the fact that the children spoke aloud yet required no response. It would be important not to interfere if the child wanted to continue the activity in solitude.

Implications for Guidance

This age group uses language creatively. They listen fairly well and understand many more words than they speak. How do we handle this explosion of words in relation to children's behavior? There are a number of implications:

1. *Take advantage of children's enjoyment of language.* Start conversations with them, listen to their stories, play word games with them. Join in when Claire begins to be silly with words and invite other children to participate, taking the focus off Claire's misbehavior and putting it on something constructive. Write down some of their inventions and send them home for parents to appreciate. *Foster a sense of language as a vehicle for creativity.*

"Claire is saying 'nitty gritty, nitty gritty.' I say, 'pretty ditty, pretty ditty.' You say '_____ .' That's right, Boris, 'city, city' rhymes. We just made up a poem. Let's write down all the words you can think of to finish the rhyme."

2. *Help them use their language to talk about their feelings and to express their anger and frustration.* It is during the preschool years that children learn to use their words rather than their fists or their tears. We must help Rosie, Frankie, and Claire to find the right words to label how they feel and to show that we understand what they feel. (See Table 6.2.) *Foster language as a way to express feelings and anxieties.*

"Rosie, are you angry with Kendra? She doesn't know why you won't let her play. Let's find some words together to tell her what you are feeling."

3. *Assist children, as needed, to negotiate the social world of the preschool.* Give children the words that help them protect their rights and maintain their unique place in the group. Claire's teachers might want to ask the group if they would help solve the problem of Claire's grabbing most of the snack. Together, they could generate alternatives and come to an agreement that Claire endorsed. Kendra needs help in asserting her rights and Rosie could use some techniques for welcoming others into play. *Foster language as a way to help children problem solve, allowing them time to sort through alternatives and figure out solutions.*

"If you had the book first, Genella, what can you say to Tony that lets him know you weren't finished?" "If Rusty makes you mad, how can you tell him without using your hands?"

4. *Let children know when their language is inappropriate.* This is an age when profanity, "bathroom talk," and name-calling are rampant. Many adults can and do ignore children's experimentation with language chosen for its shock value. In some instances, however, direct action is preferred. Remember, though, that children really do not know the meaning of many of the words they are using and have discovered that adults react strongly to certain words. Let children know where and when these words are appropriate, and tell them if you do not want them used in your presence. We must also protect children like Kendra from being hurt by other children's words when they are excluded or being called hurtful names. *Foster children's interest in trying new words but set limits when necessary.*

"Alessandro, those words hurt other people's feelings and we don't say them here." "Gracie, you may not use those words here. If you are angry or frustrated, you can choose some other words like 'Nuts' or 'Popcorn.' What other words can you think of?"

5. *Respond to children's curiosity, questions, and interest in solving problems.* Three-year-olds constantly ask "why?," fours like to give a lot of information, and fives like facts. Children are less likely to misbehave if they are engaged in activities of interest and have the attention of important adults. Teachers could challenge Rosie's problem-solving skills by introducing Kendra as the new postmistress who needed someone to help care for her baby, and ask Rosie and her friends to suggest some solutions. *Foster good behavior by meeting the intellectual challenge of children's blossoming problem-solving skills.*

"Rosie, Kendra needs some help. Can you and Tess think of a way she can be the postmistress and still take care of her baby?"

6. *Use language as a tool to get children to behave the way you want them to behave.* Children can now be controlled by language; preschoolers understand verbal commands and can match words to actions. We must realize that children of this age rely heavily on physical and social contexts to understand language. When we say, "Frankie, put your cot near the books so you can reach them while you rest," instead of "Don't put your cot there," we help him learn what it is we want him to learn from the situation. *Reinforce what children do right.* "You made up a new word, Claire! Can anyone think of a word that rhymes with 'gloppy'?" *Foster the intentional use of language as a way to help children behave appropriately.*

"I like the way you figured out how to finish writing that story before going home. That was hard."

7. *Never underestimate the adult's role as a model for language use and function.* We obviously model linguistic techniques, and equally important, we teach children to use language as a social interaction tool. Much of what we do with Rosie, Frankie and Claire is based on our intentional use of language that helps them develop the necessary verbal skills to make friends, solve problems, and express emotions. *Foster children's* *use of language by the clarity, precision, and thought of your own use of language.*

"You may not bite people. Teeth are for eating and chewing. I'll get you an apple if you want to bite something."

The Journey from Self to Others

Piaget claims that the key task of this age group is to make the shift from the self as the only frame of reference to include others. Erikson's theory says that this is a time of initiative and self-motivation crucial to healthy development. We know that preschoolers are eager, purposeful, and energetic. To successfully complete this period of growth, the child's independence, assertiveness, and interest in exploring new vistas should be supported. Otherwise, children may grow up to doubt their own abilities. In both emotional and social growth, the preschooler is all about fulfilling the tasks of those two theories.

Affective development relates to a child's self-concept: knowing and understanding one's self so one can better understand and relate to other people. Beginning at three and ending around age five, children gain a heightened awareness of themselves that now can include others. This process brings with it a variety of emotional expressions common to the young child.

Language blossoms in the early years as children learn different ways to communicate feelings, thoughts and ideas. Young children begin to shift their attention from themselves to others.

We help children master the language of emotional and social growth. We supply the labels to name feelings and support them as they learn to accept and express the feelings that sometimes overwhelm them. See Table 6.2 on page 211 for a process that helps children deal with their feelings. This is a lifelong task and one that is a primary focus of the preschool years.

The Age of Shifting Emotions

Preschoolers have a wide emotional range. If the two-year-old's byword is "No!" then the three-year-old's is "Yes!" They love to please and conform. Enter the four-year-old, who has rapid mood changes and an urgent need to test limits. "I can do it by myself!" is an emotional motto of fours as well as a physical reality. Fives close out this age group with a return to cooperation, a desire to help, and an ability to follow directions well. Emotional development is truly an up-and-down cycle for the young child.

In fact, disruptive stages tend to alternate with more placid phases of growth, even within a single year (Ames, 1992). *Disequilibrium,* as the difficult stage is called, seems to occur around the half-year: at eighteen months, three-and-one-half, four-and-one-half, and so on. Quieter, complacent stages tend to alternate with exuberant, expansive stages. The three-year-old who liked to please adults may becoming unwilling to do our bidding; this change of behavior is repeated when the well-balanced five-year-old rebels at mid-year. We can expect these cycles and not overreact when a formerly contented child becomes the terror of the classroom.

During these phases of disequilibrium, preschool children may exhibit behavior we thought they had outgrown. Bedwetting, thumb-sucking, and regression of physical skills are some of the behaviors they may repeat. If these appear, we take the long-range view and treat the behavior as the temporary phenomenon it is, support and comfort them as best we can, and know that each phase children go through can ultimately strengthen their self-confidence and their ability to cope with emotions more appropriately.

Fears

Emotionally, the preschool years could be called the age of fears, such as those Rosie experiences. Some of the most common fears are of animals, of the dark, of bathtub drains and toilets, and of people who have characteristics unfamiliar to the child, such as a beard or glasses.

These fears, although real to the child, are irrational and probably based on an aspect of transductive reasoning called *physiognomic perception.* Elkind (1994) explains that young children experience some of these

Table 6.2

Helping Children Deal with Feelings

Helping children learn to express their feelings fosters a sense of self-control and acceptance.

1. **Notice and verbalize their feelings.**

   "You look sad. What seems to be the matter?"

   "You act like you are having fun and enjoying yourself!"

   "That red face makes me think you must really be angry."

   "I see disappointment all over you."

   "Are you lonely over here by yourself or just being quiet?"

   We read the child's facial expression and body language and identify the emotion. This gives children some of the language of emotion and models for them the appropriateness of naming how they feel. Putting words on the feeling is the first step in bringing it under control.

2. **Accept the feelings expressed.** Children are comforted and reassured when a sympathetic adult says, "I know you are angry (tired, scared, hurt, embarrassed)." There is a sense of relief that someone recognizes what they are experiencing and they feel less overwhelmed by the depth of their own feelings. We make no judgments about the feelings, but simply acknowledge our acceptance that the feelings are real to the child.

3. **Provide a way to express the feeling in an appropriate way.**

   "I know you're angry and feel like hitting but I can't let you hurt other children. Here's some clay to pound. You can hit it as hard as you like."

   "Let's go find a place at the water table. You can make splashes there instead of at Janet."

   "You can yell just as loud as you like from over on that hill. Let's see if I can hear you from here."

   "Come stay by me and I will be your friend until your daddy picks you up."

   Young children hit, cry, throw tantrums, bite, push, shove, and otherwise inflict pain on themselves and others when their feelings get out of control. We must take into consideration the child's age, developmental level, and the situation, and offer an outlet for the strong emotions they express. Play is a suitable outlet for negative feelings and aggressive behavior and its role in providing an arena for free expression of a wide range of emotions cannot be underestimated.

4. **Find a suitable alternative activity if necessary.** There are times when children choose not to return to the activity that caused the problem, or they may be prevented from doing so. They may still need a further outlet for their aggressive feelings before joining a group of children. In any case, it is sometimes helpful to offer other options that meet the child's need.

   "You sure want to push and shove a lot today. I want to move these cots and it takes a lot of pushing to get them out of the way. Come and help me."

   "The garden needs digging. You seem to have a lot of energy today. You could show me how big a hole you can dig."

fears because they project their own anger onto inanimate objects, such as the monster in the closet. Rosie is unable to express anger at her mother and father for the loss of their attention, so her three-year-old way of coping is to direct her fear of loss at the monsters. One of the tasks of this period is for preschool children to differentiate between themselves and objects; when they do, some of these irrational fears disappear. We must take these fears seriously and comfort the child with reassurance of our presence and protection until they learn to talk out their feelings instead of internalizing them.

Sharing

Physiognomic perceptions also explain why sharing is such a difficult concept for the late toddler or early preschooler. By identifying themselves with objects (a doll or teddy bear), they see the object as an extension of themselves (Elkind, 1994). We must understand that by asking the child to let another child play with a cherished possession, we in essence are asking the child to give away part of herself. As they approach five, we see children shift from themselves as the focus of all transactions and become more generous in their ability to share their treasures—and selves—with others. Although ideas about and approaches to sharing vary with cultures, it is helpful to understand why it can be problematic for preschoolers.

Try It   The next time a child brings a favorite article from home, observe how other children react. What can you say to the child who does not want to share a special item? Are there rules the children could help you establish that would encourage the child to share, yet protect feelings and property? Create a time where you and the children could talk over what kind of sharing takes place at school with (1) school property and equipment, and (2) special items brought from home. Check to see if the rules and standard for sharing are age-appropriate.

Imaginary Friends

Around three years old, many preschoolers develop an imaginary friend who offers companionship and often takes the blame for the child's misbehavior. Again, the child's emotional needs are being met by transductive thinking and reasoning. As with other manifestations of the preschooler's incomplete reasoning abilities, we treat her concerns with respect and honor her requests for an extra place set at the table for her "friend." Yet we also acknowledge with her that we are pretending as we put an extra plate out. We want to help children discern reality from fantasy at the same time we recognize and accept their emotional needs.

Dealing with Feelings

How do we respond to this roller coaster of emotional states? The best preparation is to learn as much as we can about children's emotional development and understand the importance of the various phases children go through on their way to becoming adults. We must also learn to help children identify and express their emotions so that they can be in control of them. Ways to help children deal effectively with their feelings can be found in Table 6.2, which outlines four steps to help children achieve self-control.

The next step is to help children deal with the feelings of others. It begins with supporting young children in their own emotional growth. The steps outlined in Table 6.2 show how understanding adults can encourage children to become aware of their own feelings, be able to talk about them, and find a way to express them. Ultimately, as children learn to accept and tolerate others' opinions and feelings, greater cooperation and sharing can take place. A sensitive teacher can say, "I remember when you were angry this morning, Paula. Looks like Tonya feels that way now. What helped you get over being angry? Do you think it might help Paula? Let's go talk with her about it."

No discussion of preschooler's emotional growth would be complete if we omitted the value and function of dramatic play as an avenue for emotional expression. Children from three to five take on and elaborate a variety of roles as they act out emotional dramas. Rosie's interest in playing mommy roles can be seen as a direct outlet for her feelings about what is happening at home. She can identify with the mommy and act out situations that confuse or frighten her; she can control the outcome and play out solutions to real or imagined problems. Dramatic play has traditionally been seen as a way for children to work out problems for themselves and is an important vehicle for the child's emotional growth. Erikson saw such play as an avenue through which children learned about themselves and others and an obvious enhancer of their initiative. Early childhood classrooms should provide ample opportunities and a wide range of dramatic play accessories to foster this symbolic play.

Becoming a Social Being

Rosie, Frankie, and Claire each exhibit some degree of the social interactions typical of preschool children. Rosie has friends who frequently join her in dramatic play; Frankie is a popular playmate for all of the boys and girls in his class; and children tolerate some of Claire's assertiveness because of her complex social skills and ready humor.

Each child also has some aspect of social relationships he or she is working on with the adults who care for them. Rosie longs for the attention she enjoyed as an only child; Frankie is testing all the limits with his teachers; and Claire suffers the teasing of older siblings. The manifestations of these issues—bed-wetting, excluding others from play, testing limits, food fads, various forms of aggression—are all age-appropriate responses, although not necessarily socially acceptable ones.

Children need practice in learning self-control. When Quentin, a toddler, takes away another child's toy or hits a playmate, he is using his behavior as a form of language. We understand that children Quentin's age are still learning how to talk, how to play with others, and how to get what they want. Hitting, although not an acceptable behavior, is an age-appropriate response for a toddler who is still learning the rules of social interactions. We do not let children hurt one another, so we help Quentin learn other ways to express himself, even though his natural tendency at that age is to hit out at someone.

Table 6.3 lists a number of the social tasks and behaviors children learn in the preschool years. Each task affects children's behavior and has implications for guidance and discipline. It is another example of how an effective approach to discipline is embedded in a developmental understanding of how children grow.

An Emerging Sense of Self

The preschooler is becoming an autonomous person. Between the ages of three and five there is an emergence of individual identity, a sense of seeing oneself as separate from others. The picture preschoolers begin to form of who they are is based primarily on

- Physical features ("She's got curly hair.")
- Age ("I'm four and three-quarters.")
- Accomplishments ("I can ride a bike and run fastest.")
- Concrete experiences ("I was sad when my gramma died. I cried.")

Self-esteem is the act of putting a value judgment on one's self-concept and is strong in these years of initiative and mastery. Two aspects of self-esteem that are important when discussing children's behavior are *sharing*

Table 6.3

On the Road to Self-Discipline: Ages Three to Five

Social Emotional Tasks	Behavior a Child Learns
Learning self-control	Listening to others
	Accepting behavior limits
	Shifting from self as only frame of reference
	Dealing with feelings of others
	Learning to express feelings in words
	Taking turns, sharing, learning to wait
	Accepting, respecting authority
	Abiding by rules
	Inhibiting impulsive/aggressive behavior
Learning self-awareness and confidence	Liking adult companionship
	Showing off
	Accepting change and new situations
	Taking pride in accomplishments
	Verbalizing likes/dislikes
	Developing body awareness
	Forming self-identity
Becoming autonomous	Choosing own friends, activities
	Learning self-help skills
	Separating from parent
	Undertaking and completing tasks
	Initiating own learning
	Exercising judgment/making decisions
Learning to cooperate	Working in small groups
	Helping make group decisions
	Being helpful with family chores
	Enjoying group play and competitive games
	Helping adults with tasks
	Assisting with clean up
	Liking to please adults
	Becoming aware of rules
Becoming empathetic	Gaining heightened awareness of others
	Offering comfort, help, sympathy
	Being affectionate toward children
	Beginning to see how behavior affects others
	Appreciating differences in others
Becoming a problem solver	Can be reasoned/bargained with
	Can look at alternative situations
	Able to negotiate
	Talks out conflicts

(continued)

Table 6.3 (Continued)

Social Emotional Tasks	Behavior a Child Learns
Developing a moral consciousness	Seeing that behavior has consequences
	Beginning to see cause/effect relationships
	Beginning to be aware of right/wrong
	Learning from adult examples of behavior
	Understanding punishment as consequence of behavior

esteem that are important when discussing children's behavior are *sharing* and *empathy*.

Difficulty in sharing, as mentioned earlier, is related to cognitive growth and is not a character flaw in a young child. Sharing is seen by some researchers as a "positive sign of developing selfhood" (Berk, 1994), an attempt to distinguish between self and others. By shouting, "It's mine! I got it first and I'm gonna keep it!" a preschooler begins to claim an awareness as a separate being. We should affirm this attempt at self-definition rather

Alternative Approach

In the section titled The Years of Energy and Activity, we offered suggestions for dealing with Frankie's resistance by providing transitional activities and ample warning. Another way to approach Frankie is to deal directly with him, inviting him to help resolve the situation. The wise teacher does not take up Frankie's challenge of who is most powerful, but might say, "That's right. I'm not your boss, Frankie, but I am your teacher. It's my job to see that you and the others get enough rest. When you refuse to come inside at naptime, that creates a problem. What do you think we could do to solve it?" Frankie may suggest that he be left outside alone while the children nap, or other ideas that are impractical or unsafe. A creative teacher can pick up on one of his ideas. "You can't stay out here alone but you can be the last one in. Why don't you be the yard monitor each day and check to make sure everyone else is in and the equipment is stored?" Children respond more readily to solutions in which they have some choice or control, and Frankie and his teacher are beginning to negotiate some options for a reasonable, workable solution.

than stress the child's possessiveness. "That's right, Ebony. You've got the red shovel. Later, when you are finished with it, will you tell Roy? He's waiting for a turn." This response supports the child's increasing self-awareness and suggests a resolution. By letting Ebony determine the timing under for her to share, we also acknowledge her initiative and ability to accept the responsibility for notifying Roy. The same is true of Frankie when he confronts his teachers with "You're not my boss!"

In Chapter 5, we saw that children as young as toddlers exhibit some degree of empathy toward other children who are hurt or sad. This characteristic expands in the preschool years and hinges on a child's ability to take the perspective of another person. In typical developmental fashion, the ability to take that perspective is related to both cognitive growth and language acquisition. As children increase their ability to appreciate others' viewpoints, their empathy increases. We want to provide opportunities for children to express this emerging trait. We can ask them to help us attend to a child who has been hurt by finding a Band-Aid, a towel, or a cuddly toy. Children in this age group enjoy the responsibility of assisting, and offer verbal comfort and support to their unhappy playmate.

The Beginning of a Conscience: Internal Control

Most theorists agree that between the ages of three and five, the child's conscience begins to form. This is when children begin to internalize the controls and standards others have taught them. Family, society, and religious beliefs help to form a core of behaviors that the child's inner self begins to regulate.

Two particular theories are important to keep in mind as we help children learn to make judgments for themselves. Behaviorists remind us that our own actions affect a child's moral development. Modeling the empathetic and prosocial behaviors we want to see children acquire helps children learn those behaviors. When we are helpful and responsive to other people's needs, when we comfort and care for those who are hurt, when we act with kindness and generosity, when we are honest and truthful, and when we respect anothers' possessions, we are teaching moral and ethical behavior.

According to cognitive development theory, preschool children actively think about right and wrong and make judgments about the morality of an action. They can understand that there are degrees of moral reasoning and behavior, for example, when they judge that it is worse to hit someone intentionally than it is to hit someone accidentally. Preschoolers are also able to distinguish that a breach of moral conduct (taking someone else's things) is far more serious than if they forget common courtesies, such as "please" and "thank you" (Berk, 1994).

Through social interactions with others, children have the opportunities to live out their moral code and come to a more complete understanding of right and wrong. Inductive guidance techniques, as described in Chapter 3, promote children's moral development by helping them see how their actions affect others. Claire's teacher is helping her realize the consequences of her behavior by stating, "When you grab so much of the snack, Claire, other children get upset with you and sometimes hit you. You may take just one carrot for each hand." Empathy, awareness, and reasoning are brought into play as Claire struggles with her impulses and attempts to learn acceptable behavior.

Think It Over

Who do you know like Rosie, Frankie, and Claire? Does their behavior seem typical of preschool children you know? How so? Do their behaviors remind you of anything you did when you were young? What do you remember?

Guiding with Success

Developmentally Appropriate Guidance

To be developmentally appropriate, a practice must fit the general age range as well as take into consideration the individual child's history, needs, and capabilities. That is, teachers ask themselves: Is this discipline technique suitable for a four- (or six- or eight-) year-old? Does it fit with what I know about Jody? Is it likely to be successful with her? Teachers must first become familiar with developmental theories, which define children's behavior and set forth age-range expectations. This knowledge can then be applied to the specific age group and to individual children within a classroom setting. We can do something about behavior if we understand why it is happening and when it commonly occurs. We guide behavior in a developmentally appropriate way when we know what children are capable of at a certain age, and not by expecting them to behave in ways typical of older children. The methods and techniques that follow were discussed in Chapter 3.

Positive Requests and Suggestions

One of the most obvious behavior characteristics of preschool children is their need to assert their independence. This is a good age, then, for adults to learn how to frame requests and make suggestions in positive ways, providing options and choices from which children may choose. "We're going to get ready for lunch soon. When you finish your book, you can put the puzzles away or set the tables. Which do you want to do?" Commands and demands lead to resistance and tears.

Creating Alternatives

The preschool age is a time to be flexible, to be willing to negotiate and bargain, and to have alternate solutions. When there are opportunities to let the child "win" legitimately, do so. "Okay, Raoul, you have convinced me that you are really busy. You can take an extra five minutes to finish that project. We don't have to leave quite yet." As preschoolers come into their sense of self, it is important for adults to help them feel the power of asserting their needs and wants in appropriate ways. Adults who work with preschoolers should allow for testing out behaviors and become comfortable within themselves in setting limits. Review again Table 3.2 "Setting Limits" on effective ways to set and maintain appropriate limits.

Redirection and Reinforcement

Distraction as a guidance technique may not work well with older preschoolers, but redirection can be effective and demonstrate the adult's understanding of a child's curiosity and imagination. Children this age also respond to empathetic listening and attention from adults, which lets them know their fears and concerns are being taken seriously.

Positive reinforcement is one of the most useful techniques because children of this age seek adult approval and affection. Preschoolers like to please, and we can incorporate that into our guidance approach with them. As we have seen, modeling is another particularly effective strategy. Teachers can model kindness, courtesy, and fairness, in their interactions with children; they can also teach children ways to play with one another as they play along with them.

As preschoolers mature and their language skills improve, they become better able to handle problems on their own with a minimum of adult guidance. At this point, the adult role is to listen more than talk, and allow children the opportunity to figure out solutions. We want to foster the notion that differences of opinions and ways of doing things are natural and workable. In group settings, older preschoolers are able to generate

Modeling is an effective guidance tool. A sympathetic and caring adult teaches children through her own behavior.

rules of behavior and solve classroom problems through discussion and negotiations.

Inductive Guidance

Inductive guidance techniques help children become aware of the effect of their behavior on others, and are most effective for this age group because they help children understand the reasons for behaving in certain ways. "Claire, when you push other children out of the way, they don't want to play with you." This method calls on the child's emerging cognitive abilities to become sensitive to and aware of others' feelings and to see that their own behavior has consequences that affect other people. Children are encouraged to find other ways of getting their needs met without imposing on the rights of others. "What can we do to help you make sure you don't do that again?" might be asked of Claire. Induction is an important ingredient in the development of self-control, empathy, and forming a conscience.

There are many ways to guide children's behavior and the environment is one of the most powerful. Table 6.4 offers suggestions for fostering constructive and purposeful behavior through guidance procedures that work well with the preschool child.

Table 6.4

Environments That Foster Constructive and Purposeful Behavior

Include	To Encourage Children to
Physical Environment	
Low, open shelves	Help themselves and put things away when finished. Support children's initiative.
Variety of activity centers	Explore, manipulate, probe.
Materials that match the developmental level of the group	Seek out challenges and rehearse skills. Children won't be bored or reckless.
Materials in easy reach of children	Promote self-selection and independence.
Enough materials and equipment and activities	Play without creating problems of sharing. Give children alternatives/choices.
Rooms arranged without runways and dead ends	Walk from one area to the other and be able to access all activity centers.
Private space for each child's belongings	Have a sense of belonging and security for special objects.
Child-sized furniture that fits the preschool body	Sit while working.
Ample, uncrowded space	Explore variety of materials; exercise; avoids congestion.
Temporal Environment	
Large blocks of time for unhurried play	Move unhurriedly and at own pace, make choices and have a variety of experiences and participate in independent learning. Avoid being rushed, have no time pressure to cause tears.
Clean up built into the daily schedule	Take responsibility as a member of the group and work cooperatively with others.
Schedule provides a balance of quiet and active times	Pace themselves so they do not become overly tired, or overly stimulated.
Routines that encourage self-help activities	Take greater responsibility for their own care and foster a strong sense of independence (match their emerging independence).
Smooth transitions	Make choices, maintain self-control.
Interpersonal Environment	
Small group activities for three to four children	Interact with adults and other children; stress cooperation and social interaction.
Adequate number of trained teachers	Have ready access to teachers who set goals for each child and provide developmentally appropriate activities. Have opportunities for one-to-one interactions and get adequate attention from a teacher.

(continued)

Table 6.4   (Continued)

Include	*To Encourage Children to*
Teachers who deal with behavior problems fairly and consistently, are comfortable setting limits and guiding behavior.	Become aware of behavioral limits of the school setting. Establish mutual trust.
Set up for group play with three to five chairs and a table, two adjacent easels	To encourage social interaction and group participation. Use each other as resources.
Teachers who set goals for each child based on observation and assessment	Treated as an individual with unique strengths and characteristics. Mutual support and acceptance.
Activities to help children release tension, allow for body movement, exploration and manipulation of materials	Participate in activities that allow them to behave in the normal, active way their bodies demand.
Opportunities for children to help develop the rules and set guidelines	Become responsible for setting their limits, monitoring themselves as they see themselves part of a group.
Groups are balanced in size and make-up	Have a variety of playmates; become socially connected to other children.
Encourage problem-solving	Resolve conflicts themselves, self-discipline is goal.
Mixed age groups	Older children model behavior for younger ones; help teach one another skills.

The Teacher's Challenges

The challenge of this age group is immense: helping children who are becoming fiercely autonomous yet who want to be socially connected to other people. For teachers, three prominent issues related to this challenge are (1) aggression, (2) self-determination, and (3) friendships.

Aggression

Aggression is common among young children, although in the preschool years we see a distinct shift in the frequency and the form aggression takes. Between the ages of two and four, the peak years for physical aggression, the child's language skills improve and physical aggression declines. Verbal aggression then becomes the norm. In young preschool children, aggressive acts usually follow conflict with parents; in children four to eight, it most often occurs after conflict with peers (Bee, 1992). In many ways that sums up the preschool child's short journey from home to school, from the relative safety of few interactions to the broader social world of peers.

Instrumental aggression is common below the age of four, where children attempt to secure an object, privilege, or space and where there is no intent to harm another. *Hostile aggression,* on the other hand, is more typical of four- to eight-year-olds and is meant to hurt people and/or feelings. As children learn to negotiate their wants through language and acquire more sophisticated social conflict resolution skills, aggression of this type diminishes.

What causes aggression in children and why are some children more aggressive than others? Both nature and nurture seem to play a role. One of the most consistent findings over the years is that boys are more aggressive than girls, and that there is a biological basis for this gender difference (Maccoby & Jacklin, 1974, 1980). Other factors that influence aggression in children are related more to environmental influences.

It is a well-documented fact that TV violence is a significant contributor to children's aggressive behaviors (Liebert & Sprafkin, 1988). For approximately three to four hours a day (Singer, 1983), preschool children watch TV and learn specific aggressive acts. They see that violence is rewarded and that it is a successful way to solve problems. Murray (1980) found that children who watch violence on television are more aggressive with their peers than are children who watch less violent television. We also know the strength and power of adult models of behavior. The impressive data of the effect of television violence on preschoolers have serious implications for teachers and parents who are concerned about children's aggressive behaviors. Children need adults who set limits and control what they watch. Parents should be with preschoolers as they watch television to interpret what happens, help them sort fact from fantasy, and to see that they view programs that show more helpful and positive behaviors.

The family itself influences aggression in children in two specific ways: the family's own pattern of aggression, and how the family reinforces aggressive behavior. Research tells us some interesting stories about family patterns that foster aggressiveness in children. (Implications of this research are discussed in Chapters 1 and 3.)

- Children who are rejected by parents exhibit more aggressive behavior. The quality of attachment is critical (Bee, 1992).
- The most aggressive children come from families who permit aggressiveness yet also punish aggressive behaviors (Sears, Maccoby, & Levin, 1957).
- When a cycle exists where children are reinforced for their anger or aggression (that is, the parent gives into the child's behavior), aggression is actually increased (Patterson, 1980).
- Children who are punished harshly are likely to be unusually aggressive (Harris & Liebert, 1992).

Remember Frankie? His father's expectation that "boys will be boys" is another important way aggression is reinforced within families. The widely held stereotype about boys is supported through family interactions where boys are encouraged to be more physically active than girls, are given more freedom, and are rewarded for being demanding and assertive. Obviously, parental influence over aggressive behavior, particularly in boys, is an area where teachers can bring insight and knowledge and model a variety of techniques to deal with the aggression, high levels of energy, and exuberance of preschoolers.

Self-Determination

Self-determination is the second challenge teachers face with preschoolers. Over and over, as we discuss physical, social, and emotional development in the preschool child, we use the words "autonomy" and "independence" to describe what children are struggling to master at this age. There is no doubt that as children grow in self-confidence and awareness, conflicts arise within the classroom over the child's need for self-determination. Frankie said it best when he told the teacher: "You can't make me! You aren't my boss!"

As children move from dependency on adults toward being able to manage more independently, it can be helpful to look at the important social-emotional growth that occurs during this three-year period. Table 6.3 outlines some of the significant changes children experience during this time. Each task is necessary for the child to complete to achieve a level of self-determination appropriate to this age level. Each action is typical for the age and helps to form a core of behaviors critical to a child's sense of an independent self. Every behavior on the list has the potential to provide a challenge for teachers. As children embark on the road to self-determination, it is the adult's role to know and understand these behaviors as part of a developmental process. We can support emerging autonomy and independence by joining the child in the process of questioning, thinking, and solving the implications of these behaviors.

Try It Talk with a small group of children about their favorite television programs, then watch the program yourself. Be aware of aggressive action, talk, and behaviors in the shows children say they watch. How do the programs compare with your assessment of the child's behavior? Is there any correlation between the shows the children watch and the amount of aggression that they see on television?

Friendships

Friendships are very important in the preschool years. Preschoolers are determined to be independent, but want to develop friendships. They are beginning to internalize some control over their behavior. They enter the preschool years physically aggressive, and learn to replace their fists with words. Three-year-olds learn the meaning of "we" as they make friends for the first time and five-year-olds have a "best friend." A great deal of social skills have been learned in those two years. Understanding that progression helps us focus on our role in the child's developing social arena.

The young child's definition of friendship is fluid. It is common for preschoolers to make instant friends, and for the friendships to end just as abruptly. This is not surprising if we remember that cognitively, these are children of the here and now who cannot see beyond the immediate situation. First friends for the youngest preschooler are generally children who play together often, perhaps because their parents are friends or they are neighbors. Around age three, children observe other children's behavior and note that "Annie hits" or "Daniel likes to ride trikes with me." They pick

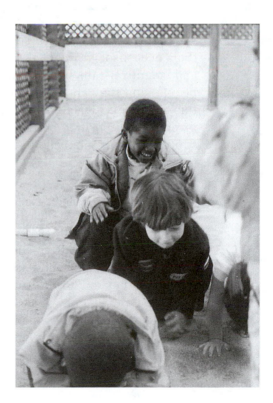

Opportunities for play promotes positive behavior in preschool children. The daily schedule should allow plenty of time for children to develop friendships and the social skills needed to thrive in a world of relationships.

playmates who are the same age and sex and who like to play in a similar fashion. They also like children who are friendly and who are good at cooperative play (Harris & Liebert, 1992).

From the preschool years through middle childhood, both boys and girls seem to prefer same sex playmates. Maccoby and Jacklin (1974) note that boys' play is more "rough and tumble" and they influence their playmates through demands or force. Girls, on the other hand, tend to make polite suggestions and are slightly more timid than boys. Understanding basic differences in the way girls and boys approach friendship is an important ingredient in influencing their social development. Chapter 4 has a more detailed discussion of these gender differences and their effect on discipline and development.

The sequence of development of social play shows us something of the progress children make during these preschool years as their play grows in complexity. Toddlers play alone (*solitary play*) or alongside but independently from another child (*parallel play*), whereas young preschoolers usually participate with other children in common activities, such as water play, art, or building with Legos, in what is called *associative play*. Conversations and interactions take place, but *cooperative play*, a more highly organized activity, doesn't begin until children join forces in planning and carrying out play activity together. Most play happens spontaneously as children select activities and play materials that meet their needs; social interactions follow. As we have seen, their language and cognitive skills have progressed along with their awareness of other people, and they are ready for the intense social interactions that mark this age period. Teachers must understand the importance of social play in promoting positive behavior, the sequence it follows, and its role in supporting peer interactions. Review the section on play in Chapter 3 for the many critical ways play supports good discipline practices and social friendships.

Teachers foster good social interaction in a number of ways. Table 6.4 contains many suggestions. Teachers also allow for plenty of free time to develop friendships and play partners; we encourage children to play with one another outside of school, if possible. Adults are resources for children, and we help them learn how to play together by modeling techniques for them on how to enter a group where play is ongoing or how to ask for help with a play idea. Sometimes we become part of the play ourselves to teach children social skills they need to develop. Throughout the early childhood years teachers recognize the unique role dramatic play has in social development, and we ensure its proper place within the schedule and curriculum.

Think It Over

Watch children's friendship patterns for a week. How do they make friends? What seems to sustain the friendships? What happens when it ends? Who were your best friends when you were a preschooler? Why did you choose certain children to play with? Do you see any similarities between you at this age and the children you observe now?

Partnerships with Families

The initial steps toward building a partnership with parents of children you teach is clearly stated in Chapter 5. Once the separation process is complete and adjustments to school are made, the challenging work of providing mutual support begins. Today, early childhood educators know the importance of providing parents with childrearing information and support to strengthen families to meet the challenges of raising children.

Building a Partnership

Ideally, parents and teachers become colleagues and co-workers in an effort to help the child develop freely and fully. This effort is enhanced when teachers:

- Help parents feel welcome at school and as part of the learning process.
- Give parents information on childrearing and provide emotional support.
- Show parents they are respected for the unique contribution they make to the child's learning.
- Make sure that their contact with parents is not limited to problem situations, but includes positive feedback as well.
- Take the time to understand the parents' cultural, social, ethnic, and religious background.
- Provide multilingual communications as needed.
- Listen to parents' concerns.
- Involve parents in meaningful ways in the classroom and in advisory and policy-setting committees.
- Are sensitive to individual family structures and needs.

Implications for Guidance

These techniques enhance mutual discipline practices as well. A level of trust is established as teachers and parents form an alliance that emphasizes a family-centered view of the child. Children know that these two important worlds they live in—school and home—relate to one another, endorse one another, and work with one another on their behalf.

Discipline problems are best dealt with in the context of the child's family. The parent's view of the child is matched with the teacher's observations and a more complete picture of the child emerges, which can help define appropriate behavior management techniques. We know that children are influenced by and have an influence on the family, and these dynamics must be considered when working with parents. To solve the problem of Frankie's nap time, his teachers need to find out if eliminating Frankie's nap may cause any hardships at home. Because Frankie's mother often works at night, she may have opinions on his daily sleep schedule that would impact the household routine. Frankie's teachers and mother should discuss his resistance to naps and together, agree on what approaches to take at school.

The ultimate result of good discipline techniques is to raise children who care for one another and who treat each other with kindness and concern.

Often, parents are uncomfortable and feel unsure of themselves when they deal with their children's teachers. They may sense social, economic, and cultural differences or have unpleasant memories of their own school experiences. Many parents of young children are just beginning to sort out the issues of discipline and authority and have not yet developed a cohesive plan for dealing with their children's misbehavior. They are afraid of being judged by their child's teacher.

Knowing this, teachers must work hard to forge a strong bond with the parents of the children in their classroom. Strategies outlined in Chapter 5 (Keeping in Touch, Communicating Your Expectations and Understandings, and Resolving Behavior Problems Together) are as important to do with parents of preschoolers as with parents of toddlers.

Today's teacher must be trained in parent relationships, in conflict resolution, and in a family support approach to meet children's needs. Parents of children with handicaps, single parents, immigrant parents, divorced parents, parents who do not speak English, gay/lesbian parents, teenage parents, and homeless parents face additional challenges as they raise their children. The teacher of the nineties must be prepared to offer them additional support as needed.

Think It Over

What do you think you could do to foster positive relations with a parent whose child is having difficulty? Are you comfortable with the idea of talking with parents about their child's problems? What makes that so?

Developmental Alerts

It is no secret that most parents see their offspring as a perfect child. They bring their precious offering to our schools and entrust us to do what is right for that child. One of the most difficult situations for a teacher is having to inform parents that there may be problems of a serious nature. At some time or another, all young children behave inappropriately and developmental norms cover a broad range of behaviors. There are times, however, when behavior persists over a period of time with no discernible change. Such a situation requires dialogue between teachers and parents. For several months the teaching staff noted that Eddie didn't respond to their directions and often seemed to ignore their greetings. They recorded this information and spoke to his parents, asking them to watch for similar responses. The teachers wanted to distinguish whether Eddie was deliberately ignoring them, or if there was a possibility of a hearing loss or difficulty with receptive language.

Informed early childhood educators keep abreast of each child's growth and development. It is part of their job to be alert for behaviors that indicate a child may need services and expertise beyond what the school can provide. This is what Eddie's teachers were attempting to find out. Most programs keep up to date about local social services where parents may seek advice in identifying problems and securing help for them. The teaching staff works with these human services/health care professionals, sharing observations and strategies.

When Eddie's teachers were first confronted with behavior that suggested the necessity for a developmental screening, they carefully looked at what developmental norms were appropriate for Eddie. With Eddie's parents, they sensitively explored what family situation might be causing the problematic behavior. Finding none, the teachers suggested Eddie be seen by a specialist.

What are some behaviors that are atypical? How did the teachers know whether Eddie's behavior was extreme? Preschoolers, as we have noted, are capable of great emotions: tantrums, aggression, crying, clinging, dependency, to name just a few. They complain of head and stomach aches, may have toilet accidents long after they have achieved bladder control, become withdrawn, develop strong food preferences, show anxiety, show irrational fears, and have separation problems. From a very early age, young children find many ways to respond to stressful situations with disruptive yet understandable behavior. Often, in young children, it is related to something that is happening at home. Most of these behaviors are common, often exaggerated, and provide a key opportunity for parents and teachers to work together. By joining forces, they bring to bear the care and concern of both school and home to make a difference in the child's life.

When symptoms persist and interfere with the child's ability to participate in normal, everyday activities (Allen, 1992), an outside consultation of behavioral experts is appropriate. So, too, if the child frequently destroys equipment and materials or in some way harms himself or others. A four-year-old's tantrum once a month is not a concern; a four-year-old's tantrums several times a day is. So is a six-year-old who bites, and a continuous thumb sucker who cannot participate in any activity requiring two hands (Allen, 1992). The main point is that the range of developmentally appropriate behaviors is so wide during these early years that caution is called for, lest children become labeled early on as "behavior problems."

Diagnosing learning disabilities in preschool children is difficult, perhaps impossible (Allen, 1992). Yet early childhood teachers are aware that many young children exhibit characteristics typical of children who are diagnosed as learning disabled later. These are also behaviors that can cause problems in a classroom setting: constant motion, difficulty in following directions, mood swings, low frustration tolerance, to name a few that can create discipline and guidance situations. Strategies for dealing with these behaviors are discussed in Chapter 3. Again, a reluctance to label young children, because of the wide range of behaviors considered developmentally appropriate, calls for teacher sensitivity to the individual needs of any child who exhibits such behaviors.

It is only through a close school-home relationship, based on trust and mutual respect, that these sensitive issues can be addressed. The wise teacher gives a high priority to developing a strong family-support system.

Think It Over

What do you think it would be like to be a parent of a child whose development is delayed or who is disabled? Is there a child that fits that description in your class? What, if any, issues are there regarding behavior? How are these resolved? Investigate what support services are available in your community to address the child and family's needs.

Summary

Preschoolers, from ages three through five, are learning new behaviors every day. They are blossoming with newfound social, intellectual, and physical power. Their behavior is a second language, communicating their unstated feelings, anxieties, and concerns.

Guidance-oriented teachers understand the reasons for children's behavior. By being attuned to the various developmental stages—the highly patterned way children grow—teachers and parents can more effectively help preschoolers learn appropriate ways to express their feelings.

Wise use of the environment alleviates many behavior problems. Children this age need challenging curriculum and materials that they can explore and manipulate, change and control. They need physical settings geared to their level of activity and interests and to their need to move about and use their bodies as they learn. Environments that support children's desire for independence and responsibility are filled with opportunities to make choices, to negotiate for their wants, and to solve problems.

The adult's role in guiding the preschooler through these years is helped by the remarkable intellectual and language development occurring at this time. Children this age use language well, understand what is being said to them, and can show empathy toward others. Teachers can take advantage of children's enjoyment of language to foster appropriate behavior in the classroom.

Although wildly emotional through these few years, preschoolers are gaining a sense of themselves, which allows them to include others in their thinking. They move from a self-centered point of view to one that can accept and tolerate others' opinions and feelings. Cooperation and sharing become more commonplace as they reach the upper ages of preschool.

Guidance and behavior issues center primarily on the child's need to assert independence during the preschool years. Testing limits and questioning boundaries is typical behavior, as is a growing ability to negotiate and learning to discuss problems. Inductive guidance measures support children's quest for independence while helping them develop an awareness of the effect their behavior has on others.

Teachers are called on to be firm yet flexible as they support children's growth during these years. Parents and teachers can share their skills and knowledge as they work together in the best interests of the child.

Observe and Apply

Do you hear children expressing fears like Rosie's? What are they? How did you respond to children when they express such fears? What do you now know about these fears that would cause you to respond differently? Read the book *There's a Nightmare in My Closet* to a group of children, then ask them if they ever had a nightmare in their closet. Talk with them about other fears they have, making a list of what frightens them and how they behave when they are frightened. Next to that, begin a list of ideas of what they might do to feel less afraid.

Review Questions

1. How is a preschooler's logic and thinking different from an adult's? How does this affect your choice of guidance techniques?

2. Why is it difficult for young children to share? Do you believe that children this age should learn to share? Why?

3. What is the role of private speech in learning self-control?

4. Write an example of a child's age-appropriate but faulty reasoning that would have led to conflict if you had not known about *transductive reasoning*.

5. Describe three techniques that help children begin to manage the strong emotions and feelings they have.

6. What documentation is there to support the claim that watching television affects a child's aggressive behaviors?

7. Describe how family patterns of aggression can influence children's behavior.

8. What are five ways teachers encourage a good working partnership with parents?

Bibliography

Allen, K. Eileen. *The Exceptional Child: Mainstreaming in Early Childhood Education.* Albany, NY: Delmar, 1992.

Allen, K. Eileen, & Marotz, Lynn. *Developmental Profiles.* Albany, NY: Delmar, 1994.

Ames, Louise Bates. *Raising Good Kids.* Rosemont, NJ: Modern Learning Press, 1992.

Bee, Helen. *The Developing Child.* New York: Harper Collins, 1992.

Becker, J. A. " 'I Can't Talk, I'm Dead.': Preschoolers' Spontaneous Metapragmatic Comments." *Discourse Process,* 11, (1988): 457–467.

Berk, L. E. "Private Speech: Learning Out Loud." *Psychology Today,* May, 1986, pp. 34–42.

Berk, Laura E. *Infants and Children.* Boston: Allyn & Bacon, 1994.

Elkind, David. *A Sympathetic Understanding of the Child.* Boston: Allyn & Bacon, 1994.

Harris, Judith Rich, & Liebert, Robert. *Infant and Child.* Englewood Cliffs, NJ: Prentice Hall, 1992.

Liebert, R. M., & Sprafkin, J. *The Early Window: Effects of Television on Children and Youth.* New York: Pergamon Press, 1988.

Maccoby, E. E., & Jacklin, C. N. *The Psychology of Sex Differences.* Stanford, CA: Stanford University Press, 1974.

Maccoby, E. E., & Jacklin, C. N. "Sex Differences in Aggression: A Rejoinder and Reprise." *Child Development,* 51, (1980): 964–980.

Murray, J. P. *Television and Youth: Twenty-five Years of Research and Controversy.* Stanford CA: The Boy's Town Center for the Study of Youth Development, 1980.

Patterson, G. R. *Mothers: The Unacknowledged Victims.* Monograph of the Society for Research in Child Development, 45, 1980.

Schickedanz, Judith A., Schickedanz, David I., Hansen, Karen, & Forsyth, Peggy D. *Understanding Children.* Mountain View, CA: Mayfield Publishing, 1993.

Sears, R. R., Maccoby, E. E., & Levin, H. *Patterns of Child Rearing.* Stanford, CA: Stanford University Press, 1977.

Singer, D. G. "A Time to Reexamine the Role of Television in Our Lives." *American Psychologist,* 38 (1983): 815–816.

7

The School-Age Child:
Five to Eight Years

Profiles

Kindergarten . . . What a wonderful world the name evokes! Two best friends, Daniella and Campbell, are looking forward to finally being in "real" school, but are a little nervous, too. Daniella thinks you learn to read the first day and get a desk of your own. Campbell is worried, thinking about how the moms can't stay. They both went to the visiting day last spring, and like the super-tall climber and really big swings. Daniella wonders, "Do you get to play outside whenever you want? Why is there only one teacher?" but Campbell thinks, "What happens if I get scared? What if I don't know something?" Daniella says that every day in kindergarten is fun, because that is what her brother and sister told her. Campbell doubts if that can really be true.

Learning to read and staying all day at school are big deals. But, then, Hiroshi is a big deal, too! He has lots of great ideas, and now he can play on a soccer team, too. Not only that, but the first graders use the big yard with the rest of the school, not the baby yard for the kindergartners. Plus, there is a computer in his room and kids get to use it after they finish their reading or math work. The only problem is, other kids want to use it, too, and some of them get there ahead of him. No fair; he wants to use it more than they do. He wishes the teacher would let him do the computer instead of spelling; the words are so easy he's bored with all the exercises.

"What I love about the Rainbow Center," muses Tasauna on the way to her after-school center, "is the way we have clubs. That way I can be an actress, because we get to put on plays." Tasauna wishes that she could go to the Rainbow Center all day. You can still paint pictures, there are art projects on the tables, and they have popcorn and movies every Friday. Her regular class is too much work, and the teacher gives them homework every week. That's the only part of Rainbow she feels funny about. They have Homework Time, she usually says she doesn't have any, even though it's in her backpack, all crumpled up. She hates doing it, and feels embarrassed that it is so messy. Besides, she doesn't always know how to do it, and doesn't want to ask for help.

Think It Over

Imagine that you are these children's teacher. What would you say or do to address the expectations and anxieties of Daniella and Campbell? Should Hiroshi be allowed to use the computer more often? Why is Tasauna having trouble with her homework, and what can you do?

Who Is the School-Age Child?

Generally speaking, the elementary school years are known as middle childhood, ages five to twelve or until the onset of puberty. This period includes the end of the early childhood years. By eight years of age, children have the foundation skills: they can move their bodies and fingers to run and climb, draw and print; they can talk and think fluently in their primary language; and they have a basic sense of themselves, their feelings, and their relationships. After these primary years, they are ready to acquire the secondary skills of the middle years, such as sports, cursive handwriting, multiplication, and making friends without adult help. Therefore, in early childhood education terms, we see the first part of these middle childhood years as the final third of early childhood. Children who are in kindergarten and first and second grades are those who are five to eight years of age . . . the school-age child in early childhood.

Although the middle childhood years are important, they are relatively calm. Physical growth tapers off and acquisitions in language and cognition are less dramatic. Still, there are increases in intellectual competence. Most important, the primary years of the school-age child are marked most by the change in relationships to others. For the five- to eight-year old, these years signal the shift in social and emotional areas from dependence on adults to connection with peers. It is in these areas that the teacher and caregiver are of most help—and are most challenged—in guidance and discipline.

In guiding the primary child, teachers help children "brainstorm" several ways to solve problems, as these kindergarteners are doing in pictures.

Growth and Motor Skills

Typically, growth and motor skills in the primary years increase significantly during middle childhood, although more slowly than in the earlier years. Strength increases more dramatically than size, and agility and coordination are refined. Gender differences in height and weight are slight at age six, although by age twelve the differences are greater. In athletic ability, however, the overall negligible differences at age five are replaced by a significant difference between boys and girls by age eight. Boys are able to throw and catch better than girls, and girls are probably better in fine eye-hand coordination, balance, and flexibility (Thomas & French, 1985; Williams, 1983). Both nature (boys are predominantly more muscular than girls) and nurture (girls spend less time outdoors than boys and are generally unwilling to compete with boys in mixed-sex situations) are clearly all at work (Harper & Sanders, 1978).

In guiding the school-age child, keep in mind that children are clearly ready for more physical challenges, and can cope with the notion of teams and sports with rules. However, establishing games that are too competitive can overwhelm many children. Games with only one winner may produce many who consider themselves "losers" and who become unwilling to participate. Mixed-sex games are especially tricky; research indicates that in a variety of cultural situations and even with highly skilled girls, girls tend to be unwilling to compete (Weisfeld, Weisfeld, & Callaghan, 1982). Finally, children entering middle childhood can be more independent, dependable, and generally have higher standards of behavior because of their increased physical and brain capacities.

Intellectual and Language Understandings

It is no accident that children around the world are given more responsibility in the primary age group. In the Piagetian view (see Chapter 2), the preoperational period of cognition gives way to the period of concrete operations around age six or seven. The transition is gradual; children improve from age five to nine in their ability to take another's point of view and to judge how much information people have and might need. For instance, ask a five-year old to tell you how it felt to a classmate to be left out, and you may get a blank look. Ask a nine-year old, however, and you see the understanding of hurt feelings in both face, word, and deed.

In guiding the school-age child, this means that a child can be counted on to consider two things at once, but not necessarily to play out alternative possibilities with any detail. In daily teaching, teachers can get the children involved in a dispute to "brainstorm" several ways to solve the problem, but may need to help them talk through the alternatives to find a mutually acceptable one. Additionally, a chart of "rules" that the children help generate can be referred to by a child or teacher and serve as an effective reminder, because children can now actually keep in mind a set of rules, and use graphic language as a prompt.

The concept of real and imaginary gradually changes, too. Five-year-olds are convinced that a dream is actually in the room for anyone to see; by seven, they realize that others cannot see the dream, although it may still be in the room; by nine or ten they finally localize their dreams as "in your head" (Piaget, 1929). *In guiding the primary child,* the teacher takes into account that fears can still overwhelm a child; the "stubborn" one who won't walk along the creekbed during a field trip may be ruled by the dream of drowning. Acknowledging the perceived "reality" of the fears, the teacher can help the child move through them, rather than scoffing or discounting them.

During middle childhood children gradually improve in their ability to estimate duration of time. They also become better at locating themselves within time periods; for instance, they can tell where in the week or year they are. It is not until second grade, however, that most children can correctly name the days of the week or months of the year (Friedman, 1986), so teachers cannot expect children either to fully understand or keep track of what they are supposed to do within a certain time period. Furthermore, there is great variety in familial and cultural use of time. *In guiding the primary child,* keep in mind that the concept of time is still fluid and under the influence of both family and culture. Teachers must remain concrete in their directions to children about what to do and when to do it: say "in a few minutes" only when referring to between two and five, not between one and twenty; give a warning to help those who do not respond well to abrupt transitions; and actually teach organizational skills so children can learn to accomplish a task sequentially.

In language development, children now have a firm, adult-like grasp of their primary language. Children raised in a bilingual atmosphere now begin to catch up with their single-language classmates, attaining a complete knowledge of the dominant language while retaining their first one. Because the school-age child is now working on developing graphic language, the teacher can use this well. *In guiding the primary child,* reading and writing can be used to make "contracts" or agreements between adult and child about behavior or intentions. Finally, few areas of school-age development are as apparent as in the use of language for humor. Of course, toilet humor and jokes about sex are eternally popular with these children, but also jokes may be less about pure silliness than double meanings or even puns. Popular children in elementary school are often those with a good sense of humor (Masten, 1986).

Affective Development

Unfortunately, it is the affective side of early elementary children that is sometimes ignored or left to fend for itself. Social acceptance and self-concept are of major importance to the school-age child, and are the two affective areas that have direct impact on guidance.

The social development of the child at this age shifts from dependence on adults to a "sociocentric," or peer-related emphasis. Moreover, as Elkind (1995) tells us, "the child who is active and social, and is an initiator of activities in nursery school or daycare, is likely to continue his leadership ways in elementary school. . . . Likewise, the child who is on the sideline of activities in the early childhood program tends to perpetuate this role after he attends elementary school. Remarkable individual changes can and do, of course, occur. Some children 'find' themselves in school and blossom out socially in a manner that would have been hard to predict from their preschool shyness. Contrariwise, because of unseen circumstances, such as a death or a divorce in the family, a child's interaction patterns may change for the worse." For instance, look at Campbell, one of our kindergartners in the opening profile. His initial fears nearly overwhelmed him during the first few weeks of school. As time went on, however, he found that he knew most of what was asked of him, and he began to bloom in the exciting social stimulation of his class and his new special friend, a third-grade "buddy" who visits him every week. Although he remains a "watcher" in new situations, he is becoming more of a participant as he gains social experience and familiarity.

The "culture of childhood" that the child enters in the elementary years is one marked by more independence from adults and higher expectations from them. This puts the child in conflict, between the desire to grow up and a wish to remain a child forever. On the one hand, the five- to eight-year old wants to grow up and enjoy the freedoms of adult life, such as getting to and from a friend's house alone, staying up late, and understanding more of the adult world. On the other hand, such knowledge and responsibility is scary, and many children want to keep their childish options of whining and quarrelling. *In guiding the primary child,* teachers are likely to see both, sometimes almost simultaneously. Being prepared to deal with these two competing desires includes being able to listen carefully to children's feelings without overindulging them with too much sympathy or "bailing out" techniques, such as giving a child all the answers or eliminating all the hard tasks so that they never feel discouraged (or challenged). At the same time, teachers aren't surprised or punitive about whining, but simply make it clear that the child needs to use a "regular voice" and "tell me your good ideas, because I know they are in you." Chapter 3 offers more techniques for dealing with quarrelling and whining behavior.

Children also experience less adult supervision in developing friendships, bringing a newfound freedom from controls and some anxiety about social acceptance. Intellectually, children from kindergarten to third grade are beginning to take the other child's point of view, thus gaining in empathy and caring. In the world of friendships, however, this ability does not always hold. Children in this period still think of friendship as a matter of playing together, of agreeing to do the same things, or sharing toys. With time and maturity, children come to see friendship as shared activities and values. For now, however, the rule more often is "We are friends because she shares her toys" or "He's my friend because he does what I want." *In guiding the primary child,* refer to Table 7.1 on page 242, which outlines the stages of friendship, common problems, and guidance suggestions.

A second major task of the primary years is self-discovery. Children find themselves in an increasingly wide array of activities. Academic, recreational, and playground experiences all give the child information about "Who am I." Children's home experiences also come into play: Daniella's perception of herself as the youngest of three is different from Campbell's perceptions as a single child. The structure of the family can affect a child's self-concept, too. Children in a stressed household may see themselves as taking on more responsibility. Children with older parents, such as Hiroshi's, may offer different experiences and expectations than those who are younger. Ethnic background and socioeconomic class are also determinants of a child's view of self.

Research (Elkind, 1995) suggests that it is the minority group—whichever that group might be—that experiences lower self-esteem than does the majority group. This is true whether it is black children who are a minority in a white school, or Jewish children in a predominantly Christian school, or Catholics in a largely Protestant school. It is *minority status,* rather than race or ethnicity as such, that has a lowering effect upon self-esteem.

In guiding school-aged children, it is useful to know their position in the family and the age separation between the siblings. It is helpful to have a sense of how the family is structured and how it operates. And besides the direct effects of racial, ethnic, or economic status upon the child's self concept, there are indirect effects as well. The values and expectations of parents vary greatly. The teacher who takes such influences into consideration

Table 7.1

Stages of Friendship in the School-Age Period

Age	Stage	Characteristics and Common Problems	Guidance Implications
Preschool to kindergarten	Playmateship	Similarity of interests Proximity (playing in same place, with same toys) Momentary (at same time) Friendliness and "me, too" as valued qualities Problems: sharing materials, space, playmates; waiting, getting started, letting another play	Offer variety, point out similarities Mix the groupings frequently to give close encounters Offer friend ideas Teach cooperation and inviting skills
Early school-age	One-way assistance	"Tit-for-tat" (doing what is asked) Is known better (others' likes and dislikes) Friends can have different viewpoints Problems: taking another person/viewpoint into consideration; opening up friendship groups; allowing friends to differ, diverge	Teach listening skills Give shared experiences such as workgroups, field trips, teams Teach conflict resolution skills
Later school-age	Fair-weather cooperation	Awareness of reciprocal nature of friendship Willingness to adjust to another Problems: Difficulty keeping friend if arguing, loyalty often questioned	Point out appreciation of differences Notice deeper qualities rather than judgment Teach responsiveness Teach perspective-taking skills

Adapted from material by Selman (1981), Galinsky (1988), and Ramsey (1991).

better understands the children's self-perceptions, which affect their behavior greatly. Chapter 4 discusses such issues in greater detail.

Finally, moral concepts in children are developing now. As the child moves through the primary years, the concepts of right and wrong become solidified. The child has many more opportunities to exercise judgment:

what happens when the bell rings and I want to play ball longer? What do I do when a bunch of big kids ask me for my bus money? The works of Piaget, Kohlberg, and Gilligan (see Chapter 2) all indicate that, for the young child, the morality of *unilateral authority* is still in place. That is, authority is derived from adults; they set the rules and enforce them. The amount of "badness" of a deed is associated with the amount of damage done. In this time period, however, children are beginning to take the person's intentions into account. This marks a shift into a second form of morality, that of mutuality. Rather than just looking at "badness" as the amount of damage, the child's intention of doing good or bad makes a difference. And children throughout this age grade personal injury as more punishable than property damage.

For instance, Tasauna's dilemma about the crumpled homework page is an interesting case in point: she wrestles less with the morality of the ruined sheet of paper than with hurting or angering her parents or lying to the after-school caregiver. *In guiding the primary child,* teachers must have a few clear guidelines and maintain the atmosphere of authority. That is, the children need to know that you are in charge (which is not the same as being a dictator), and that, even as you participate with the children in their work and play, you still are "the grown-up" who maintains the appropriate limits and deals with out-of-bounds or unjust behavior.

Typical Behavior Patterns

There are many ways in which the development and behavior of the school-age child guides the teacher in matters of discipline. Table 7.2 on page 244 outlines several implications; the issues of peers, authority, and the self are three others that are unique in the primary years.

Peer Issues

In the social realm, the primary child is quite self-sufficient. One of the most notable traits of this age is activity, so children engage in a lot of boisterous play as well as verbal jokes and attacks. Still, it is far easier to dish it out than to take it, so many of the conflicts children have with each other is about getting hurt, including feelings.

The kindergartener, moreover, may be still unable to know when or how to stop; roughhousing and some clumsiness as well as trying activities beyond their abilities can bring tears of frustration and hurt. Children often pair up with a "best" friend, leaving others out. On the playground, children may exclude others from a team game if they are clumsy or overly bossy. Pairs change more frequently with the five- and six-year old than with older children, and the dominant trend is in same-sex friends.

Table 7.2

How School-Age Children Develop Guides Teachers toward Effective Discipline Techniques

Development Related to Guidance	What Teachers Can Do About It
Five-Year-Olds	
Has to be right; persistent Sensitive to ridicule	Avoid methods that point out the child as wrong, humiliated
May get silly, wild Enjoys jokes and riddles Sometimes roughhouses, fights	Set clear limits, stop them before it gets out of control, expect high behavior, use humor to defuse
Aware of rules, may define for others Insists on fair play Accepts, respects authority	Involve children in setting rules, point out issues of equity, fairness around exclusion, hurt feelings
Uses words to give/receive information Takes turn in conversation	Reinforce turn-taking, introduce social problem-solving with everyone's ideas solicited
Insists "I already know that" Likes to display new knowledge	Ask children to tell you what they feel, know, think should happen when problems arise
Wants to know "how?" "why?"	Allow time in schedule for questions
Six-Year-Olds	
Know-it-all Free with opinions and advice Rigid gender-role stereotypes	Avoid "one-up-man-ship" on who knows more; ask for their ideas Set mixed-gender groupings often, watch for male dominance
Measures/tests self against peers Proud of accomplishments	Point out efforts as valuable, not just results; avoid comparisons, help establish goals for self
Likes to roughhouse, may get hurt	Provide legitimate channels for high energy, keep supervised
May cheat, change rules Believes in rules except for self	Stay consistent in the limits, explain your differences in consequences
Learning to read	Make contracts, charts available
Seven-Year-Olds	
Talks *with* rather than *at* adults	Discuss alternatives rather than tell what to do
Boisterous, enjoys stunts	Provide social times using motor skills
Can consider others' viewpoint	Offer "Talk it Out" social problem-solving opportunities
Learning to print, write	Have them record rule-making sessions, small groups' brainstorming of problems, solutions, consequences
Can conceptualize, sequence Winning/losing are difficult	Read/work regularly with children's literature for social and moral dilemmas

Adapted from material from Gordon & Browne (1992)

The end of the primary years is marked by an increased inwardness, with a heightened sensitivity to others' reactions and an increased sense of self. The boasting and tattling of kindergarten and first grade give way to withdrawal so as not to expose oneself to criticism and complaints about being treated unfairly. Children who run scared of a bully at age five may simply try to leave the scene rather than make a fuss or risk others' disapproval. These children may worry about what other children, teachers, even parents say and do about them. They often fret about perceived slights or snubs and wonder if people like them. In guiding primary children, teachers must be especially careful of embarrassing children when dealing with unacceptable behavior. Although the primary classroom is a public place, a more private handling of the problem preserves a child's persona and therefore makes a change in behavior more likely.

Authority

As we adults shift our view of the child from one of dependence and innocence to one of competence, we need to look carefully at how we teach children rules and limits. Sometimes this shift causes adults to abdicate their

"It's not fair!" is a common complaint of the school-age child.

responsibility in setting limits; unfortunately, the result is unruly or undis-ciplined behavior. Children of this age try to resist authority as they push for increased autonomy. And they deal with the authority (or lack of it) of teachers in much the same way they deal with that of their parents.

Additionally, five- and six-year olds are often dawdlers, finding end-less ways to "stall" and get off-task. Still needing to be at the center of things, they have less patience with other's demands to wait than with their wish for others to wait for them. By age seven, adults often find more will-ingness to help, and to take on responsibilities: children even become more polite. Still, complaining does persist, and the comment "it's not fair" is common at this age. A lack of clear limits can exacerbate this, as children

Alternative Approaches

Inclusion and Exclusion in Friendships

Do children have the "right" to choose their own friends? If so, do they also have permission to leave others out? These two teachers have different viewpoints; which do you think is best?

Include Everyone

When children come together, we have to try and form a kind of mini-world for them, one in which there is some fairness and justice. It may not always be the "real world," but then we don't allow guns or gangs into the school to be more realistic. I agree with Vivian Paley (1992) that children then have to work with the others who enter their world. If the boys invade the dramatic play house where the girls are, they don't just get to say, "Get out. You can't play here"; they have to reckon with the energy and ideas the new children bring.

Besides, children are often excluding others because they like the feelings of power and bullying that it brings. I don't think that's something I particularly want to encourage. I think I give my children other ways to feel powerful, and one way is to really make them have to deal with others of power who come along. There is surely enough unkindness in childhood without inviting it into my class.

respond to a vacuum of authority. For more details, see Chapter 3 for how to handle authority as a teacher.

Public versus Private Self

A hallmark of the primary years is the development of a private self. Since preschool, children have been creating an internal world of fantasy. The process of private speech that begins at the end of the very young period seems to be part of the internalized process of language and thought. Nevertheless, it is in the school-age child that the more complex aspect of a "private self" emerges.

This is manifested in two ways. The first comes from the child's internal clock in terms of cognitive and self-concept development. As a very young child, the child thinks, "I AM the universe." The preschooler ex-

Let Them Decide

School is a place where children are forced to come together, and I don't think it is appropriate to force children's friendships on each other as well. I think of the center as a kind of "human relationships laboratory" (Read, 1971) and children need to have experiences of all kinds to grow competent. We cannot shelter children from disappointment and hurt feelings, and we shouldn't. What we can do is help them deal with the reality of being left out, and figuring out what to do with the feelings and with yourself. Also, we need to give children some right to choose their friends, and to learn to deal with how to handle others' strong reactions to being left out.

Children exclude for a number of reasons. Sometimes, children say "No, you can't play with us" simply to make others feel bad—what power there is in words! The one left out, then, needs to learn to be assertive, to say, "I don't like you calling me names," or "I can TOO play here" or "Then I'll find somebody ELSE." But sometimes children are trying to be protective of a new, budding friendship, or they don't feel strong enough themselves to keep the friend they already have if another, more attractive person enters into the play. Also, with children who are in groups all day long, I think we need to allow children private spaces and some intimate, private time with just one friend, safe from interruption. It seems to me that this richness, and complexity, is all wiped out with a blanket rule preventing children's choices.

pands on this notion to declare "I am the CENTER of the universe." The school-age child comes to see that "I am PART of the universe." It is a sobering but still more expansive view of the self. In guidance terms, the teacher can now explain the effects of a child's behavior on others and expect to be understood. At the same time, teachers must be careful to avoid humiliating a child in front of peers.

The second way the child changes is as a result of personal experiences of schooling and adult expectations. As society expects more self-direction from the child, the child takes on more and becomes aware of a broader range of expectations and roles. The child becomes more capable of taking on responsibility, and more pensive and internal about what is happening. Teachers and parents sometimes lament that this period "starts like a lion and ends like a lamb": that is, that the five- or six-year old who exclaims, "Look at me! I'm pretty good, huh?" and can be "read like a book," becomes the seven- or eight-year old who is inscrutable and private. In guidance terms, the child who appears aloof or unconcerned when corrected may very well be seething or cringing inside. Adults may need to work harder and be more creative in the ways they stay in touch with this private self.

Think It Over

Do you remember your "first friendship"? Do you recall how it felt when you were starting a new school year? The feelings of "firsts" as a school-age child, with some consciousness about your self and your own awkwardness, can be flooding emotionally for a child, and can mask good behavior—or bring out the negative. To remind yourself, try reading the *Ramona* series (Cleary) or *First Day Blues* (Anderson).

Guiding the School-Age Child

The old adage that "an ounce of prevention makes a pound of cure" is as true for primary children as it is for the younger set. Whether you teach kindergarten, a primary grade, or an after-school group, setting up an age-appropriate environment is essential for preventing the unnecessary problems of boredom or overcontrol. Programs with enough interesting and

Peacemaking activities that teach cooperative learning will help primary children learn tolerance.

challenging materials and activities, and with an environment and schedule that respond to the development and individual needs and interests of the five- to eight-year old child, can eliminate many of the difficult behaviors and repetitive problems that beset teachers.

Developmentally Appropriate Discipline Techniques

What Still Works

Remember that many, though not all, of the strategies suggested for the other two age groups are appropriate for school-age children. School-agers behave for the same reasons as do younger children: they want to belong, their behavior is purposeful, and they are growing in their understanding and skills based on both maturation and experience. The skilled teacher provides an appropriate environment and observes behavior closely. By watching and listening, the teacher can find out

- The intent (what the child wants to accomplish),
- The content (what the child does), and
- The context (what the situation was before and after).

Using Dreikurs' recommendations (see Table 2.2), a teacher can evaluate the situation and develop a guidance strategy.

For example, Hiroshi has just screamed "NO FAIR!" for the third time today; his teacher then reflects that each time it has been around the computer, so Hiroshi's intent each time has been to protest, and hopefully change, the situation in which he has no access to the computer. He screams and usually pushes the other child aside. This happens when he has had a turn and doesn't want to end it. His misbehavior, the teacher concludes, is for power; to check, she asks Hiroshi, "Could it be you want to be

Try It   Next time a child misbehaves—for instance, disrupts during group time, swears, or yells at another during class, or hits another child—try to use the technique of *Active and Reflective Listening*.

1. Stop the aggressive behavior (with words if possible or actions as necessary) and allow everyone to cool off. ("It's not OK to swear; practice cooling off by taking nine deep breaths and walking along the back of the room.")

2. Find a time to talk together in private. If this cannot happen right away, make a specific plan with the child ("Right now, you need to sit at the far table; when the group starts math time, we will talk it out.")

3. Set the ground rules and your availability. ("I want to know what happened and how you felt about it. I won't interrupt and get you in trouble; you can trust that I will hear you.")

4. Establish eye contact. Get at the child's level, stop other tasks, and give the child your attention. Look directly at the child who is talking; nod your head and keep your comments to "Uh-huh; I see; Oh, and then . . ." as prompts.

5. Now, hear and define the feeling you think the child felt, and pair it with what else they told you ("So you feel *angry* because he *teased* you.") This formula, "You feel _____ because _____" can be done with less structured statements, but reflective listening requires you to do just that: listen, then reflect the feelings and reasons.

6. Stay active; after the child feels heard and understood by you, the last step is to move forward with a plan of some sort. ("Now I understand. What can we do to solve this?" or "OK, I see why you don't like group time; how do you want to fix this?" or "I can tell how you don't like teasing; but because I can't let you hit, what else could you do next time?")

the boss of the computer?" The answer is a resounding "YES!" so now they can proceed: ask Hiroshi to "use his powerful brain" to think up six ideas of how he can get turns at the computer and the other kids can, too.

In addition to this process, several strategies from Chapter 3 are especially useful with primary children. Teachers use the indirect methods of *labeling problems* and *guiding with suggestions* to help children get focused on the matter at hand without embarrassing them by getting them into trouble or looking poor in the eyes of their peers. More directly, teachers must *be clear on what behaviors they expect* and *give encouragement for such positive behavior.* When children tattle or complain, the teacher can *use active listening* to help a child feel heard and understood without solving the problem for them.

Now, more than at earlier ages, teachers can use the two techniques of "natural and logical consequences" and "social problem-solving" with the older child. Increased social experience enables most primary children to engage in sustained interactions with others. At the same time, the school system demands that children wait, do what is asked of them, and not always get what they want. Not only that, they need to do what is asked on their own, with less direct intervention or assistance from an adult. This is true of classrooms, schoolyards, and after-school centers.

The first technique deals with "misbehavior," or those behaviors that the adult wants to decrease or eliminate. Helping children live with the **natural or logical consequences** of their actions allows them to experience the world firsthand, which goes along with their increasing abilities to do so. A natural consequence of "fooling around" during lunch time is not eating; the child who is hungry today is more likely to eat tomorrow than one who is nagged and cajoled by a teacher to eat, or even sent to the bench to eat alone at playtime. The logical consequence of leaving the homework notebook at home is not having it in class. The parent who always brings it because the child forgot is preventing the child from experiencing the direct discomfort of such forgetting. Of course, the teacher may not need to implement any further consequence than the child feeling left out or being the only one without the spelling sheet.

The second technique is of crucial importance to a child's sense of competence, critical thinking, and self esteem. Their more mature intellectual and language skills allow them to talk out problems easier than their preschool counterparts. Therefore, a *social problem-solving* or "talk it out" approach gives children the responsibility to use these skills in emotionally troubling or socially difficult situations (see Chapter 3 for the full explanation of this technique).

For instance, our kindergartner Daniella ran outside to the ball box and grabbed a ball at the same time as another child. The two shouted, "I've got it!" and a pushing match ensued. The teacher followed the same steps as the chart, and here's what happened:

1. *Stop. Cool Off.* Teacher: Hold it, kids! I'll hold the ball while you decide what to do.

2. *Talk and Listen.* Teacher: Daniella, you start . . . I see. Now, Roger, it's your turn. . . . So, there are two kids and one red ball. What can we do to solve this problem?

3. *Brainstorm.* Teacher: Daniella thinks she should have the first turn, and Roger thinks he should have it first. What else can two smart kids think of? Roger says no one should get it. Daniella, you say play a choosing game?

4. *Pick the One You All Like Best.* Teacher: So which one do you like best? The choosing game?

5. *Make a Plan; Go for It.* Teacher: All right, I'll do "One Potato, Two Potato" and the one who is out first will get the first turn, and the second one out will get it second. Great! You figured it out! Let's see those potatoes!

Starting Off on the Right Foot
. . . and Staying There

Planning for a good beginning takes thought and consideration. But the efforts pay considerable dividends for both adult and child. In addition to setting up the proper physical environment and using several key techniques with school-aged children, teachers make appropriate rules and procedures for their classrooms or centers. Teachers who set clear rules and limits may not avoid all resistance, but in the long run, deal with it more effectively. Teachers who understand the child's natural inclination to resist authority as a self-assertion are less likely to overreact by either not enforcing the rules or applying a heavy-handed punishment that engenders hostility or fear.

There is no simple answer to the question of what rules to set, because the programs for school-aged children, as well as personalities and styles, differ greatly. Moreover, there are a multitude of ways to teach rules and routines. Table 7.3 outlines some of these ideas.

Table 7.3

Creative Ways to Teach Rules and Routines

School-age children can be taught effective self-discipline by using common teaching techniques to focus on classroom management skills.

1. *Rule Unscramble:* Have the rules stated in phrases. Mix up the words in the phrase, and have the children put them in the correct order so that they make sense.

2. *Hug or Handshake:* When the teacher or other children "catch" someone at following the rules, ask them if they want a hug or a handshake and reward them with their wish.

3. *"Oops, I Goofed!"* Conduct a class discussion on how children feel when they break a rule. Ask them to share a personal experience when they goofed in their behavior, then say what they might do next time. Focus on the idea that we all make mistakes and it is OK if you learn from a mistake and don't repeat it.

4. *Rule Bingo:* Make Bingo cards with the rules listed in each square. Have the student or the teacher act out the rule. Children cover the square if they have the rule listed that is being acted out.

5. *Picture Signals.* Have pictures as signals for each classroom rule. For example, ears for the rule "we listen politely" or chair for "sit in your chair." Then use the pictures to signal students if they are not following the rule, allowing silent management rather than telling children when they are doing wrong. *(Authors' note: see Chapter 3 Table 3.5 for "Talk It Out" as an example.)*

6. *Hidden Rules.* Fold paper. On the inside, write the class rule. On the outside, give clues to the rule. Children read the clues and guess the rule inside, opening the folded paper to see if they were correct.

7. *Wheel of Fortune.* Play the game where rules are the puzzles to be solved. Students guess the letters of the puzzle and try to guess the rule in the puzzle.

Adapted from Jones & Jones, 1990

In general, this *authoritative teaching* is more effective than either permissive or authoritarian teaching. Three principles of authoritative teaching (Elkind, 1993) provide guidelines for establishing rules and staying on the right foot with the primary child.

1. *Start tough and ease up later.* Begin a school year or program with clear rules and limits about nearly everything regarding children's behavior. After they learn the rules, more freedom or flexibility is easy for them to incorporate. For example, start the year with a firm "No shouting" rule even during grouptime or free play; over the course of the year you may allow children's enthusiasm to expand the volume.

2. *Allow the children a voice in decision making.* Just as with the "talk it out" method of problem-solving, giving children a voice gives them an investment in making a decision succeed. The teacher may have the final say, but the children have a chance to be heard and to make their ideas part of the process. Be sure to incorporate these ideas; children learn quickly if it is an empty exercise. For instance, when Daniella and Roger both want the ball, a teacher helps by allowing *all* ideas, not just the reasonable ones. If the teacher dismissed Roger's idea of "No one gets it" in any way, Roger wouldn't want to resolve other conflicts by participating.

3. *Try to take the children's viewpoint when they complain.* When they claim rules are too oppressive, or our expectations are too demanding, it helps to see how it might look or feel to them. The Try It box in the section on Teacher's Challenges is an example of this technique.

Rewards and penalties are effective with primary children. Behaviorists describe how to encourage positive behavior (See Chapters 2 and 3). Teachers help children move toward prosocial and productive behavior by being encouraging, through praise or other rewards. The key to rewards is to know the children and find out what is rewarding to each one. Daniella likes a lap, Campbell an approving look, and Hiroshi an extra turn on the computer. Tasauna is thrilled if she can decide which play to perform this week at the after-school center, but would be overwhelmed if given that same attention in the second grade classroom.

As for penalties, we are reminded by the social discipline theorists (see Chapter 2) that the primary child's self-concept can be damaged by too harsh punishments. The techniques of natural and logical consequences may be a sufficient penalty. Primary aged children can also engage in contracts with adults. These may be implicit or explicit, and those with teachers involve reciprocal expectations and standards. The most effective teachers are those with both warmth and standards. Teachers work with children to have the "punishment fit the crime." A loss of privileges is the most common form of penalty; a "fine" or activity to make amends for damage done can also be used. Teacher-child contracts can often involve the child in setting both reward and penalty, thus helping the child learn self-discipline.

There are more activities that promote *peacemaking* and conflict resolution available than ever before. Teachers usually begin with some cooperative learning activities and cooperative games, finding such success in terms of increasing motivation and promoting tolerance that they increase their repertoire of such activities quickly. "Most people use cooperative learning because it's more effective," says Slavin of Johns Hopkins University. "The nice thing about it is that for free, along the way, you also get improvements in race relations and self-esteem" (Ladestro, 1993). Several organizations have started in the United States in the last three decades, most notably the "Nonviolence and Children Program" and "Educators for Social Responsibility." Learning the skills of peacemaking involves incorporating activities about the self, conflict with others, children's family and cultural roots, improving communication skills, articulating feelings, and teaching both tolerance and cooperation. The bibliography at the end of this chapter includes several excellent resources for peacemaking activities at the primary level.

The Teacher's Challenges

With the Child

The primary child is centered more on peers and less on adults. Because of this change in focus, school-age children begin to experience pressure from the *peer group* and internal pressure about the perceptions of the peer group.

Teachers are challenged to deal with this in constructive ways. They must be aware of a child's place in the peer group to understand the child's developing self-concept. At the same time, they have to be more indirect and less intrusive in the daily interactions of children to allow the child the freedom to develop friendships both independently and in relative privacy. Setting up cooperative games or activities with pre-set classmates gives children the "excuse" of having to deal with others that they would not or could not otherwise choose in front of friends. Balancing this teacher-imposed structure with opportunities for self-selection gives children the experience of selecting for themselves as well as the problem-solving opportunity of inclusion/exclusion, and allows the teacher to witness the various skills and challenges of the group without being noticed.

What the teacher must address is group behavior contagion. The five- to eight-year-old group can get both very silly and overly charged. Teachers who substitute "warm, fuzzy" kindness for a sense of authority and limits can find themselves overwhelmed by out-of-control and hostile behavior.

Finally, children may need a teacher's private help, but not public rescue, on peer pressure. Children and adolescents who are pressured to go

Try It   You are reading a story to a group of children. Several of them begin to complain that they don't like the story, and start chanting, "That's a stupid story, that's a stupid story." What can you do?

1. Stop reading and explain that it's your turn to read and their turn to listen.
2. Pick another story, telling them that if they don't like the story they can just tell you and you will do another one.
3. Bargain with them, saying this time you chose the book, and next time they can.
4. Just say that you can see they aren't interested in stories right now, and dismiss them to the next event.
5. Tell the ones who started the chant that they can take a time-out, and make them sit away from the group.
6. Talk to everyone about how hurtful the word "stupid" is and have them find another way to talk to you.

Which one do you like best? What will the class learn from each choice?

along with the crowd are sometimes unjustly categorized as part of the gang by adults. Teachers cannot expect a child to openly disagree with friends; it does happen, but adults who think it is easy to buck the crowd need only to think about the social pressures they themselves feel to conform.

Perhaps the biggest challenge to the primary teacher is simply the reality of *more children and fewer adults.* Because children are developing increasing abilities to be independent and engage in activities without direct adult intervention, most programs in the United States have larger group sizes. Whether a soccer team or classroom, whether an after-school center or academic setting, children in this age group are probably with more peers. Additionally, there are fewer adults around. Team teaching is the exception rather than the rule in elementary schools, and recreational and after-school centers have fewer adults for the group than their preschool counterparts.

All this makes it particularly important for adults to have a clear sense of purpose and of their own authority. As Elkind (1995) reminds us, "Teachers and children hold reciprocal expectations of one another. If one party to the contract [for instance, the teacher] does not hold up their end, the other party [the child or children] may feel no corresponding obligation to fulfill their side of the bargain." Teacher-child contracts, in an unspoken way, revolve around competence-respect, fairness-cooperation, and achievement-support. If the teacher is not prepared or competent, children do not accord them respect. A "teacher's pet" is a blanket condemnation of the teacher's lack of fairness, and as such undermines the children's wish to cooperate. Finally, the teacher who gives support for children's attempts and actual achievements is apt to be liked. Feeling that the teacher likes you becomes particularly important to the first- and second-grader.

With the Parent

Now that the child has become more independent, staying in touch with the parent is harder, because there is usually a parallel withdrawal of parental involvement in the child's programs. Elementary school systems generally support this separation, having fewer contacts with parents directly and making less of an effort to get parents involved. However, the teacher and caregiver must make regular efforts to establish some kind of relationship with the family, because the family and culture still exert a strong influence on the child.

What teachers need from parents has changed somewhat from the early years. Now, teachers need to hear parents' expectations of both the child and the program. What parents need from teachers has changed over time, too. The parent who wondered "What's next?" for the toddler and "How do I take charge?" for the preschooler, now wonders, "What should I be doing?" Again, children's increased competence and societal expectations can lead the involved parent to take too much of a "hands-off" approach. Teachers can tell parents more about normal development, what kind of behavior is tolerable or unacceptable, and techniques for dealing with children that increase self-discipline rather than those that either abandon children or overcontrol them.

With the System

The teacher of the school-aged child has a new role, both in the child's life and in the development of the child. A teacher is a guide and resource, not a parent substitute. Teachers may also find, with certain children, that they serve as a confidante or springboard for an adult reaction to certain feelings and ideas. By and large, however, children begin to move away from adults and toward other children and themselves.

Expectations shift depending on the system in which the teacher operates. Academic classrooms often ignore areas of affective development:

children's behavior on the playground or with friends is not their concern. Coaches focus on a child's physical and motor skill, not necessarily on self-concept. After-school personnel may take a supervisory rather than participatory role. The curriculum, rather than the child, is often at the center of the program.

As early childhood specialists with a bias toward child development, however, we assert that adult's roles and expectations of the primary child *must* line up with the child's total development, not just one piece. Taken out of context, a child's skills may ignore the individual profile. For instance, simply working with Hiroshi's increasing cognitive skills on the computer may leave out an essential part of his learning to take others into consideration, or make friends, or even play outdoors. Because what we have learned about development in the primary years indicates a crucial psychological aspect of the development of self and of peers, we conclude that any developmentally appropriate program for school-aged children must take into consideration these affective areas of development.

Furthermore, guidance and discipline are intimately tied to social and emotional growth. It is our conclusion that if you are in charge of children, you must include as part of the system dealing with children in these ways.

Think It Over

Do you remember being left out or snubbed? How about telling someone they couldn't play with you and your friend? Which "side" were you most often on in childhood? How have those experiences affected your teaching when children exclude others?

Working with the Family of the School-Age Child

Learning the Family Components

As mentioned earlier in the chapter, learning about the families of the children you teach is not easy. Still, "research has shown that parents and family are critical factors in children's education, particularly for those who are at risk . . . Numerous studies demonstrate that the influence and support given by the family may directly affect the behavior of children in school" (Haley & Berry, 1988). Any amount of direct parent participation helps you learn about children's families. For instance, Hiroshi's interest in computers prompted his teacher to send a note home, telling of his special interest and asking how he got so skilled. A follow-up phone call revealed that Hiroshi's mother was a computer programmer, and was willing to visit the class and show the children some fancy graphics on their in-class model. This positive connection made it easier for the teacher to address Hiroshi's behavior with his parents.

Communicating Your Expectations and Understandings

Whether parents participate in the school-age program, enter the room only briefly for pick up, or attend an orientation meeting, they need to know your expectations and understandings, both about their child and about the program. Although teachers and caregivers often put their philosophy and procedures in writing, the interaction about these expectations usually comes in the form of a parent-teacher conference. Parent-teacher meetings are often the only direct contact parents have with teachers. Unfortunately, it is often a negative experience. This is due, in part, from parents' anxieties about getting "bad news" and from teachers' tensions about talking to parents instead of children.

For instance, remember Tasauna and her homework? Well, not turning it in has become a problem, and when her second grade teacher calls home, her mom and dad are surprised. They didn't know Tasauna even had homework. Tasauna squirms and says she "keeps losing it." Two weeks later, the homework sheets that do get home are so upsetting that the entire family is in an uproar. Her parents tell both the second grade teacher and the after-school director to figure it out. The two educators speak on the telephone, then plan a joint meeting with all the adults. As a result, the school personnel find out how upset Tasauna's parents are, and the parents hear why the school wants homework and how the after-school center deals with it.

The true "guidance" comes as these adults all hear each other and make plans for Tasauna: the teacher to put stickers on all homework turned in; the after-school center to offer homework time first and Tasauna's favorite "clubs" time afterwards; and her parents to keep the television off during the weekdays. "But we all love 'Martin,' " they protest. "Then by all means watch it together," laughs the teacher, "*after* the homework is done and in her backpack!"

Developmental Alerts

When students' behavior is unacceptable or their performance indicates that they are not doing well, more serious measures may be needed. The teacher's first question is: "Is this behavior atypical—beyond normal variation?" A child who is misbehaving—tattling, being rude to the teacher or others, avoiding work, even being aggressive against others occasionally—needs the attention of both teacher and parent. Tasauna's homework is one example of such a problem; Hiroshi's domineering behavior around being a "big kid now" is another.

But what if the teacher senses that a child's behavior indicates a deeper disturbance or that someone's skills are seriously delayed? There is such a wide range of "normal" and such an array—and varying degrees—of special needs that identifying developmental problems or delays is a complicated affair. Still, there are clear evaluative procedures and services for the school-age child. Table 7.4 gives a teacher of five- and six-year-olds a list of developmental alerts, which can help a teacher see if a difficult behavior is simply that or needs more attention.

An example of this decision-making process around guiding a child comes from one of our opening profiles. It is now nearly winter in the kindergarten. All the children are quite comfortable in class now. Campbell

---

Table 7.4

Developmental Checklist for Five- and Six-Year-Old School-Age Children

Developmental alerts for this age range from the physical to intellectual, linguistic, and affective areas. Teachers watch for regular signs of growth, and talk with the child's parents if they have concerns.

Check with a health care provider or early childhood specialist if the child does NOT:

Speak in a moderate voice; is either too loud, soft, high, low, or monotone

Follow a series of three directions in order ("Stop, pick up the cup, and bring it here.")

Use four to five words of the primary language in acceptable sentence structure

Cut on a line with scissors

Sit still and listen to an entire short story (five to seven minutes long)

Maintain eye contact when spoken to (unless this is a cultural taboo)

Play well with other children

Perform self-grooming skills independently; brush teeth, wash hands, comb hair

---

From Allen & Marotz, 1993

"I'm gonna hit you!" When a child is misbehaving, the teacher must decide if the behavior is atypical or within the boundaries of normal variation.

cannot even remember when he was worried; why, he can already read his name and the words "Stop, No, and Exit"! Daniella, however, is another case altogether. She came in so bubbly and excited in September; now she droops her way into the class, and often fusses about rugtime. The child who was first to dance in front of the nursery school class now frowns at storytime and won't say her line in some of their rhyming chants. The teacher sees all this negative behavior, and finds it escalating even as it is dealt with daily.

Daniella's contrary behavior could have been mistaken as that of a wayward child in need of sterner discipline. Parents pushed too fast might have decided the problem was a bad teacher who asked too much of kindergartners. A teacher might have misjudged nervous parents as neglectful ones who don't expect enough. Instead, the teacher talks with the parents to get the child evaluated first by a speech and language specialist. As it turns out, Daniella has a moderate hearing loss in one ear. A hearing aid is now installed on a child who is, once again, enthusiastic, participating . . . and singing along on the rug!

Summary

The school-age child, in early childhood terms, refers to the five- to eight-year-old who is usually in kindergarten, or first or second grade in elementary school and may be in a mixed-age after-school program. Developmental changes are more subtle and complex than those observed in the preschooler, but are profound in their implications for independence and guidance. Growth and motor skills in this period give children physical strength and coordination for more advanced individual feats and team sports. Care must be exercised, however, in creating overly competitive situations that could create emotional problems of inferiority or incompetence. Intellectually, children entering the concrete operational stage of thinking and graphic stage of language development will be able to remember more, play out alternatives, estimate time better, and make agreements about behavior. The two critical areas of affective development are social acceptance and self-concept. The egocentric preschooler gives way to a more sociocentric primary-age child, and more intense peer issues emerge. Children learn more about themselves and have more of a consciousness of a self, including a sense of responsibility and right-and-wrong.

In guidance terms, the teacher remembers that school-agers behave for the same reasons as do younger children, and several discipline techniques still work, such as indirect suggesting and direct rule-setting, as well as encouraging positive behavior. New techniques include establishing consequences of misbehavior and using a social problem-solving method for conflict resolution. An authoritative teaching style coupled with peacemaking activities are effective tools for the teacher of these older children. There are several challenges unique to this age: more children and fewer adults in a group, less direct parental involvement or contact, and a system that may not focus as much attention on social and emotional development.

Observe and Apply

Observe a group of children at recess or at a playground with relatively little adult involvement. Watch how the children establish what to play, who may play, and what the rules of the game are.

1. Who is the leader? What behaviors do you see that tell you this? Would you want the children in your care to learn these skills? How might you teach them?

2. Do the "followers" do so because (a) the ideas are good, (b) they don't have any good ones of their own, (c) they are bullied and have no real choice in the matter, (d) they actively participate and have decided to cooperate on their own? How can you tell?

3. What can you do to help followers develop leadership skills, and help leaders become cooperative followers, too?

4. What kind of language is used? Is there reasoning, threats, bribes, humor? What kind of "body language" do you see—such as positioning, posture and gesture, voice inflection and volume? How does this tell you what you can do with children to change their behavior?

5. How can this activity help you understand the school-aged child? How can it give you clues to what might or might not work with them?

Review Questions

1. Below are examples from this book of the developmental milestones of the school-age child. Give an example of children's (mis)behavior and how you might deal with it.

Development	Behavior	Solution
Example: Gender differences in athletic abilities.	Boys play rougher in contact sports.	Keep sexes apart for such sports; have lots of other games for both together.
Great improvements in memory		
Adult-like ability in primary language		
Increased independence from adults		
Friendships become primary force		
Children still get "carried away" emotionally		

2. List three guidance techniques from the preschool period that still work with the school-age child.

3. Match the technique with its definition.

Social problem-solving
Rewards & penalties

Peacemaking
Natural/logical consequences
Authoritative teaching

When you leave your homework at home, you don't have it to turn in

Talking it out, a way to involve all disputants in identifying a conflict and generating ideas for its resolution

Techniques that involve starting tough and easing up later

Being encouraging by knowing what is rewarding to each child, and being careful not to be too harsh

Developing cooperative learning activities, including those that improve communication skills

4. Finish each sentence.

The teacher's challenges with the school-age child include _____ _____ .

Group behavior contagion can be addressed by _____ _____ .

Staying in touch with parents can include _____ _____ .

The teacher's role with the school system of the older child shifts to _____ .

"Talk and listen to one another" applies to working with children and _____ .

Bibliography

Allen, K. E., & Marotz, Lynn. *Developmental Profiles.* Albany, NY: Delmar Publishers, 1993.
Anderson, P. K. *First Day Blues.* Seattle, WA: Parenting Press, 1992.
Croft, Doreen. *Be Honest with Yourself.* Belmont, CA: Wadsworth Publishing, 1976.
Dinkmeyer, D., McKay, G. D., & Dinkmeyer, J. S. *Parenting Young Children (STEP Program).* Circle Pines, MN: American Guidance Service, 1989.

Drew, Naomi. *Learning the Skills of Peacemaking.* Rolling Hills Estates, CA: Jalmar Press, 1987.

Elkind, David. *A Sympathetic Understanding of the Child.* Boston, Allyn & Bacon, 1995 (3rd ed.).

Evertson, Carolyn M., Emmer, E. T., Clements, B. S., Sanford, J. P., & Worsham, M. E., *Classroom Management for Elementary School Teachers.* Englewood Cliffs, NJ: Prentice-Hall, 1989 (2nd ed.).

Friedman, W. J. "The Development of Children's Knowledge of Temporal Structure." *Child Development,* 57 (1986): 1386–400.

Galinsky, Ellen. *The Preschool Years.* New York: Times Books, 1988.

Haley, Paul, & Berry, Karen. *Home and School as Partners: Helping Parents Help Their Children.* Washington, DC: Office of Education, Research and Improvement, 1988.

Hareven, T. K., & Adams, K. (Eds.). *Aging and Life Course Transitions: An Interdisciplinary Perspective.* New York: Guilford, 1982.

Harper, L. V., & Sanders, K. M. Preschool child's use of space: sex differences in outdoor play. In M. S. Smart & R. C. Smart (Eds.), *Preschool Children: Development and Relationships.* New York: Macmillan, 1978.

Jones, Vernon F., & Jones, Louise S. *Comprehensive Classroom Management.* Boston, Allyn & Bacon, 1990 (3rd ed.).

Judson, Stephanie (Ed.). *A Manual on Nonviolence and Children.* Philadelphia, New Society Publishers, 1984.

Kreidler, William J. *Creative Conflict Resolution.* Glenview, IL: Scott, Foresman, 1984.

Kreidler, William J. *Elementary Perspectives 1: Teaching Concepts of Peace and Conflict.* Cambridge, MA: Educators for Social Responsibility, 1990.

Ladestro, Debra. Teaching tolerance. In *Teacher Magazine Reader,* Boston: Allyn & Bacon, 1993.

Lutz, C. Goals, events, and understanding in emotion theory. In D. Holland & N. Quinn (Eds.), *Cultural Models in Language and Thought.* Cambridge: Cambridge University Press, 1987.

Masten, Ann S. "Humor and Competence in School-Aged Children," *Child Development,* 57, (1986): pp. 461–73.

Miller, S. A., Shelton, J., & Flavell, J. H., "A Test of Luria's Hypothesis Concerning the Development of Verbal Self-Regulation." *Child Development,* 41 (1970).

Paley, V. G. *You Can't Say You Can't Play.* Cambridge, MA: Harvard University Press, 1992.

Parenting Press. *The Decision Is Yours.* Series for children 7–11, Seattle, WA: Parenting Press, 1988.

Piaget, J. *The Child's Conception of the World.* New York: Harcourt Brace Jovanovich, 1929.

Porro, Barbara. "Talk It Out: How to Help Children Resolve Conflicts." Elementary teacher and parent education classes and personal communication, 1990–present.

Ramsey, P. G. *Making Friends in School.* New York: Teachers College Press, 1991.

Read, Katherine B. *The Nursery School: A Human Relationships Laboratory.* Philadelphia, WB Saunders, 1971 (5th ed.).

Richards, D. D., & Siegler, R. S. "Children's Understandings of the Attributes of Life," In *Journal of Experimental Child Psychology,* 42, pp. 1–22 (1986).

Selman, R. The child as friendship philosopher. In S. R. Asher and J. M. Gottman (Eds.), *The Development of Children's Friendships.* New York: Cambridge University Press, 1981.

Shure, Myrna B. *I Can Problem Solve: An Interpersonal Cognitive Problem-Solving Program.* Champaign, IL: Research Press, 1992.

Shure, Myrna B., & Spivack, George. Interpersonal cognitive problem solving. In R. H. Price, E. L. Cowen, R. P. Lorion, & J. Ramos-McKay (Eds.), *14 Ounces of Prevention: A Casebook for Practitioners.* American Psychological Association, date unknown.

Siegler, R. S. *Children's Thinking.* Englewood Cliffs, NJ: Prentice-Hall, 1991 (2nd ed.).

Thomas, J. R., & French, K. E., "Gender Differences across Age in Motor Performance: A Meta-Analysis." *Psychological Bulletin,* 98 (1985): pp. 117-134.

Tietjen, A. M. The ecology of children's social support networks. In D. Belle (Ed.), *Children's Social Networks and Social Supports.* New York: Wiley, 1989.

Weisfeld, C. C., Weisfeld, G. E., & Callaghan, J. W., "Female Inhibition in Mixed-Sex Competition among Young Adolescents," *Adolescence,* Vol. 18 (Fall 1983): pp. 695–708.

Williams, H. G. *Perceptual and Motor Development.* Englewood Cliffs, NJ: Prentice-Hall, 1983.

Index